THE
SWASTIKA

MATERIAL CULTURES
Interdisciplinary studies in the material construction of social worlds

Series Editors: Daniel Miller, Dept of Anthropology, University College London; Michael Rowlands, Dept of Anthropology, University College London; Christopher Tilley, Dept of Anthropology, University College London.

MATERIAL CULTURE AND TEXT
The Art of Ambiguity
Christopher Tilley

ARCHAEOLOGICAL THEORY IN EUROPE
The Last Three Decades
Edited by Ian Hodder

EXPERIENCING THE PAST
On the Character of Archaeology
Michael Shanks

THEORY AND PRACTICE IN ARCHAEOLOGY
Ian Hodder

TECHNOLOGICAL CHOICES
Transformation in Material Cultures since the Neolithic
Edited by Pierre Lemonnier

ARCHITECTURE AND ORDER
Approaches to Social Space
Edited by Michael Parker Pearson and Colin Richards

GIFTS AND COMMODITIES
Exchange and Western Capitalism since 1700
James G. Carrier

THE
SWASTIKA

Constructing the Symbol

Malcolm Quinn

London and New York

First published 1994
by Routledge
11 New Fetter Lane, London EC4P 4EE

Simultaneously published in the USA and Canada
by Routledge
29 West 35th Street, New York, NY 10001

© 1994 Malcolm Quinn

Typeset in Garamond by Intype, London
Printed and bound in Great Britain by
Biddles Ltd, Guildford and Kings Lynn

British Library Cataloguing in Publication Data
A catalogue record for this book is available from the British Library

Library of Congress Cataloging in Publication Data
Quinn, Malcolm
The swastika: constructing the symbol
p. cm. – (Material cultures)
Includes bibliographical references and index.
1. Swastika – History.   2. National socialism – Germany.
3. Symbolism (Psychology) I. Title. II. Series.
DD256.5.Q56 1993
302.2'22 – dc20   94–4683
ISBN 0–415–10095–X

When the bones of King Arthur were digged up, the old Race might think, they beheld therein some Originals of themselves; Unto these of our Urnes none here can pretend relation.

(Sir Thomas Browne, Urn Burial, 1658)

CONTENTS

CONTENTS

ILLUSTRATIONS

FOREWORD

For too long, the archaeology of knowledge about the swastika has been confined to books and part-works which belong roughly midway between Nazi nostalgia and the occult. Malcolm Quinn's well-argued study helps to re-locate the swastika within a variety of fresh contexts: the parallel histories of archaeology, colonisation and design; polemics about the ways in which symbols work; analysis of the rhetoric of the image. The point, as he says, is 'to break the chain of reference from image to image, the means by which the symbol is constructed'. So this book is about symbolism, rather than Nazism, and it represents an important and even courageous contribution to the study of visual culture since the late nineteenth century.

Christopher Frayling
Royal College of Art

PREFACE

This book is about the construction of the archaic within the modern, and the fabrication of the swastika as a sign of identity in an era when personal and collective identities were being rapidly displaced. The construction of the swastika as the icon of a supposedly immemorial and indivisible race identity began in the mid-nineteenth century and reached its height in the Nazi period in Germany; its echoes are unfortunately still with us, despite the fact that the gulf between the representation of identity and its quotidian social dissolution grows ever wider. High on the list of the duplicities attributable to National Socialism was its use of the swastika as an emblem of the sense of self-definition and community which capitalism was rapidly eroding. In fact Nazism, under the sign of the swastika, subsumed the 'organic' and historical model of the nation state within a totalitarian scheme based on the expansionist and market-led notions of territory and social geography which had succeeded the organic model.

This book shows that a similar paradox also informed the construction of the swastika as a sign of the 'Aryan race' in the nineteenth century. The myth of an Aryan race re-assembled the archaic in the image of the modern, and its mythology of structure was derived from the study of Indo-European comparative linguistics, which also presaged the ahistoric, structural and modernist linguistics of Saussure. 'Aryan man' was a creature born of abstraction and deracination; and the swastika, a globally distributed mark with no discernible point of origin, was his heraldic device. In the nineteenth century, the swastika was used as both Aryan sign and Aryan evidence, place and race in one, and was adopted by Nazism in the twentieth century in its violent erasure of the historical links between people, place and praxis. From 1889 to the present, the display of the Aryan swastika as a symbolic locus, identifying mark or point of reference has also signalled dislocation, displacement and at worst, the Nazi terror.

It is for these reasons that the modern and Occidental swastika presents a particular set of problems to the analysis of material culture 'in context', since it must be simultaneously read as contextually placed and displaced, as presenting meaning and identity and at the same time deferring and

xi

postponing it. Insofar as the term Aryan (where used in an academic sense) has historically represented an unresolved problem of material evidence in the gap between Indo-European language theory and archaeology, the swastika as a supposedly 'Aryan sign' has instead been used as a substitute for and evasion of the archaeological problems of accurate representation, reference and material evidence. In 1880, the German scholar Rudolf Virchow ruled the swastika out of court not simply as evidence of the Aryan race but as archaeological evidence *per se*, suggesting that its wide spatial distribution rendered it useless for the determination of time: for Virchow, a liberal politician, a rigorous scientist and sceptic on the Aryan issue, the swastika was trivial, marginal and unreadable. However, the obstacles which the swastika presented to an orthodox archaeological reading must be set against the construction of the Aryan symbol, with its placement and displacement of meaning from sign to identical sign across an immobile space and a frozen time. Nazism, in its turn, employed the swastika as the sign of a race identity legitimated not in the historical dimension and 'sense of place' sought by the nineteenth-century nation state, but through the conquest of new territories. This book begins by looking at the 'Aryanisation' of the swastika in the Bismarckian period; but it was not until 1933 that this migratory image with no link to geographic place or historical time could be used as the 'national symbol' of Germany.

Whilst I would not deny that this has been a difficult book to write, I do not see my work on the swastika as part of an heroic discourse of reclamation and salvage. Instead, I hope to show that philanthropic notions of a 'change of meaning' for the swastika only serve to divert attention away from the Nazi strategy which used the symbol to demarcate, divide and control social space. Ultimately, however, my concerns are not with Nazism nor, in a sense, with the swastika itself. I believe that the Aryanisation of the swastika provides a paradigmatic example of the attempt to construct, in a secular era, an inviolable and immutable symbolic space between a living tradition on the one hand, and the constant flux of the market on the other. The end result of this attempt to transcend time was that the Aryan swastika caricatured tradition as an identical repetition, and that the Nazi swastika became the commodity sign *par excellence*.

April 1994

ACKNOWLEDGEMENTS

My first debt of thanks is to the staff of the Humanities Department at the Royal College of Art, for giving houseroom to such an unlikely project. I am also indebted to Daniel Miller at University College London. Without his advice and support, my research would never have become a book, and without his critical acuity it would have been a poorer one. Thanks are also due to Andrew Wheatcroft, Heather McCallum and Caroline Cautley at Routledge, for seeing this book patiently through to completion. I am grateful to Valerie Holman and Christopher Tilley for reading parts of the manuscript, and to Sabina Ubil for her patience, generosity and help with translations of eccentric texts written in bad German. Thanks especially to Susan Dinsmore for reading and editing the manuscript, and also for putting up with a year of 'Daily Life in Swastika City'.

A version of the introduction was presented as a paper to the Material Cultures Discussion Group in the Department of Anthropology at University College London on 6 May 1993.

I would like especially to acknowledge my debt to Jan Murton at the Royal College of Art slide library for the girls' hockey team photograph. (Plate 3). I am also grateful to the Süddeutscher Verlag, who gave permission to reproduce and provided the photograph for Plate 5, and the Hirmer Verlag for permission to reproduce the image shown in Plate 11. Plates 1, 4, 6, 7, 9 and 10 are reproduced by permission of the British Library. Plate 19 is reproduced by permission of the Designs and Artists Copyright Society.

Every attempt has been made to obtain permission to reproduce copyright material. If any proper acknowledgement has not been made, we would invite copyright holders to inform us of the oversight.

INTRODUCTION
Reading the swastika

The swastika ... could not be confused with any other symbol.
(Paul Virilio, *War and Cinema: the Logistics of Perception*, 1989)

This book begins with a warning against the consequences of misappropri-
ation. It was a warning which came too late, but which nonetheless is still
relevant today. This caveat was issued in 1880 by the philologist Max
Müller in a letter to the archaeologist Heinrich Schliemann, then known
throughout Europe as the excavator of Troy. In his letter, Müller warned
Schliemann that he should be wary of confusing the word 'swastika' with
an archaeological 'found image', and that to do so would sever the links
between the symbol and tradition:

> I do not like the use of the word *Svastika* outside India. It is a word
> of Indian origin, and has its history and definite meaning in India. I
> know the temptation is great to transfer names, with which we are
> familiar, to similar objects which come before us in the course of our
> researches. But it is a temptation which the true student ought to
> resist, except, it may be, for the sake of illustration. The mischief
> arising from the promiscuous use of technical terms is very great.[1]

In one sense, Schliemann had already taken heed of Müller's warning, by
substituting images of the left and rightward-turning 'swastika' for the
word in his texts (Plate 1). On other occasions, these same images were
matched with others in order to construct plausible theories for the
migration and dispersal of Schliemann's 'Aryan' ancestors. In this book, I
have eschewed Schliemann's expedient of using drawings, and have instead
included the word swastika as a 'flag of convenience'. The word, therefore,
does not imply a particular form of the image, but should in each case be
seen to refer to the specific instance under discussion. I stress this in order
to avoid the identical repetition of the symbol and the iteration of the
gesture which have conspired to keep the swastika in the public eye. When
I began the research for this book, the swastika had already resurfaced as
an emblem of the far right in a reunified Germany, and as I was completing

1

it, a British national newspaper carried the photograph of a swastika daubed onto a postbox in London, following the election of a member of the British National Party to a local council seat.[2]

The BNP had secured this victory using the slogan 'rights for whites', and the swastika is again being employed across Europe not simply with reference to Nazism, but as an image which unites various groups promoting a racist creed. The 'lineage' of the swastika which can be traced from 1880 to 1994 is not a tradition, but in the name of race it has appropriated the lineaments of a tradition, one established by the repetition of the sign and a chain of identical images. From the late nineteenth century onwards, there developed a set of practices that sought to maintain the integrity of the swastika as a symbol of race. This usurped and reversed an order of meaning in which cultural practices are represented by a material symbol. An 'Aryan' lineage of the swastika was established by referring to the self-identity of its form over time, not by linking the image to a continuity of custom or ritual praxis. This separation of the symbol from tradition and the attempt to construct a 'tradition of the symbol' in its stead is the trajectory linking the Aryanist and swastikaphile Michael Zmigrodski, who organised a swastika exhibition in Paris in 1889, to the anonymous neo-Nazis who sprayed the swastika on war graves in Nijmegen in Holland on 11 August 1993.[3] In both cases, the preservation of the 'race' is expressed by adding yet more images to the chain of identical forms bounding the Aryan corral.

My search for this tradition of self-identity and self-evidence has required an ethnography of texts, and the study of the swastika as the site not just for conflicting interpretations, but for different cognitive frameworks and 'ways of seeing'. The type of micro-history and close textual analysis employed in this book has ruled out the more usual encyclopaedic or 'travelogue' approach to the swastika, and in fact I am proposing that the compilation of a list of the meanings attributed to this image in a variety of geographic locations is an exercise which succeeds only in reifying a deracinated 'tradition of the symbol' and does nothing to draw the sting from Nazism. The exotic locations for the swastika in this text are book covers, terracotta whorls, maps and a set of drawings that have been kept in a drawer at the Musée de St Germain-des-Prés since 1889. On the occasions on which I do resort to a broad cross-cultural comparison, it is to show how the swastika functions spatially and to study the distribution of the motif over a variety of surfaces, not to compare and contrast one attributed meaning of the image with another.

Nor is the travelogue method appropriate to an understanding of the recent history of the swastika. In the popular imagination, the swastika begins with Hitler, and this historical paralysis needs to be addressed as a phenomenon in its own right, rather than simply being dismissed as an aberration. I believe that the best way to approach the swastika is to show that the atrophy of history and the deracination of tradition has a history and a tradition of its own. Unfortunately, many anti-Nazi and anti-fascist strategies have succeeded only in reinforcing the stasis of the swastika, rather than making it fully historical. This holds true for one of the first pieces of 'de-Nazification' legislation passed in the closing months of World War II. Early in 1945, after the Allied Expeditionary Force had crossed the Rhine and occupied Southern Germany, and before the surrender of the *Wehrmacht* shortly after midnight on 9 May that year, a set of regulations was issued abrogating Nazi law in the occupied territory. The purpose of these regulations was to 'eliminate from German law and administration... the policies and doctrines of the National Socialist Party'. The first Nazi policy to be repealed was the 'Law for Protection of National Symbols' of 19 May 1933.[4] This set of regulations, issued on the authority of Josef Goebbels' Propaganda Ministry, had been concerned with safeguarding the 'dignity' of the Nazi swastika and preventing its unauthorised commercial use.

That the first 'de-Nazification' regulations to be introduced in 1945 revoked laws specifically protecting the swastika, shows that the Nazi party and its symbol were seen as indivisible, a recognition which the years since World War II have done nothing to diminish. The image of the swastika, and the word Nazi have become both interchangeable and, in a sense 'onomatopoeic': they are linked to their referent in a way in which the words National Socialism are not. As the film director Sergei Eisenstein once suggested in an open letter to Josef Goebbels, the words 'National Socialism' are a self-cancelling 'mongrel of lies' of purely rhetorical and propagandist application.[5] However, the use of the swastika as a 'National Symbol' that also stood as the symbol of a 'race' aggregated and gave a chilling sense to the contradictory messages, the patched-up ideology and the performative statements of Nazism. The embracing sign of race functioned as the symbol of both a 'national' boundary and a 'social' group, and translated the redundant rhetoric of nineteenth-century nationalism and the radical politics of socialism into a populist language of race consciousness and 'national awakening'.

This discourse of awakening and 'coming to consciousness' has led me to include the swastika within another tradition, that of the romantic idea of the symbol. In the writings of Goethe and Schelling, of Coleridge and Novalis, the symbol is defined not so much as a representation as an event, a sudden revelation which restores the alienated subject to a richer, fuller existence. The romantic symbol contains this fullness and plurality within the singularity of the catalytic and visionary image. J. W. Goethe, in a letter to Schiller in August 1797, had written of symbols as 'eminent examples, which stand, in characteristic multiplicity, as representatives for many others, and embrace a certain totality.'[6] The Nazi swastika at once completed and extinguished the romantic concept of the symbol by

3

presenting it in the form of a monumental and static image of 'awakening' (*Erhebung*), and expressing Goethe's 'certain totality' in the form of a signifying field of self-identical imagery. The diachronic 'lineage' of the Aryan swastika became synchronic in Nazism, as the supposed preservation of a racial essence over time was translated into the conquest of an 'Aryan' space in the project of *Lebensraum*.

The swastika and the memorials at Dachau, Auschwitz and elsewhere are now the most familiar mnemonics of the Nazi regime, and both the swastika and the perimeter of the camps define spaces that cannot be rehabilitated and used for other purposes. In 1945, Germany could be de-Nazified by the removal of swastikas, but the swastika itself could not: the laws which once policed the public display of the swastika were abrogated, but that same abrogation recognised the indivisible links between the swastika and Nazism. I do not wish to claim that these links can be severed in the foreseeable future, but I will suggest that the historical problem of 'reading' the swastika both pre-dates and structures the totalitarian injunction which now confines this image to a single interpretation. This book has evolved from the attempt to resolve the problem presented by the impossibility of an 'objective' or completely de-Nazified reading of the swastika, a problem I first encountered when I began to study the uses of this image as an ornamental motif in 1989. I soon realised that the swastika had presented difficulties to a rationalist and objective analysis in the nineteenth century, when Max Müller had described the swastika as a 'troublesome puzzle', and when Count Goblet D'Alviella claimed that 'there is hardly a symbol which has given rise to more varied interpretations'.[7] What began to interest me was the possibility of a link between this storm in a hermeneutic teacup and what the historian Ian Kershaw has termed the 'intellectual impossibility' of an adequate explanation of Nazism in the face of Auschwitz. Kershaw sees this inadequacy as resulting in a polarisation of 'Hitlerist' and 'structuralist' interpretations of the Holocaust, with neither model providing a satisfactory explanation. His own suggestion is that the historian should look to the way in which the Holocaust functioned in 'sustaining the momentum of escalating radicalisation around "heroic", chimeric goals'.[8] In other words, we should examine the question of a Nazi 'self-representation'. What links the image of the swastika directly to the camps is the 'mission' and the goals which Adolf Hitler had outlined in *Mein Kampf*: 'In the swastika [we see] the mission of the struggle for the victory of the Aryan man, and, by the same token ... the idea of creative work, which as such always has been and always will be anti-Semitic.'[9] Hitler's 'definition' of the party emblem shows that it is worth asking exactly how Nazism might be said to be explained or represented by its chosen image of the swastika. In naming the swastika as the symbol of 'the victory of the Aryan man' Hitler described an heraldic device announcing an absent referent, the signal for an event which had not yet taken place. In a more direct sense, the swastika 'stood for' the Nazi party; but the party also facilitated the 'mission' of the swastika, which was to unite a racist (anti-Semitic) image with an Aryan racial identity. The concentration camps are the monuments to this attempt to produce a race from the sign of racism, the phantom Aryan from the murder of the living Jew. As Ian Kershaw suggests, the accepted frameworks for a historical exegesis are inadequate to Auschwitz, a word which at once evokes the stark brutality of recorded facts and lets those facts stand as an inexplicable symbol, a non-negotiable boundary. The swastika is now the visual equivalent of the word Auschwitz, but its institution in Europe as an Aryan and anti-Semitic sign preceded both the concentration camps and Nazism itself. In this instance, the problem of a rational and adequate explanation does not begin with Hitler. Nor was Hitler the point of origin for the discourse which attempted to establish a referent for the Aryan swastika through a negative definition and rejection of all that the Aryan was not.

The present and long-standing tension between rationalist 'interpretations of' the swastika and fetishistic 'reactions to' the image suggests that a 'decoding' of the swastika is a partial answer at best. With the swastika, what is particularly noticeable is the interrelationship of interpretation and response, of the search for a symbolic cause which then becomes part of the swastika's symbolic effect. Over the past 120 years, this has resulted in a redoubling and accumulation of 'effects' and the corresponding institution of the swastika as an apotropaic object rather than a readable sign. The swastika is not so much read as reacted to, and has assumed a causality in its own right rather than being seen as an image whose presence can be accounted for with a viable explanation. This talismanic or apotropaic phenomenology pre-dates Nazism, and therefore throughout this book, I have included interpretations of the swastika within the category of 'uses for' the swastika. This reverses the tendency of certain discourses to reduce the study of symbols to the interpretation of symbols. Interpretation sees symbols as produced by a cultural context, but it is also the case that symbols can themselves be seen to have 'produced' the contexts in which they are encountered, as well as catalysing the interpretative project itself. The passive representative role which is given to the symbol in a 'decoding' operation should also be seen as an *active* function which displays, defines and objectifies that which it represents. This is particularly noticeable in those cases where symbolic images are used to construct identities such as nation, speech and race. The symbol 'identifies' these identities as incomplete: it represents not what has been, but what must be done. In 1891, when Michael Zmigrodski defined the swastika as the armorial shield of the Aryan race,[10] his heraldic metaphor was apposite in several senses: the Aryan swastika was both the precursor heralding an absent or delayed referent meaning, and also its defensive shield. It was also heraldic insofar

5

as the 'tradition of the symbol' and the repetition of the sign was a mimesis of racial lineage and pedigree. In this 'heraldic' form, the swastika itself does not 'mean', it produces meaning by announcing it on the one hand and obscuring it on the other. Throughout this book, I have chosen to discuss this simultaneously 'presentative' and defensive role for the symbol, rather than seeing in the swastika a hieroglyph which can be translated into an equivalent textual interpretation. In this regard, it is significant that whereas the swastika has historically proven to be intractable to rational analysis and a one-to-one decoding, subjective explanations of the image are voluminous. I believe that defining the swastika as an 'object for' discourse rather than as the 'subject of' an explanation is the only viable way to deal with the problems of an objective reading whilst not lapsing into an unselfconscious subjectivism.

It must be admitted, however, that anyone who writes a book 'about' the swastika finds themselves in disreputable company. Not the company of Adolf Hitler, who devotes only a few lines in *Mein Kampf* to the subject, but that of writers such as Edward Butts of Kansas City, Missouri, who in 1908 produced the self-published *Statement Number 1: The Swastika*. This book, which was provided with Butts' mailing address and a blank page for the reader's notes, begins, like many similar texts, with the seductive narrative of a lost origin:

> Away back on the horizon of our records, seemingly a little beyond their limit, an emblem we recognise as the swastika came into existence. Of the past history related to this little emblem we desire to know more ... To our minds it appears much like a beautiful cloud that once floated above a setting sun, tinted with brilliant colours – now scattered by the 'four cardinal giants' here and there over the earth.[11]

Butts' scene-setting eulogy is then followed by a complex numerological theory for which the swastika provides the template and, ultimately, the *raison d'être*. The contemporary writer is confronted not only with a mainly eccentric discourse on the swastika, but with the sobering realisation that the image has frequently provided otherwise directionless texts with a legitimate goal and object. However, this reifying role does allow for an immediate distinction between the phantom value of what the swastika might 'mean' and concrete examples of how the swastika has been used, since, as Butts himself points out, the image 'must have been a more useful device and of very necessary application to have forced itself into the needs of so many widely distributed localities'.

In Butts' book, the swastika is an object which is used for writing, whilst ostensibly acting as the subject of a discourse attempting to decode or dissolve an image into a textual meaning: but a study of the canon also reveals that only certain kinds of books are 'written with' the swastika. As well as Butts' text, there are such curios as *Swastika: The Symbol of Religion, Physiology and Medicine Known to Man Some Thousands of Years Ago* (1943) written by N. Ramasvamayya, a retired judge from Madras, who interpreted the swastika as a 'diaphragmatic' symbol, and a pamphlet written by the Reverend Norman Walker in 1939 (Plate 2) who asserted that the swastika was a symbol of the supreme god in ancient India, Anatolia, Europe, China and America,[12] as well as numerous texts published during the Nazi period in Germany which mainly consist of outlandish attempts to establish a specifically Germanic racial provenance for the sign. The bad company I have been keeping over the past few years has constantly brought me up against the question: why has the discourse on the swastika been so relentlessly eccentric? Consequent upon this question was another: what kind of representational grotesque was the swastika that it could continue to meet the demands of popular occultism, antiquarianism, pornography and racism simultaneously? The concept of the aberration or grotesque flies in the face of an orthodox structuralist reading of the image 'in context', and deconstruction is also of little help, since the types of scandal its adherents prefer are dramatic and transgressive, a 'thinking of the other of Western philosophy', rather than the compromises and counterfeits of representation that interested me. Somewhere between absolute knowledge and a postmodern absolute uncertainty lies the kitsch semiotic of the swastika, a form of ersatz or tabloid transgression whose fitting emblem is the swastika carved into the murderer Charles Manson's forehead.[13] It is also interesting to note that Manson figures as the demonic aspect of 'alternative' culture in much the same way as Hitler was the figure who transformed romanticism into tawdry and sinister kitsch. Charles Manson is to the hippie commune as Adolf Hitler is to the *Volksgemeinschaft*, the 'national community'. What connects Hitler, Manson and the consumer of the Nazi 'sensation' in its variously mediated forms is the occult device of the swastika, which has put in long service as the degree zero of the cheap thrill. In pulp fiction and sensationalist journalism, the swastika is not so much a pornographic image as a device which occupies the place of the obscenity which cannot or should not be represented: the Manson murders, Gestapo cellars, Nazi atrocities.

In theory, the swastika is a moveable grotesque, since it stands not as the representation of a particular forbidden act but is instead a substitute for the act of representation. In practice, of course, all uses of the swastika in Europe post-Nazism, including Manson's, inevitably refer back to 1933 as their point of origin. However, within Nazi Germany itself, the swastika was substituted for an image and a definition of the Aryan. It was at once acknowledged as the sign of race, and occluded and dissimulated all that was done in the name of racial purity. It is this 'occult' order of reality which connects both Manson and Hitler with the swastika-lore of the theosophist Madame Helena Petrovna Blavatsky, and which links popular occultism with the romantic tradition. This line of descent might be termed the history of a misrepresentation, since in occultism, contra Wittgenstein, what cannot be spoken about is not passed over in silence, it is spoken of as the unspeakable and seen as the unseen. The same 'heraldic' strategy which at once precedes and announces the revelation of meaning and obscures and delays meaning precisely by *not* revealing it, is used in Aryanism, occultism and Nazism. In Kenneth Anger's film, *Invocation of My Demon Brother* (USA 1969) the swastika is used as one element of an occult ritual inspired by the 'Magick' of Aleister Crowley, but precisely which magical transformation the swastika effects is less important than the prior knowledge that the swastika is symbolically effectual. Anger has commented that the swastika was 'a psychic power pack' and claimed that 'Hitler couldn't have done it without the swastika'.[14] One is tempted to add that Anger couldn't have done it without Hitler. It is this genealogy of uses of the swastika which allows for a definition of the occult not as a secret doctrine or particular set of practices but as an order of meaning in which the symbol is rationally understood as the barrier to a rational understanding. Occultism does not subvert representation, instead it institutes a domain of representation and one of repressed desire, two realms separated by the hygienic device of the symbol.

The occult sign is also the Freudian 'fetishised object' and in the first section of this book I have referred to Homi Bhabha's psychoanalysis of Eurocentric thought as one model which can be used to understand how the 'Oriental' sign of the swastika was fetishised within an Aryanist discourse. The fetishised sign signifies a strict division between the Occident of the known and the Orient of the unknown, where the occult symbol functions as the border image whose visual aspect is material but whose 'content' is metaphysical. It dissimulates the anxiety caused by a loss of centre in the form of a fixed point which represents that loss, rather than allowing the absence of meaning to realise itself as a free associative flux. In the case of the Aryan swastika which eventually became the Nazi emblem, the response to the loss of a stable tradition and a secure reference was to develop a strategy of self-reference. In this way a sign of doubt, of nostalgia and loss was instituted as the certainty of a reference from image to image. When tradition is lost as a continuity of practice, of custom and culture, it is replaced by the repetition of the sign and the repeated acknowledgement of the sign. Both racism and the racist image or gesture signal the loss of a power to re-enact or recreate a community. Instead, they institute the passivity of a visual acknowledgement, the recognition of a form (whether that form is a shared skin colour or a swastika) which substitutes for the absence of a more tangible connection or mutality. In Nazism, communal action was directed towards preserving the continuity of the *representation* of tradition, in direct opposition to the communist ideal of mutually constructive action in response to the decline and subsequent overthrow of tradition. The hammer and sickle was a device which invited an act of construction both visually, as a dialectical argument, and socially, as mutual labour. The swastika, on the other hand, invited the passive acceptance of race identity as a form which had existed over time and which had to be 'awakened', *reconstructed* and preserved. In *Mein Kampf*, the swastika is identified as an image of 'creative work', which by Hitler's own definition is labour directed towards the maintenance of a race representation.

Although the Nazi swastika can be seen as one version of the Aryan swastika, its transformation of doubt into certainty, and of a marginalised sign into a dominant one, represents a radical shift of emphasis. In the nineteenth century, the swastika served as both an Oriental sign standing at the border and limit of a rationalist discourse, and as an 'orientation' device, an anchoring object for the wayward, anxious and subjective discourses of occultism and Aryanism on the margins of rationalist thought. If the swastika was an image which had functioned as the mnemonic for a lost object, a lost referent or ancestral 'ground' then Nazism can be said in one sense to have supplied the answer to this questioning and yearning with its discourse of 'national salvation'. However, Nazism simply extended the 'tradition of the symbol' and the fetishisation of the image spatially and synchronically, by instituting the swastika as the border of an ever-expanding Nazi space, threatening a colonisation of the West under the sign of the East, and using the image to set limits to the space of a *Lebensraum* which was at once colonially inclusive and racially exclusive. In a contemporary context, the swastika now appears as a barrier between democracy and the Nazi terror, in which the threat of the fascist space which was once mapped by a swastika on every street corner is held in check by constant vigilance. What all these swastika-delimited spaces have in common is not what they contain, but that they all exist as notional, projected or 'metaphysical' schemes: even *Lebensraum*, despite being dissimulated as a geographic and national boundary, was essentially schematic. This contrapuntal relationship between a definite bounding image and an indefinite bounded space has made it impossible to provide any resolution of the swastika into the paired values symbol/content or symbol/meaning. My own task has been to keep discussion of the swastika within this book focused on the question of the boundary or limit, thus avoiding the temptation to construct an architecture of meanings supposedly contained within the image itself.

That a given image will always mean the same thing or be encoded in the same way is a simple argument to refute, and in describing the swastika as a 'boundary' sign I do not intend to succumb to the same fallacy by assuming that the swastika has always and everywhere been used for this purpose. The word boundary instead here defines the *symbolic* form of the swastika, and thereby suggests a particular model of the symbol which will be used throughout this book. I make no claims for the originality or fashionability of this model, only for its applicability in the present instance. Its basis is in a cognitive, spatial and visual concept of the symbol, as a device for annexing and containing a set of meanings, and therefore as a *means* to organise and control social space. This cartographic function of the symbol has been identified by the anthropologist Dan Sperber, who in his *Rethinking Symbolism* suggested replacing a Western model which compares symbols to words, with one in which the symbol can be seen as a landmark or orientation device which 'serves cognitively to organise our experience of space'.[15] The landmark functions as a kind of lens through which we are directed towards a particular view of the surrounding landscape: the symbolic device, similarly, focuses and channels our construction of sense and meaning without itself being 'meaningful'. In a more free associative or eccentric vision, the symbol is used as a specular or 'speculative' device for magnifying first one set of texts, then another.

An anti-interpretative theory of the symbol might appear to be a contradiction in terms, but I am here suggesting that the symbol functions as a 'structuring absence' whose lack of interpretable meaning is cognitively recognised as the boundary between one set of meanings and another, or as a heraldic device for the possibility of a meaning which is not known. The boundary-line of the symbol establishes space by dividing it, including those texts which are its 'meaning' and excluding other texts not proper to that meaning. This is the defensive or shielding aspect of the heraldic device. However, in order to function as a recognisable limit of both this 'inner' and 'outer' context, and to prevent any textual miscegenation, the chosen material symbol must be a non-text or non-sense. The relevant question then becomes 'why is this message symbolically constituted?' not 'what does this symbol mean?' In other words, it is necessary to enquire how the symbol foregrounds and magnifies one set of meanings whilst diverting our attention away from others. In this sense, the symbol directs us to interpret only within its boundary, but the error is to read the boundary as something coextensive with the interpretation. This error occurs if it is suggested that the swastika means x in context y. Instead, we should rather say that the swastika is used in y as the 'symbolic vehicle' or focusing device for encoded message x. In this instance the swastika becomes a way of subdividing the context, of isolating a particular message from its ambient system of reference.

Whether the swastika is used to divide sub-texts from contexts or subgroups from groups the principle of symbolic difference is constant. Plate 3 shows the Edmonton, Alberta, girls' ice-hockey team in 1916, wearing identical swastika sweaters. In this instance the sign has been adopted from native American culture, and the image of the swastika is used to divide the Edmonton Alberta team from the class of all ice-hockey players. The less the chosen image has to do with ice-hockey, the more clearly will this division be effected. The swastika here functions as a kind of 'outline' which is used to separate off an area of homogeneous space using a heterogeneous element, in much the same way as a landmark is read *against* the landscape. In the case of the ice-hockey team, there is also the construction of a 'metaphysical' sub-group using the received wisdom that the swastika confers good luck on the wearer, a felicity which is not possessed by the opponent. The ease with which the 'symbolic vehicle' of the swastika was shifted from native American culture to ice-hockey bears witness to its symbolic utility and its visual heterogeneity: the swastika is strongly self-identical and not easily confused with anything else. It is therefore not surprising that so many examples can be provided of the swastika being used symbolically in a variety of cultural contexts from India to the Americas. Aryanism was to collect these individual instances of symbolic utility and gather them into a grand design, in which the swastika took on the role of representing its own self-identity as a sign of absolute difference. The morphological cohesion of the swastika was then used to express the survival of a racial essence over space and time.

My reading of the swastika 'against' context denotes a shift of emphasis from the more familiar notion of a reading 'in' context, whilst preserving the necessary emphasis which this method places on relative rather than absolute definitions. Without context, analysis can become a set of prejudices and opinions, but with it, the tendency is to 'read off' symbols simply as the product of a meaning or system of differences, and not as meaning-*producing* agents in their own right. A reading of the swastika as a 'symbol in context', with reference to the use of the swastika in punk iconography, has been proposed by the anthropologist and archaeologist Ian Hodder.[16] Hodder has argued that punk used the swastika with inevitable reference to Nazism, but in order to effect a change of meaning by placing the image in a new context:

> While the distant origin of a particular trait may be of little significance in a present context, the more immediate history is relevant. The total history of swastikas is less relevant to the present meaning of this sign than its more recent associations. In general, the choice of a symbol as part of a present strategy must be affected by at least its immediately previous use. But as soon as a symbol is used in a new context its meaning and history are altered.[17]

Here Hodder rejects a trivial reading of the swastika as a list of meanings in favour of a more complex structuralist/semiotic one. The approach he criticises is accurately represented by the 'Dictionary of Symbols' genre, which despite the customary diligence and accuracy of its research, cannot avoid the temptation to construct an interpretative travelogue in which Nazism is the exception which proves the rule. To quote an example:

11

Those who know the swastika only as the Nazi *Hakenkreuz* (Hook Cross) may be surprised to learn that it is one of the oldest, most widely distributed religious symbols in the world. Swastikas appear on Palaeolithic carvings on mammoth ivory from the Ukraine, dated ca. 10,000 b.c. Swastikas figure on the oldest coinage in India... Sanskrit *svastika* meant 'so be it' or 'amen.'[18]

This account of the swastika lists some twenty or more examples in sixty-four lines of text. Such abundance of meanings serves to distract us from the impossible goal of an ultimate 'true meaning' for the swastika, whilst comforting us with a diffuse sensation of just how meaningful it seems to be as the sum of its various parts. Here the swastika is still an alien sign, removed by a ten-thousand-year history and the radioactivity of Nazism from the present tense.

However, Ian Hodder's contextualism, despite being far removed from an encyclopaedic interpretation, still bases its method on the ascription of meaning to the symbol. Rather than suggesting that the 'meaning and history' of the symbol are altered in a new context, it could rather be argued that in punk a twentieth-century 'symbolic history' or genealogy of the swastika is being preserved. Punk used the swastika as a term of absolute opposition rather than as the first stage of a recontextualisation. Nor did punk include the swastika in a 'context within context' of its own. The swastika did not exist within a punk 'set' along with the safety-pin and tartan trousers, but instead it functioned as the barrier between contexts (punk and civilised, rational behaviour) not as something existing meaningfully within them. The symbol marks the limit of context, and punk did not use the swastika as a way of opening debates on the image, but instead as a device for slowing down its own assimilation into the wider culture. The anarchic stance of punk may now be an occasion for seventies nostalgia, but the swastika remains where punk found it and used it in the first place: on the outside. As Paul Gilroy suggests 'Sixteen years after punk, there are no residues of art school situationism to make [neo-Nazi] appropriation of the swastika an ambiguous gesture.'[19] What remains unanswered, however, is precisely how the 'unambiguous gesture' of the racist swastika was constructed in the first place.

Those who have attempted to justify the use of the swastika in sub-cultural situations, on the grounds that in this way the sign can be gradually rehabilitated or its meaning altered, are not allowing for the way in which the swastika has functioned as a portable token of bona fide sub-cultural status, one calculated to put civilisation and decency on the defensive. The swastika does not *contain* a meaning susceptible to change, instead it *arranges* meanings, regroups and shapes them into recognisable formations. We 'draw the line' at the swastika. That the swastika is still being used as a symbolic boundary rather than as an interpretable text is the view of

Axel Honneth, Professor of Philosophy at the Free University of Berlin. When asked about 'strong reactionary sentiments' in a reunified Germany, Honneth suggested that Nazi symbolism was employed by the skinhead movement in Germany as a token of opposition and aggression:

> it has a lot to do with the situation of jobless youth, a generation which has no other cultural means to find an identity except by using certain symbolic elements of the German past, which they know can produce certain provocations... Now the members of the youth generation are in a situation in which their opposition to what's going on in Germany can only be made ... in this way.[20]

Honneth claims that the simple opposition of fascism to leftism does not adequately account for the new use of the swastika, and suggests that the real danger occurs when skinhead symbolism comes in contact with right-wing ideology: 'It could happen that the fascist explanations make a more consistent, biographically more convincing, sense of the cultural symbols that the younger people are using.' However, Honneth's view of Nazism as a fascist 'ideology' which could explain the symbol perpetuates the left/right opposition he criticises, and identifies Nazism as Marxism's ideological 'other'. Nor does the danger lie in convincing explanations. The Roman fasces is certainly an image of the fascist state: the swastika as a racist sign cannot be explained simply in fascist terms. There is not a current use which can be accounted for on the basis of a previous ideology, but a continuity of forms which 'acts out' a racist paradigm by re-inscribing the swastika.

Descriptions of the swastika as fascist, anti-communist, reactionary, militarist and right-wing all dissimulate its racist imperative. Even the term 'Nazi swastika' to some extent disguises the history of this image. It is therefore in the true interest of both sub-culture and mass culture that the swastika should *remain* Nazified: for sub-culture as an image which defines a barrier, and for the mass media as a shorthand for Nazism. Both these uses avoid the issue of race which the Nazi swastika at once proclaimed as its ahistoric 'mission' and concealed as symbolic and historical praxis. In neo-Nazism, the interests of sub-culture and the mass media coincide, since the neo-swastika of a group such as the South African AWB is clearly an attempt to annexe the media space and prompt recognition afforded by the Nazi sign. Gestures towards the 'rehabilitation' of the image are not only futile and nostalgic, they at once imply that the problem of the swastika is one of corrupted content, and also serve to corral Nazism within the *cordon sanitaire* of a linguistic rather than spatial concept of the symbol. Changes at the level of meaning are overpowered by the 'higher authority' represented by the Nazi swastika, and renaming it will not contain the authoritarian imperative so much as attempt to replace it with a weaker version of itself. Even the word swastika, and the word Nazi, carry considerably less weight than the image, which rather than being a representational sign is an apotropaic and repulsive object. The 'promise' of the heraldic device, of an Aryan race or a national awakening, is now reflected as the threat of a new 'rise of fascism', a phrase which ironically preserves Nazism's expansionist trajectory.

The Nazi swastika was at once an emblem of expansion and conquest and one of absolute immobility. The 'dromological' and kinetic aspect of Nazism has been described by Paul Virilio, whose description of fascist strategy as being symptomatic of the colonialist impulse of Western culture in general accounts for his lack of interest in the 'little sadico-museographic or commercial trifles' that remain of Nazi iconography itself.[21] Yet in his discussion of the swastika, Virilio is content to rely on the Proustian model of an image which releases 'potent affective associations' in the viewer, adding 'Hitler himself is said to have had a certain power of hypnotic suggestion'.[22] In fact, the paralysis of the spectator's gaze which the Nazi swastika still effects is a paralysis *of* reading, rather than the hypnotic power to initiate new associations or 'suggestions' *for* reading. It is more pertinent to examine the monopoly the Nazi swastika holds over the field of vision, and its tendency to interpose its own image between all other forms of the motif.

This paralysis of the gaze is most clearly seen in cross-cultural travelogues of the swastika. In an informative article on what he refers to as the 'Symbol of the Century', Steven Heller provides 'alternative' examples of the swastika, such as the diamond-studded swastika lapel pin of the Girls' Club of Philadelphia, which was advertised in the club magazine with the legend 'what every girl wants – her own swastika'.[23] Without the invisible presence of the Nazi sign, this amusing contrast would be merely mundane, but the 'innocent' example only highlights the gulf between the Philadelphia maidens *circa* 1916 and the Gestapo. All the alternative uses of the swastika which Heller cites are seen through the framing device of his Nazi 'Symbol of the Century', which is both the image which precedes all post-war discussions of the swastika, and the 'after-image' which remains disturbingly within view after all other examples have been forgotten. This fixity is its 'hypnotic' power. Several authors from Ernst Gombrich to Siegfried Kracauer have attested to the stultifying effect of the swastika on the gaze, and it is often included, along with a pair of 'piercing blue eyes' in Hitler's personal bag of tricks.

To suggest, as Virilio does, that Nazism carries implications for our culture which extend beyond the perimeter of the camps is salutary; but on that basis to leave intact those representations which form that perimeter and boundary line perpetuates the problem. The representations themselves are an embodiment of the strategy which spatialises and totalises power rather than containing it in the form of the 'meaningful' symbol. In Nazism, power and the image of power cannot be separated. The phenom-

enological or poetic freedom implied by Virilio's idea of 'affective associations' is replaced in the Nazi swastika by a parodic and deterministic
variety of that same romantic plenitude in the form of an endless repetition.
And when Virilio describes the swastika as having an 'arresting power',
this generalisation can be tied to the specific way in which our gaze is
transfixed at the level of the image, restricting a movement forwards in time
towards a meaningful dialogue or backwards towards a fixed structural/
contextual point of reference.[24] In the Nazi swastika, the authority of the
precedent is not implicit, but manifest: the sign is fixed before our very
eyes, and freedom of movement is forestalled. The paralysis of the gaze
and the constriction of free association which the Nazi swastika can still
effect also relies upon the strong self-identity of the image. This has
historically resulted in a proliferation of 'versions' of the swastika which
gravitate towards a recognisable type of symmetry group: conversely, the
meanings attributed to the swastika are so numerous and diverse that they
can only be referred back to the image as their point of origin. The Nazi
swastika is now a kind of anti-archetype or template for all other swastikas
and all other interpretations of the swastika.

If not meaning and interpretation, then what? This book proposes that
it is more pertinent to ask how first the Aryan and then the Nazi swastika
gave space and definition to a race concept and conceptualised a racist
space, which was to become the 'killing zone' of *Lebensraum*. It must also
be asked how in 1933 the new national symbol reconceptualised existing
national boundaries. In Chapter 2, this question is pursued through a
definition of the swastika as a piece of Germanic typography that authenti-
cated and included the text 'Germany'. The inclusion of German language
within Germanic rhetoric parallels the transformation of a German *Heimat*
into an Aryo-Germanic *Lebensraum*. *Heimat*, a word whose original meaning was that of family home or local community, had already been enlarged
to include the concept of the nation-state when the Nazis came to power,
but the expanded concept of an expanded space had retained the definite
'sense of place' that the term implied. The German film director Wim
Wenders is quoted as saying that 'In America . . . mobile is said with pride
and means the opposite of bogged down . . . [whereas] what *makes* it a
home in the German language is the fact that it is fixed somewhere.'[25]
What Nazism did was to retain the notion of *Heimat* as a defensible space,
and expand it into the concept of *Lebensraum*, a 'living space' which put a
siege mentality on the move. This is somewhat different from the American
'mobile home' whilst sharing the colonising intent of a 'frontier spirit'.
The concept of *Lebensraum* exceeds the geographic boundaries of Germany
in a colonisation which proceeds from the centre outwards. This logic
subsumes a geographic German space within a notional Germanic space
whose boundary is theoretically limitless. As the larger space of *Lebensraum* began both to supersede and redefine the previous limit of the

Heimat, so the swastika as the symbol which marked the extent of the new Germanic boundary began both to include and occlude the text 'Germany'.

The shadow of this occlusion still persists in the tabloid shorthand which allows for the reading 'swastika equals German' as an unconscious extension of the interpretation 'swastika equals Nazi'. The principle of 'fixity' or steadfastness which Wenders attributes to *Heimat* was retained in the form of the swastika as an absolute opposition to the non-Aryan and non-Germanic; but the dynamic of *Lebensraum* instituted an ever-expanding exclusion zone, and a two-front war both within this zone and without. The perfidious logic of *Lebensraum* proposed a region which was simultaneously inclusive (of new territories) and exclusive (of the 'non-German' populations within them). These overlapping principles of *Lebensraum* for the Aryan and an exclusion zone for the non-Aryan form articles three and four of the programme of the National Socialist German Workers' Party, issued in Munich in February 1920. Article three calls for 'the requisition of territories ... for the resettlement of our surplus population' and article four for the restriction of German citizenship to compatriots (*Volksgenossen*) and for the exclusion of those of Jewish blood.[26]

As a globally dispersed image, the swastika is an example of a migratory sign which Nazism adopted as its own, only to transform it into the signifier of an absolute national 'character'. It is also significant that this nomadic and anonymous sign, existing at once everywhere and nowhere, should have become interchangeable with the figure of Hitler, the self-appointed representative of a 'people' and a 'race' with indefinite historical, textual and geographic boundaries. The liminal or marginal image of the swastika effectively represented the limits of the projected space of an Aryo-Germanic *Lebensraum* without signifying anything material about Germany itself, its history or culture. *Heimat* as *Lebensraum* was Wenders' defensible German space set into motion, the German castle in the form of a Panzer tank. The militarised form of the 'Aryan' armorial emblem of the swastika was as an apotropaic motif on warplanes and tanks, whose presence indicated the current limits of the Nazi advance. However, this symbol of limits collapsed a Germanic symbol of difference into the German text so that the two became one: *Lebensraum* then *was Heimat*.

This is also the reason why the swastika has proved so difficult to 'reassign' since Nazism, since there is no space between image and text into which a new meaning for the swastika could be inserted. Instead, the logic employed by the Allied Expeditionary Force in 1945 which decreed that to eliminate the swastika was to eliminate Nazism is still viable today. Attempts to reassign the swastika also have a tendency to gravitate towards the discourse of colonisation and conquest. In Sam Fuller's film *Verboten* (USA 1958), a wounded American GI is tended by a young German girl in the ruins of her home. Pointing to the swastika armband on a portrait of Adolf Hitler, he says 'That's an old American Indian sign that Hitler took from us'. When the girl stares at him, uncomprehending, the GI points to his epaulette and says 'The 45th Division used to wear the swastika right here. We had it long before little Adolf got the idea.'[27] *Verboten* presents the American de-Nazification programme as victorious over 'little Adolf' and the remnants of the old regime, and its self-conscious attempt to reclaim the swastika is part of this project. However, in identifying the swastika as an 'old American Indian' sign which had been subsequently adopted and militarised by white settlers, Fuller rehearses the colonisation which 'Aryanised' the swastika in the first place.

In *Verboten*, Fuller attempted to place the swastika back into its global context, and instead established that the limits of the globe were the limits of European expansionism. Well before the advent of Nazism, the swastika was being included within an anthropological discourse of diffusionism which, with its model of an origin or single source from which all examples of a particular phenomenon could be derived, followed the imperialist logic of global conquest. Diffusion is the theme which informs the longest text ever written about the image, *The Swastika, the Earliest Known Symbol and its Migrations*, a 250-page swastika 'encyclopaedia', written in 1894 by Thomas Wilson, curator of prehistoric anthropology at the US National Museum (the Smithsonian). Wilson's book gathered together illustrations and interpretations of one image from a range of sources including native American designs and the Persian rug in his bedroom, all of which were presented so that 'philosophers who propose to deal with the origin, meaning, and cause of migration of the swastika will have all the evidence before them'.[28] The terms 'symbol' and 'migration' in the title of Wilson's book immediately introduced a paradox of which the anthropologist was only too aware: in his judgement on this image, how could he reconcile a symbolic locus with a migratory movement? Was the swastika the dissembling witness of some causal and definite 'meaning' or mute material evidence of the passage of persons and objects? The idea of a cross-culturally recognisable symbolic image without a congruent identity of meaning was anathema to Wilson, since a diffusionist model of the swastika supposed a centre of diffusion, a centre implied an origin, and an origin a meaning. This may account for Wilson's vehement denial that the swastika was an autokinetic 'moving image', whilst contradictorily listing it as 'turning to the left' and 'turning to the right' in his index, and providing his 'map showing distribution of the swastika' which charted a supposed migratory curve extending from Murmansk to São Paulo (Plate 4). This map represents the conquest of space over time which was the basis of the diffusionist paradigm, a theory which also proved useful to 'Aryanist' theories of the swastika. Wilson wished to reverse diffusionism to arrive at one swastika and its original meaning, but eventually had to resign himself to a decentred field and a missing origin.

Most revealing of all is Wilson's description of the swastika as a manifestly purposeful image, distinct from the 'more easily made' straight line, circle and cross, embodying 'a definite intention and a continuous or consecutive meaning'.[29] Wilson supports his idea of 'continuous meaning' as a visual trace across diverse cultures by the introduction of a theological 'argument from design' through which at some point in the remote past, an original and concealed word became swastika. His encyclopaedia, however, demonstrates the opposite argument, namely that once it is itself identified as a point of origin, the image of the swastika can generate a surfeit of interpretative speech. And even though Wilson allows all parties their say, the parliament or democracy of exegesis that an encyclopaedia presents only serves to demonstrate the impossibility of competing interpretations coexisting under its roof. One authority would state that the swastika was 'solar', another that it was 'generative' but the only thing the swastika really seemed to generate was further speculation.

To understand the modern and Occidental swastika we must refer to Wilson's map, and therefore to the relationship between the single image and the spatial and temporal area which it is intended to 'symbolise'. This is the cognitive and spatial dimension of symbolism which Wilson could not have reconciled with his own search for meaning and origin, since it necessarily includes 'interpretations of' the symbol within the category of 'uses for' the symbol. At the risk of attempting long-range psychoanalysis, it could be suggested that Wilson realised that the discovery of a definite meaning for the swastika was a closure which would have frustrated his true project, which was to use the swastika to marshal and regiment meanings and construct neat divisions within the global space of anthropology. The map was a side-effect of this regimentation, but the fact that it appears to us now as a grotesque foreshadowing of Hitler's conquests is no accident, since it accurately represents the 'tradition of the symbol' which Aryanists such as Zmigrodski were building in the nineteenth century. Here the swastika is deracinated and disconnected from tradition, and accorded a lineage and conquests all its own: a totalising scheme which only became possible with the elevation of the synchronic and global and the corresponding diminution of the diachronic and local which characterises the modern era.

Under the conditions set by advanced capitalism, the symbol has only an ephemeral and contingent existence. Rather than collective representations, we have representations which collect meanings, objects or people into groups, often in ways which are overlapping, interpenetrative and occasionally self-contradictory. A British National Party member, for example, might dress her/his family in articles of clothing made by Benetton, a company which has advertised its products under the globalising anti-racist slogan 'United Colours of Benetton'. The symbol divides, but its divisions are contingent and permeable. The Nazi swastika attempted to transcend these economic conditions by constructing a socio-cultural space on the basis of an absolute division and an uncrossable boundary. After 1933, the Nazi *Gleichschaltung* sought to organise all other groups within society relative to this boundary line.

This attempt to set one sign above all others and to institute a racist 'sovereign law of value' can be seen in Plate 5. This photograph, taken in Berlin in 1934, shows policemen shouldering arms in the shape of a Nazi swastika. In this formation, the swastika does not contain the group as in the example of the Alberta ice-hockey team mentioned earlier. Here the human group is contained and marshalled within the form of the swastika. And although this is an example of paramilitary regimentation, it is paradigmatic of the way in which the Nazi swastika functioned as a racist sign. The recognisable and graphic difference of the image, its symbolic utility, was used as a value in its own right to signify the race consciousness preceding and containing all thought and action. The representation thus dissimulates itself as a non-representation, as something non-referable and non-transferable, existing beyond interpretation and preceding use. My own task in this book has been to use a micro-historical discourse and a theory of how symbols are constructed and recognised to refute the ahistoricism and absolutism of the Nazi sign. The Nazi swastika cannot be renamed or 'resymbolised' in the short term, but it can be 'desymbolised' by making it historical. The paradigmatic example of this strategy at its most effective is John Heartfield's *Blood and Iron* photomontage of 1934 (Plate 19). Heartfield's achievement was to have put a Marxist spanner in the works of the Nazi 'symbolic vehicle'. His four bloodstained axes in the shape of the swastika added history to the ahistoric and reality to the occult illusion. By supplying the Aryan sign with its missing referent, Heartfield revealed, by a kind of 'X-ray' technique, the machinery of a race representation. The blood shown on his axes can be substituted for the Aryan blood promoted by Nazi propaganda, suggesting that racist violence does not guarantee or legitimise the notion of a race. Heartfield's intentions were specifically pro-communist rather than generally anti-racist, but his iconoclastic strategy carried a wider significance which is, unfortunately, still relevant today. If this book can also be said to have 'X-rayed' and grounded the Nazi swastika (albeit by following a different historical route), it will have achieved at least one of its aims. Another is to shift the debate on symbolism away from interpretation and decoding and towards the visual and perceptual concepts of liminality, repetition and recognition. I am aware that these two aims may appear to be mutually opposed, but I am proposing that a desymbolisation and textual examination of the swastika will provide clues as to how symbols are constructed and how the symbolic mode functions.

This book is divided into three chapters: the first takes archaeology and the construction of the Aryan symbol as its theme, beginning with the swastika signs discovered by Heinrich Schliemann in his excavations at Troy. It draws a distinction between a cryptological/rationalist approach to the swastika and the Aryanist attempt to match form with prehistoric form as the symbol of an ancestral speech. The second chapter looks at the legacy of romantic theories of symbol and ornament in the Nazi swastika, placing it in the anti-classical tradition of a Germanicised and quasi-expressionist 'Gothic'. My description of the swastika in this section as Gothic and Germanic typography is developed in Chapter 3 into a comparison of the swastika with the contemporary logo, using the image to unravel the paradoxical term 'corporate identity'. A comparison of swastika and corporate logo is predicated on their common ambition to institute 'trans-economic' values. Both swastika and logo are seen as having deliberately moved away from the completion or exchange represented by the sign and towards a 'first-person' type of representation, which as well as describing the unbounded geography of the self is now glorified as the apotheosis of the 'corporate personality'.

All three chapters of the book are brought together by the model of a symbol which announces and presents a fragmentary or incomplete aspect. In Chapter 1, the swastika is seen as deracinated and rendered incomplete by being set apart as the sign of the Aryan ancestor. Its missing referent is then established not as internal and textual but external and somatic: a recognition of race consciousness heralding a race identity. In Chapter 2 this link between image and identity is explored through the tropes of romantic aesthetics and the half-life of the 'Gothic'. In Chapter 3, the logo is seen as effecting a pseudo-exchange between the corporeal and the corporate, supporting rather than transcending the exchange of commodities. Like the phrase 'corporate identity', the Aryan swastika denotes an exchange which in fact has already taken place, and for which the body is merely the conduit and the agent of reinscription. This completion is the exchange of sign for sign in the 'tradition of the symbol'. In the vain and empty repetition of racism, the swastika preserves and contains nothing, but the only possible continuity of the 'race' lies in the continuity of the image. This race is always a race against time, against the end of the proclamation and the non-arrival of the Aryan. Like those religious zealots who climb mountains to await the second coming, the racist lives under the doubly 'recurrent' sign of the swastika in the knowledge that although his Sisyphean labour will never be rewarded, it may be indefinitely prolonged. The appropriate response to this indefinite nightmare, as John Heartfield showed, is to break the chain linking image to image. Heartfield's critique, precisely because it was historically specific and anti-iterative, is unrepeatable, but it shows that there is a right and a wrong way to approach the Nazi swastika. My own history of the swastika begins, as Heartfield's did, with the Bismarckian era, but I have chosen Heinrich Schliemann and not Bismarck himself as its starting point. The historical route from Bismarck to Hitler is direct, well-trodden and follows a certain logic: Hitler himself laid claim to it in his design of the Nazi flag. The swastika, the symbol of the new Reich which Nazism added to Bismarck's flag of 1866, named a different ancestor: the Aryan, whose lineage was constructed from a set of absences concealed by the repetition of a sign.

1

SYMBOL

This is what we were once ourselves in those immemorial times when
Tacitus described us: unique, free of all taint, like only unto itself.
(Friedrich Gottlieb Klopstock)

Since we took myths seriously, literally, we found Troy, quite real,
under the rubble of history. We have the debris of the history of
Hitler, and now we have to seek the myths underneath.
(Hans Jürgen Syberberg, *Hitler, a Film from Germany*, 1982)

Visitors in search of diversion and instruction at the Paris Exposition of
1889 might have been intrigued by an unusual display at the Palais des
Artes Libéraux, where a Polish librarian named Michael Zmigrodski had
arranged drawings of over 300 objects, each bearing a swastika or, as he
put it 'an ornament which I believe to have a swastikal origin'.[1] This
tableau, in which the swastikas were arranged in groups labelled 'Prehistoric', 'Pagan' and, unusually, 'Christian' was afterwards deposited in the
St Germain Museum of Prehistory.

Over and above Zmigrodski's sub-classifications stands the embracing
taxonomy of 'objects bearing swastikas', and it was not simply vulgar
showmanship which led him to direct his audience to a sudden recognition
of the swastika as it magically appeared amongst a group of inscriptions
or in an ornamental band. A contemporary commented that '[Zmigrodski]
has made it his special study to show that this cross had everywhere a
symbolical, and not merely ornamental value'.[2] The expedient of using
drawings, rather than providing the objects themselves for inspection,
turned the swastika into an exhibit whose two-dimensionality in fact
negated the principle of an exhibition 'in the round', since the spectator
was not asked to consider and interpret the object from all angles, but
simply to recognise a distinctive and repeated sign. However, the donation
of these drawings to the Musée des Antiquités Nationales reified this
pseudo-exhibition as material evidence in its own right. That this was
possible indicates the overwhelming popularity of 'Aryan' theories of
ancestry and race in Europe at that time; Zmigrodski the librarian and

swastika-hunter was also an anti-Semite, whose self-appointed task was to promote the swastika as the heraldic device of the Aryo-Germanic family. He compared the swastika to a fly trapped in amber, its unchanging form representing the preservation of a racial essence over time, and his declared aim was to prove that 'in a very ancient epoch, our Indo-European ancestors professed social and religious ideas more noble and elevated than those of other races'.[3]

In August 1889 Zmigrodski addressed both the first International Congress of Popular Traditions and the tenth International Congress of Anthropology and Prehistoric Archaeology on the subject of the swastika.[4] The committee and correspondents of the latter contained a number of Aryanists and swastikaphiles from around the globe. Alex Bertrand, the director of the St Germain Museum of Prehistory who acquired Zmigrodski's drawings, was vice-president of the Congress. Delegates to the conference included Thomas Wilson, Heinrich Schliemann, and the anti-Semite Emile Burnouf, who in a letter to Schliemann in 1872 had noted that 'the swastika should be regarded as a sign of the Aryan race. It should also be noted that the Jews have completely rejected it.'[5] Also present was Professor Ludwig Müller of Copenhagen, an advocate of the theory that the swastika was the emblem of the supreme god of the Aryan race. Britain was represented by A. H. Sayce, who had contributed to Schliemann's dissertation on the swastika in the archaeologist's *Troja* of 1884.

In Zmigrodski's conference papers, exhibition and published texts, recognising and naming the image of the swastika became a way of claiming kinship and assuming race identity, and the visual discrimination of a 'sign-object' was made equivalent to discrimination on the grounds of race. The Aryan is thus provided with a way of seeing and a 'programme for perception'.[6] Zmigrodski's technique is similar to the racial morphology, the 'fingering of skulls' described by Ernest Renan in 1882,[7] since it attempted to define an Aryan aesthetic of forms, which are set apart from those other forms previously designated as undesirable. In Zmigrodski's exhibition, the swastika was recognised and cognitively 'recovered' from all that it was *not* (many-armed, contextually-coded, ornamental, Semitic, etc.), and the chosen emblem, like the chosen race, existed in a condition of 'negative visibility'. The symbol is made visible *as* a symbol by a process of selection and exclusion: it stands alone and represents itself. The opportunity which the swastika presented to a racist discourse in the nineteenth century, and which was to be seized and fully politicised by Nazism in the twentieth, was provided by an image which was strongly defined as a self-identical image but which had repeatedly eluded a positive textual identification. A rationalist discourse found itself frustrated by the swastika, the 'troublesome puzzle' described by Max Müller and one example of the uncanny 'world of problems' which Hegel had seen in Indian art.[8] Since the swastika could not be satisfactorily and finally decoded within the available categories of the meaningful symbol or the meaningless ornament, it could begin to function only as the image of a negative value and of a purity established in opposition to definitions of the unclean. In 1894, Count Goblet D'Alviella wrote of the swastika that 'there is hardly a symbol which has given rise to more varied interpretations'.[9] The swastika thus exposed the fallacy of an attempted closure and final decoding which, as theorists such as Jacques Derrida have suggested, can only indefinitely replicate itself. D'Alviella, however, had already solved this problem by naming the image as the sign of its own unsignability.[10] The swastika defied definition, but it was precisely this quality which allowed Zmigrodski to confer on the swastika the status of a pure form, racially apotropaic and repelling all contact: 'it stands in isolation and is set within a frame, in modern terms a votive image.'[11] Such an image could be recognised and acknowledged, but it could never satisfactorily be 'read' and then translated by all races.

Zmigrodski's interest in the 'Aryan' swastika had been prompted by the discovery of swastika-bearing objects by the archaeologist Heinrich Schliemann at the hill of Hissarlik in Turkey, which Schliemann firmly believed was the site of Homeric Troy, the realisation of the boyhood dream of discovery described to sentimental effect in the introduction to his book *Ilios*. Schliemann's treatment of the swastika exemplifies the process by which a symbol can become deracinated from tradition and replaced within a tradition of the symbol. In another sense, it continued the discourse on ruins and the narrative elaboration of prehistoric fragments which characterises the Homeric myths themselves.[12] However, in employing the swastika as the device which could include his heroic Trojan thesis within an even grander Aryan scheme, Schliemann disturbed the integrity of the traditions represented by his chosen Homeric and Vedic texts. In defining the swastika itself as an Aryan ancestral sign, he constructed a lineage preceding history and tradition, a continuity of visual forms which were seen as the trace element of a race.

It should be pointed out that Schliemann's theories generally presented Aryanism in its broadest, least anti-Semitic and most Asiatically-oriented form: methodologically, however, the archaeologist's politics of interpretation set precedents for others and for the future. His expedient of using images of the swastika instead of words, instead of preventing a misrepresentation and safeguarding a tradition, confirmed the swastika as a self-representation, a symbol referring not to a set of meanings or practices but only to a set or distributed group of similar signs. This set of swastikas was then constituted as a material trace of the Aryan race, as Schliemann attempted to turn Indo-European phonetic comparisons into archaeological evidence. Where phonetic comparison looked for constant factors across diverse languages, the swastika came to represent the undiversified and self-contained system of an Aryan *Ursprache* (original speech), a unity established by recognising similarity and eliminating difference.

Zmigrodski's exhibition, together with his two books in which the swastika is the leitmotif, illustrate how two discourses on language were being brought together in order to establish the swastika as an image of race purity. These two discourses were that of Indo-European language theory and a debate on and around the German language itself. What united them was the theme of the original, untainted, self-generating and self-identical unit, represented in Zmigrodski's texts by a swastika 'of pure form'. This obscure object of desire was arrived at by a process akin to that used in panning for gold; Zmigrodski's analysis of the swastikas excavated by Heinrich Schliemann at Troy sifted through the 'many hundreds' recognised by the archaeologist to arrive at sixty-five representatives of quintessential Aryanism:

> Dr Schliemann's atlas contains around six hundred objects adorned with a swastika. We find there:
>
> sixty-five swastikas of pure form.
> one hundred and fourteen crosses with the four points or [nail holes].
> one hundred and ninety two swastikas with three branches, known as triquetrums.
> eighty-six swastikas with four branches.
> sixty-three with six branches.
> [total 520][13]

This list highlights the similarity and the differences between the methods of Schliemann and Zmigrodski. While both were keen to identify as many Aryan swastikas as possible, Zmigrodski conducted a purge on Schliemann's less commited and less racially motivated Aryanism, narrowing down the field of vision and discrimination from the 'many hundreds'[14] of images mentioned by the archaeologist. Thirty years later, this list was shortened even further by Albert Krohn and Adolf Hitler, who removed all but one rightward-turning black swastika 'set apart' in its white circle on a red background, an image intended to remain unchanged and self-identical despite its reproduction in all forms of mass propaganda.

In 1886, however, Zmigrodski had to deal with the various forms of 'swastika-like' or rotationally symmetrical signs encountered at Hissarlik, and was obliged to construct a theory of sign reproduction for the swastika which explained variant or badly-executed forms on the grounds that the 'pure' swastika was so well known to the inhabitants of Troy that even a bad example would be immediately recognised. Yet even here we can see the beginnings of the 'sign field' created by Hitler, for in Zmigrodski's Neoplatonic scheme, each visible image is encountered as a more or less effective representation of the ideal swastika form rather than as the

25

representation of some signified meaning. In other words, there is no positive value for which the image of the swastika is the ersatz or stand-in: its 'meaning function' is to be anti-Semitic, and this is achieved when the swastika is most alike to itself, and purged of a reference or a likeness to anything else.

FROM REPRESENTATION TO RECOGNITION

This ritual purification of the 'Aryan' swastika was conducted within a discourse of Indo-European language theory which was itself methodologically informed by dialogues of recognition, and by the isolation and annexation of elements which were then used to construct pure, self-regulating synchronic systems. The basic method of cross-linguistic comparison had been available since 1598, when Lipsius listed nearly thirty-six identical words in Persian and German;[15] however, Lipsius explained these similarities using the idea of mutually loaned words, revealing an emphasis on vocabulary which was to be sustained throughout the seventeenth and eighteenth centuries. Thus, as Foucault has pointed out in *The Order of Things*, the distinct character of nineteenth-century linguistics cannot be accounted for on the grounds of new *discoveries* such as the system of Sanskrit grammar,[16] but rather is more accurately explained by employing the idea of a paradigm shift from diachrony to synchrony through which 'language began to fold in upon itself, to acquire its own particular density, to deploy a history, an objectivity, and laws of its own'.[17] Language as a self-consistent abstraction began to replace the word as concrete particular.

The way in which the swastika began to function as an Aryan sign was dictated by the qualities of the Aryan myth itself, and its strange existence as a duo-temporal 'mythology of structure'. This meant that the methodological approach of Indo-European linguistics, which looked for synchronic constants across different languages such as Latin, Sanskrit, German and Greek,[18] was linked to a diachronic vision of the ancestors. This combination allowed for the concept of a pure origin, pure because the addition of synchronicity meant that the racial/linguistic essence remained *constant over time*. Other races and other languages suffered entropy and decay; only the Aryan, it was argued, remained distinct and unaffected.

It is this theory to which Zmigrodski subscribed when he identified the swastika as a form victorious over the vicissitudes of time, a self-generating 'mother' image which had survived the maleficent influence of other forms. It was also this ideology which contributed to an emphasis upon the recognition of identity by the systematic elimination of elements of variation, and the sleight of hand through which an immeasurably ancient sign can also be seen to herald a present awakening or renewal.

This Aryanist discourse on the swastika clashed with a cryptological approach to the image, which saw it as the obdurate and frustrating barrier to a rational and textual explanation. Into this latter camp falls the tragic swastikology of Dr E. Brentano, who in a letter to Heinrich Schliemann attempted to refute the archaeologist's 'Aryan symbol' explanation of the swastika and supplant it with a theory that the image was a form of writing, and that this swastikal alphabet was evidence that the artefacts found at Hissarlik were 'historic' and not ancient.[19] Brentano's letter was only one of the disputes which troubled Schliemann at this time, the most persistent of his detractors being a retired German army officer named Ernst Bötticher, who claimed that Hissarlik was not Troy but a necropolis, and a site of ritual immolation.[20] Brentano's more pedantic criticism focused on an illustration in Schliemann's book *Ilios*, which showed thirteen forms with 'swastikal' symmetry in a band around the equator of a terracotta sphere (Plate 9). This was, Brentano claimed, evidence both of a form of writing and a knowledge on the part of the inhabitants of Hissarlik of 'the globular form of the earth', a realisation that had only dawned, according to Brentano, around 360BC. He further berated Schliemann for omitting the swastika from the chapter on 'inscriptions found at Hissarlik' in *Ilios*. Schliemann's reaction to this criticism was characteristically contemptuous: he called Brentano's interpretation of the swastika as an inscription a 'sufficient reductio ad absurdum' and cheerfully concluded his reply with an epitaph:

> Using, as I needs must, all requisite freedom in refuting the arguments of Dr Brentano, the tone of just severity is restrained by his sad end. While these pages are in the press, he has died by his own hand in a fit of insanity, on the twenty-fifth of March, 1883.[21]

The Schliemann of *Troja* was in a bellicose mood, and his text reaffirms, through the testimony of the enlisted authorities A. H. Sayce and R. P. Greg, that the swastika was fingerprint evidence for the passage of the Aryan race.[22] *Troja* also contains a dissertation by Karl Blind, Schliemann's emissary in England, on 'The Teutonic Kinship of the Trojans and Thrakians', which shifted the axis of the Aryan myth away from India and towards Germany:

> the Trojans . . . were of the Thrakian race; [that] the Thrakians were of Getic, Gothic or Germanic stock; hence [that] the Trojans were originally a Teutonic tribe . . . Can, then, this *prima facie*, this 'largest of nations' be any other race than that which afterwards pushed forward in the Great Migrations?[23]

Schliemann's indignant reaction to Brentano's theories suggests that the essential difference between a cryptological and an Aryanist treatment of the swastika is that which stands between the reading or sequential decoding of writing on the one hand and the instant recognition of (racial) character in a specimen of *handwriting* on the other. For Schliemann, the swastika came to represent not one part of a language but a whole vanished speech and race, which formed the bond between the Vedic and Homeric mythologies that he wished to unite.

Foucault's assertion that the two poles of the nineteenth-century linguistic *episteme* were logical algebra and Indo-European language theory may usefully suggest what place the swastika occupied amongst the corrupted discourses which lay between these disciplines, discourses belonging to neither yet co-opting elements of both. Foucault stresses the methodological similarity of comparative grammar and symbolic logic, in which representation and the 'act of knowing' found a new and more confined space.[24] These two elements of structure and logic are united by the fact that they both exist in their pure form 'outside' language: meaning becomes constituted in the form, not in the word. Both these approaches were to inspire hybrid theories, and hybrid conceptions of meaning: the comparison of kindred structures that established the Indo-European language group was to form the basis for the racial mythology of Aryanism, and the logic that informed cryptology, with its tendency to attract nonsense answers, contributed its own mythologies and pseudo-solutions, which in the case of the swastika corresponded to the cryptological non-starter of a supposed hidden meaning. Unlike Champollion's decoding of the Rosetta stone, no translation of the swastika could be final and irrefutable, thus allowing the process to carry on *ad infinitum*.

As Brentano's equation of writing with history suggests, the Rosetta stone, with its three equivalent texts of Greek, Demotic Greek and the Hieroglyphics that were now accessible to translation, stood at the outer edge of the discipline of history as it was constituted in the nineteenth century. The undecodable swastika, however, was necessarily defined as prehistoric or ahistoric, and began to be used as the sign of a pre-scriptural Aryan speech. In the Aryan discourse, the swastika became the material symbol of an unwritten law of race identity, and a prehistoric precedent for written languages. Empirical methods that had revealed structural links between the Indo-European languages appeared to the Aryanists to point to an original, proto-Indo-European language from which they had all emerged. Since the methodology was abstract, this structurally derived proto-language was necessarily invisible, and in reality nothing more than an idea. The attempt to rebuild an invisible language from an immaterial structure was to be criticised with cogency and wit by Max Müller, who coolly observed: 'we cannot reconstruct what never existed, and we cannot, therefore, build up a uniform Proto-Aryan speech.'[25] Recanting his former enthusiasm, Müller was equally dismissive of the evocation of an Aryan race out of whose mouths the proto-language had issued: this he regarded as 'downright theft' on the part of ethnologists from philologists, and consequently as absurd as the notion of a brachycephalic grammar. However, Müller was still ready to contradict himself by referring to an Aryan 'noble speech' and to acknowledge the lure of the idyll:

> The actual site of the Aryan paradise will probably never be discovered ... new theories, however, have their attractions, and I do not wonder that some patriotic scholars should have been smitten with the idea of a German, Scandanavian, or Siberian cradle for Aryan life.[26]

In the minds of less clear-headed authorities than Müller, the excavated swastika possessed all the necessary materiality of the evidence, the 'hard facts' that were needed to prove the Aryan hypothesis.

Müller's identification of an unholy alliance of materialist science and patriotic speech in the Aryan 'brachycephalic grammar' also reveals an absence; the absence of writing. Foucault argues that the comparative grammar of Rask, Grimm and Bopp that cemented Indo-European language theory also shifted the central linguistic axis towards the phonetic element of speech and away from inscription and writing:

> The whole being of language is now one of sound. This explains the new interest, shown by Raynouard and the brothers Grimm, in non-written literature, folk tales and spoken dialects ... By means of the ephemeral and profound sound it produces, the spoken word accedes to sovereignty. And its secret powers, drawing new life from the breath of the prophets, rise up in fundamental opposition ... to the esoteric nature of writing, which, on the other hand, presupposes some secret permanently lurking at the centre of its visible labyrinths.[27]

Foucault's 'on the other hand' is resolved in the rhetorical figure of the Aryan swastika, a labyrinthine *inscription* shielding and preserving the secret 'inner identity' of race and an ancestral speech. The primal value of the spoken element had been elaborated by Johann Gottlieb Fichte, in the public lectures published as his *Addresses to the German Nation* of 1807–8, which were primarily concerned with Teutonic ancestry, origins and language.[28] Fichte, on whom Goethe and Schiller had pinned the epithet of 'the Absolute Ego', delivered his lectures whilst Prussia was occupied by Napoleon's armies. He sought to inspire a Germany which was as yet a collection of principalities with a vision of a people united by a superior language, employing the topical and potent idea of a pure and essential speech distorted by miscegenation. Fichte evoked the image of a Teutonic *Ursprache* through which not men, but Nature had spoken, contrasting the ancestral with the pernicious influence of a foreign speech: 'in an organ of speech thus affected by the conditions mentioned there necessarily arises, not the one pure German language, but a derivation therefrom'.[29] This is the same logic that Zmigrodski employed in his presentation of a pure and original swastika, freed from any 'derivation therefrom'. Fichte argued that the German language, with its ancient and essential connection with nature, was superior to those whose mechanisms of representation were not equipped to deal with the 'sensuous images' that it was the privilege of the Teuton to understand and express: at one point in his *Addresses* he compared German speech to the soaring of an eagle in the empyrean, and that of the foreigner to the buzzing of a bee. Fichte also drew parallels between such a 'sensuous' language and the capacity for intellectual development. These comments presage later and more elaborate comparisons between spoken language and racial characteristics. He also presented the paradoxical image of the palaeontology of a 'living' language, a language living because it is spoken, in which he believed past strata might be more easily revealed:

> an idea that likewise is not arbitrary, but necessarily proceeds from the whole previous life of the nation. From the idea and its designation a keen eye, looking back, could not fail to reconstruct the whole history of the nation's culture.[30]

Fichte's concept of a 'living palaeontology' clarifies the Germanic cultural significance of the swastika: it became the emblem of a lost but still echoing speech, not the fragment of a dead script. Prehistory in the nineteenth century thus found itself caught between the desire for an evocation of the past as something which was still present and potent, still 'speaking' (often undertaken in a nationalist spirit) and the first tentative steps towards a systematic and empirical reclamation of vanished and redundant material culture through archaeology, a rationality attempting to grapple with, and often frustrated by, evidence that was pre-linguistic, and therefore appearing by extension to be pre-rational, primitive and archaic.

OSTKOLONISATION

The notion of a Germanic *Ursprache* or original speech does not simply denote a proto-German language, since for several centuries German had been identified as the original language *per se*. In the twelfth century, the mystic Hildegard of Bingen suggested that German was the language of Adam and Eve[31] and many authorities since had elaborated upon this theme of an Adamic German *ursprünglich Sprache*. The notion of a pure origin depends heavily on the model of a self-sustaining and self-generating form, and both the morphology of the swastika itself and the methods by which it was interpreted found a *raison d'être* in this scheme. Léon Poliakov has pointed out how often the construction 'Abstammung aus sich selbst'[32] (self-genesis) has been applied to the German language as a way to emphasise its purity, and he goes as far as to suggest that this principle continued to manifest itself in the way that loan words such as 'television' and 'geography' are self-consciously Germanised.[33] Whilst both this idea, and Poliakov's emphasis on *furor tutonicus* ('Germans with assertive or megalomaniac temperaments') may be over-determined, the geneaology of auto-genesis, and its role in the construction of 'the Aryan myth' from Johann Jakob Grimmelhausen[34] through to Fichte and beyond, is manifest. In interpretations of the swastika, this theme manifests itself as the appreciation of the swastika itself as an autokinetic form (Guido von List[35]), as the recognition of autokinetic forms in general as specifically Germanic (Wilhelm Worringer[36]) but also as the recognition of self-identity already referred to (Zmigrodski), which is a closed and self-generative signalling system. In this system, if you are Aryan you will recognise and name the sign of the swastika: if not, you will see nothing but a 'hasty bit of decorative work with no religious meaning at all'.[37] For the Aryan, however, this recognition does not constitute an interpretation or understanding of the swastika, but simply the acknowledgement of its reoccurrence. As a method of reading material culture, the search for self-identity leads to a filtering out of inconvenient contextual, visual and ornamental 'noise' so that the act of symbolic re-cognition or self-identification may take place:

> I recognise at the first glance the 'suastika' [*sic*] upon one of the three pot bottoms which were discovered on Bishop's island near Königswalde on the right bank of the Oder, and have given rise to very many learned discussions, while no one recognised the mark as that exceedingly significant religious symbol of our remote ancestors.[38]

This passage appears in Heinrich Schliemann's *Troy and its Remains* of 1875, the account of the archaeologists' initial excavation work at the hill of Hissarlik in the Dardanelles in the years 1871–4. The narrative of these excavations and their consequences has been rehearsed elsewhere, resulting in Schliemann being identified as a kind of *idiot savant*, somewhere between the clumsy potato-digger reviled by Mortimer Wheeler and Hugh Kenner's cosmos-altering genius.[39] The terms of the debate on the general import of Schliemann's excavations have remained largely unchanged for a hundred years. The archaeologist's 'Homeric fundamentalism' with regard to the site of Hissarlik was being placed in doubt even by the popular press of his era. A reviewer for the *Illustrated London News* of 5 January 1878, discussing the Trojan finds which were then on display at the South Kensington Museum, cautiously commented that:

> Dr Schliemann has certainly discovered, by his recent excavations at Hissarlik, the remains or traces of several important layers of buildings (so to speak) which may be considered, in his opinion, to show

the successive evidence of four ancient towns, built directly on top of one another.

In contrast to this Victorian circumspection, when the London *Times* of 24 February 1993 carried a report on recent excavations at Hissarlik by Manfred Korfmann *et al.*, its author confidently declared: 'Archaeologists at the modern day Troy, in Turkey, have found remains that indicate that Homer's Iliad was less a flight of fiction and more historical fact. The discoveries . . . indicate that the site supported a bigger city than supposed.'

The terms of this simmering debate were temporarily changed in 1991. On this occasion, *The Observer* of 24 March that year carried a front-page tableau in which pictures of Hitler and Goebbels were flanked by photographs of Schliemann and his wife, and some of the 'treasures' of Troy. Above the photographs ran the headline: 'Nazi art loot discovered in Russia.' The presence of the swastika on Hitler's armband, however, was in this instance an entirely fortuitous but nonetheless revealing link with those uncovered at Troy. This time, the crucial issue was the debate over national rights to the Trojan material taken from the Berlin Museum at the end of World War II and newly discovered in post-Soviet Russia. Significantly, the article discussed competing German and Russian claims to the objects, without addressing the claims of Turkey, the country from whose territory the objects had been originally excavated.[40]

The savage irony that the Aryan swastikas which Schliemann so enthusiastically embraced as an ancestral sign at Hissarlik in Turkey should now be put to use in Germany in racist attacks against Turkish *Gastarbeiter* points to a broader definition of what we now know as the 'Nazi' swastika. It suggests that the language of totalitarianism can be considered in many instances as an aspect of the language of colonialism. This idea has been proposed by writers such as Frantz Fanon and Paul Virilio, for whom Nazism and its *Blitzkreig* is the return of the colonial principle to haunt the Europe which exported it: 'Fascism . . . in other words the institution of a colonial situation on the European continent.'[41] Through the swastika, we can observe the entire trajectory of colonialism from the nineteenth-century annexation of the Oriental sign in the first instance, through to the Nazi *Ostkolonisation* of Germany itself. The first stage of annexation employs a logic of displacement, the logic through which an amputated sign can subsequently function as the receptacle of nostalgia for lost contact. In order for the signifying image of the swastika to represent this loss or absence, it had first to be cut free of its moorings in the 'native soil' of a referent system of context, object and environment. First it must be colonised (this is Zmigrodski's 'setting apart') and only then could it be effectively *Germanised*.

Setting the Nazi swastika within this wider context avoids the unconscious construction of another spurious ancestry and origin myth, in which

32

Schliemann and Zmigrodski appear in Nazi uniform, and also refutes the single-minded Stalinist orthodoxy of the Lukács of *The Destruction of Reason*, for whom German culture is a series of paths leading directly to Hitler.[42] Schliemann's biographer, Leo Deuel, has suggested that had the archaeologist completed a separate volume on the Aryan swastika as he planned, this might have earned him 'honourable citation by the latter day racist apostles of Nordic supremacy'.[43] In fact the directness of this criticism may skirt the wider issues: although there is little evidence to suggest that the swastikas of Troy were the direct antecedents of those of Nuremberg, (this idea simply reinforces a myth of origin and colludes with a 'tradition of the symbol'), Schliemann's politics of interpretation can in many ways be seen to set precedents for the Nazi course of action. First amongst these precedents is the element of 'recognition' already remarked upon: in the Nazi state, the act of recognising the swastika as a party political sign and as a mirror of the ancestral self became one and the same. In a wider context, however, there are also good reasons for suggesting that Schliemann's attitudes were generally colonialist and Eurocentric rather more than specifically anti-Semitic or proto-Nazi. The archaeologist was certainly no model German patriot, and his attitude towards the land of his birth underwent several transformations in his lifetime. After having been somewhat pro-French during the Franco-Prussian conflict of 1870–1, Schliemann became a late convert to German nationalism, donating many of the excavated artefacts of Troy to the German National Museum in 1881 in exchange for the conspicuous public honours of honorary citizenship of Berlin and the Prussian Order of Merit. The following year, writing in response to criticism of his methods of excavation from the Scottish scholar R. C. Jebb (whom he referred to as 'that raging English slanderer Jebb'), Schliemann declared that his views were 'those of any German archaeologist', evidence both of a newly acquired *Vaterlandsliebe*, and an uncharacteristic tolerance for German academic opinion.[44] His book *Troja*, with the Karl Blind essay promoting Germanic autochthony, was published in 1884. Previously, the businessman turned archaeologist had felt badly treated by many authorities in Germany, which may account for his desire to confound cautious scholarship with a sudden and dramatic embrace of the ancestral swastika.

THE CONSTRUCTION SITE

Schliemann's freebooting excavation methods unsettled some of his contemporaries; similarly, his treatment of classic texts angered eminent Victorians such as Matthew Arnold, who compared him unfavourably to the 'noble' Homer.[45] It is this disrespect for established traditions and correct methods that identifies Schliemann as the archetypal modern venture capitalist, and Hissarlik as an example of that 'immense construction site of traces and residues' that Gianni Vattimo has described as the true legacy of modernism:

> In the process of homologation and contamination, the texts belonging to our tradition, which have always served as the measure of our humanity (the 'classics' in the literal sense of the term) progressively lose their cogency as models and become part of the ... construction site.[46]

Hissarlik was as much a construction as an excavation site: Schliemann's reputation was made there, his personal myth assembled from a *bricolage* of the 'classical' myths of Homer and the Vedas. It is significant, however, that the collage of texts which made up popular Aryanism was regarded by Schliemann in *Troy and its Remains* as a pure, given and original value, and the swastika as its equally untainted emblem. In other words, the tools and the agents of assembly are alone regarded as sacred, whereas the Homeric and Vedic 'material' comprising the Aryan myth is unceremoniously thrown together:

> Upon a ball, found at the depth of 8 meters (26 ft) there is a tree ... surrounded by stars, opposite a [swastika,] beside which there is a group of nine little stars. I therefore venture to express the conjecture that this tree is the tree of life, which is so frequently met with in the Assyrian sculptures, and that it is identical with the holy Sôma tree, which, according to the Vêdas ... grows in heaven, and is there guarded by the Gandharvas, who belong to the primeval Aryan period, and subsequently became the Centaurs of the Greeks.[47]

Here Schliemann employed the swastika not so much as an Aryan emblem, but as the key device of the 'Aryan method' which cuts through textual and discursive complexities to arrive at the obvious and immediately recognisable *gestalt* by which an Indian tree becomes a Greek centaur. The swastika here acts not as a part of the associative chain of images, but as the image which allows the transformation to occur at all, a kind of mythological aggregate. The archaeologist Chris Tilley has advanced this model of an 'aggregation site' in his study of the prehistoric rock carvings of Namförsen, proposing an interpretation of the carvings in which they act as mediating values between mythical and quotidian worlds, 'forging social and cosmological cohesion through establishing an ontology of resemblances', a space in which familiar objects are homogenised and magically transformed into versions of each other: in the Namförsen carvings, images of elks become boats become people.[48] Tilley also notes that there are 'elks with everything' which suggests that the elk, rather like Schliemann's swastika, was working as a key device allowing mythological transformation to occur.[49] The alchemy at work at Hissarlik transformed mundane material excavation into the substance of myth, and Aryanism was the modern myth within which this change could be accomplished, with the swastika functioning as both Aryan sign and Aryan archaeological evidence. This construction was not peculiar to Schliemann; writing on the Trojan finds in the *Archaeological Journal* of 1877, Bertram Hartshorne noted that the presence of the swastika 'would seem to indicate the common Aryan descent of all the successive inhabitants of Hissarlik'.[50]

Not only Schliemann's Troy, but Germany itself, was a site for mythical reconstruction in the 1870s. The new Reich sought historical legitimation for its newly acquired statehood, a process described by Eric Hobsbawm as 'the invention of tradition':

> Since the 'German people' before 1871 had no political definition or unity, and its relation to the new Empire (which excluded large parts of it) was vague, symbolic or ideological, identification had to be more complex [than the French] and ... less precise. Hence the multiplicity of reference, ranging from mythology and folklore (German oaks, the Emperor Frederick Barbarossa) through the shorthand cartoon stereotypes to definition of the nation in terms of its enemies.[51]

Hobsbawm has defined 'the invention of tradition' as a ritual 'which seeks to inculcate certain values and norms of behaviour by repetition, which automatically implies continuity with the past', and has suggested that, where possible, history is employed in these rituals, but that material from periods preceding written history may also be used. For Hobsbawm, the growth of nationalism in Europe in the period 1870–1914 was an entirely new phenomenon which had to invent tradition in its own image:

> It is clear that plenty of political institutions ... not least in nationalism – were so unprecedented that even a historic continuity had to be invented, for example by creating an ancient past beyond effective historical continuity, either by semi-fiction ... or forgery.[52]

These criteria also applied to the discipline of archaeology in the mid-nineteenth century. Linguistic theory had swiftly become grist to the mill of invented tradition; nineteenth-century Aryanism, however, was encumbered by the fact that the language and material remains of the proposed root-race were absent. This may explain why prehistory was so quickly enlisted to the cause: the malleable, compliant and mute prehistoric artefact, with none of the intractability, but all of the materiality of the written historical record, was ideally suited to the process that Hobsbawm defines as 'identification'. The 'tradition of the symbol' established in the Aryan swastika also fulfilled the conditions for an 'automatic continuity' with the past.

Patriotic and opportunistic manipulation of the prehistoric record was eventually to aspire to an elevated status and a systematic methodology: Gustav Kossinna, in his book *German Prehistory, A Pre-eminently*

National Discipline (1914)[53] made scientifically respectable an archaeological approach with a distinctly Germanic bias that sought to link the distribution of remnants of material culture (particularly the form of pottery known as 'corded ware') with the dispersion of 'peoples' and 'tribes'. Kossinna's book was reprinted nine times, the seventh edition with a foreword by Adolf Hitler, who spoke of the need for national pride in the fact that 'the Germans already one thousand years before the foundation of Rome had experienced a cultural prime'.[54]

In the mid-nineteenth century, scientific rigour, or the semblance of it, was a less essential component of archaeological endeavour: Schliemann's approach to archaeology was neither cautious nor methodical, and his methods of interpretation displayed a similar exuberance. And the swastika, although less accessible and appropriate to twentieth-century methods of archaeological analysis than Kossinna's 'corded ware', was at once more seductive and more malleable evidence to the 'Aryo-Germanic' apologists of the nineteenth century. The very dullness and prosaic nature of what now constitutes bona fide prehistoric evidence presents the modern archaeologist with a problem: 'the prehistorian is witness to the sad fact that the ideals perish, and it is the cutlery and chinaware of a society that are imperishable.'[55] Glyn Daniel's statement that Schliemann had 'created a fresh chapter in the human past, had himself written prehistory'[56] is revealing, since it implies that the task of the archaeologist is to 'write the unwritten' and give names to the nameless. Yet the transformation from silence into speech, or from the unwritten to the written, is not strictly speaking an encoded *translation* from one language into another. At Hissarlik, Schliemann was unencumbered by the materialist archaeologist's hierarchy of ideal and prosaic: he had a *tabula rasa* on which to inscribe the past as he wished. He was assisted in the invention of his Aryan ancestors by the fact that he had a degree of freedom to invent his archaeological approach. The swastika, Schliemann had said, was 'of the greatest importance', and in this way the figure was confirmed as a significant and meaningful symbol.

In Schliemann's account of the swastika, it is possible to discern a parallel between the binary opposition made between instant recognition and laboured scholarly discussion on the one hand, and Homeric poetry and prosaic archaeology on the other.[57] There is an impatience with the thickets of scholarship, and a preference for the revelation by which one 'finds things' already referred to. Paradoxically, in Schliemann, this imaginative faculty was linked to a punctilious taxonomic instinct, which seems less unusual when one considers the average UFO enthusiast's enthusiasm for the careful cataloguing of 'sightings' of apparently isomorphic phenomena. The swastikas which Schliemann had found inscribed on spindle-whorls and terracotta spheres in the third or 'burnt' city of Hissarlik functioned throughout his Trojan campaigns as a device which sutured together various discourses: Homeric Troy to the 'Aryan' Vedas, Schliemann's exiled status to a Germanic ancestry, but most importantly, of material evidence to its textual exposition:

> All that can be said of the first settlers [of Hissarlik] is that they belonged to the Aryan race, as is sufficiently proved by the Aryan religious symbols met with in the strata of their ruins (among which we find the [image of swastika]) both upon the pieces of pottery and upon the small curious terra-cottas with a hole in the centre, which have the form of the crater of a volcano or of a *carrousel*.[58]

That the swastika performed a vital link ('These crosses... are of the highest importance to archaeology'[59]) between excavated object and explanatory text is demonstrated by the way in which the image represents itself as interpolated 'evidence' in Schliemann's books, not just in illustrations but by replacing the word 'swastika' in the body of his texts. The swastika formed the conduit between a silent piece of terracotta and a verbose myth of origin, something which could at once serve as the starting point for a discourse and its reifying agent. As with Zmigrodski's drawings, the image is assumed to constitute both sign and material evidence, which conveniently allows it to function *as evidence for itself*. Schliemann was at pains to invest the image with both a 'symbolic' and a religious status as one of 'the most sacred symbols of our Aryan forefathers',[60] a position that was sometimes defended through recourse to minor acts of fakery, such as when an actual leaden 'goddess' figure was adorned with a spurious swastika in Schliemann's *Ilios*.[61] The catalogue of the Schliemann collection in the Berlin Museum, compiled in 1902, twelve years after the archaeologist's death, notes that this leaden object was 'falsely shown with a swastika on the [pubic] triangle' in *Ilios*.[62] Here an excavated object has been enlisted in support of a pre-named 'sign-object': however, the predominance of the swastika on quotidian material culture such as spindle-whorls suggested an awkward shift away from Aryan epiphany and towards functionality, which could more plausibly be defended as a 'votive offering',[63] if a sacred context for the image such as the leaden goddess 'Artemis of Chaldea' could be established as well. The fairly clear evidence of a spindle-whorl industry at Hissarlik producing more-or-less identical objects was ignored in favour of the commodifying identity of the swastika sign, advertising Aryan ancestry from the Oxon to the Rhine. A reviewer for the *Illustrated London News*, in discussing the exhibition of 1877, noted that:

> One object appears to have been found in all four cities [of Troy] – i.e. the so-called whorls, round pieces, chiefly of terracotta, with a hole through the middle. According to Dr Schliemann, these were not used for spinning, hardly any of them showing traces of friction

or usage, but were votive offerings. These are ornamented with suns, stars, altars, animals and various unknown symbols. Specimens of these whorls almost fill one case; *they are arranged according to patterns* [my italics].[64]

In the following month's edition of the same periodical, 'various unknown symbols' have become 'mystic characters and figures' and the whorls are referred to as 'portable tokens or badges . . . held by privileged lay worshippers for their admission to the most solemn religious rites'.[65] Schliemann's display of these whorls according to their 'symbolic' markings rather than their object status was evidently having the desired effect. Once the religious stamp is identified, the object appears as merely its vehicle, the whole forming a 'portable token'.

QUEST, FERMENTATION AND SUBLIMITY

Eric Hobsbawm's leitmotifs of abstraction, ideology, false continuity and 'negative definition' all apply to Schliemann's construction of the swastika. However, what also needs to be examined is the nature of the relationship between India and Germany which allowed this remythologising of the image to take place. Karl Marx, in his letter on 'The Future Results of the British Rule in India'[66] of 1853, declared that 'Indian society has no history at all, at least no known history' a phrase that he might have been loath to apply to German society, despite his suggestion that his native land had theorised, rather than acted, itself into existence.[67]

In his letter on Britain's Indian colonies, Marx proposed a theory which he was later to revise, advocating the Westernisation of India in order that the necessary conditions for proletarian revolution should come about. The guiding principle of Marx's thought was that 'History' in the Hegelian sense is proper to Europe, and that India had not evolved towards dialectical perfection, but was an 'unresisting and unchanging society' whose fate was to be invaded and ruled, preferably by the Briton rather than the Turk, the Persian or the Russian.[68]

Despite this particularly broad and inviting path laid out by Marx, the British often had a problem grasping the sheer 'otherness' of Indian culture and its cognitive systems. Whereas Hegel, despite his opinion that Indian culture was irredeemably static, could find a *raison d'être* for what he saw as the surplus or 'inadequate' irrational element in its symbolism, other writers such as George Waring, in his *Ceramic Art in Remote Ages*, were frustrated by the perceived lack of consonance between the image of the Indian swastika and its absent meaning:

But neither in the hideous jumble of Pantheism – the wild speculative thought, the mystic fables, and perverted philosophy of life among the Buddhists – nor in the equally wild and false philosophy of the

Brahmins ... do we find any precise explanation of the meaning attached to this symbol, although its allegorical intention is indubitable.[69]

One of the better known examples of British incomprehension in the face of Indian art was John Ruskin's reaction to the Indian Mutiny of 1857. In his *The Two Paths* of 1859, Ruskin proposed a psycho-graphological equation between the abstract quality of Indian ornamental design and the alienated and savage mentality of its makers: '[Indian art] never represents a natural fact ... it will not draw a man, but an eight armed monster; it will not draw a flower, but only a spiral or a zig-zag.'[70] Later in his text Ruskin noted that 'ornamentation of that lower kind is pre-eminently the gift of cruel persons'. His opinion was not shared by design innovators such as Owen Jones and Henry Cole, who saw in Indian ornament the ideal opportunity to unite abstract flat pattern with British manufacturing methods. For Ruskin, however, both India and Industry represented soulless alienation from the 'natural fact', and for him, as Partha Miller has noted, the self-referential spiral of Indian ornament was equivalent to the cog-wheels of the machine:

The dire warning given to the manufacturers was that, instead of basing themselves on a study of nature, if they designed decorative ornament 'either in ignorant play of their own heartless fancy, as the Indian does, or according to the received application of heartless laws, as the modern European does ... there is but one word for [them] – Death'.[71]

This equation of abstraction with death recurs as one element of Wilhelm Worringer's hybrid and race-romantic conception of the Gothic, which will be examined in the following section. But for the present, it is sufficient to note that Ruskin's analysis of an Indian morphology baulked at the very same element of abstract 'meaninglessness' that George Waring saw in the Indian swastika. Ruskin's appeal to a reference in an objective natural fact is the same appeal that Waring makes to an 'allegorical intention' hidden by the image.

In contrast, the German romantic tradition of the symbol celebrated this autonomy of the signifying image from a direct and definite reference. A reading of Hegel's *Aesthetics* and his treatment of the 'symbolic' art of the East reveals how a romantic semiotics would possess many of the dialectically remedial characteristics which Hegel identifies as proper to the Oriental symbol, namely the qualities of 'quest', 'fermentation' 'mysteriousness', 'sublimity' and what can be read as an indefinite (mediating between finite and infinite) temporality.[72] Hegel's own definition of the romantic, it must be noted, did not fall into this category, since its transcendence was not that of the visible/individual to the invisible/sublime, but as Charles Karelis has noted 'the unity of the whole objective realm with the common factor of individual subjects'.[73] However, Hegel saw a surface similarity between the romantic and symbolic realms, with the essential distinction that 'in romantic art, the Idea, the deficiency of which in the symbol brought with it deficiency of shape, now has to be *perfected* in itself as spirit and heart'.[74] In other words, attempting to visualise the Absolute is a fruitless task. The 'deficiency' or 'inadequacy' of the Oriental symbol to the goals it has set for itself typifies the nature of the symbolic signifying image in general, which transcends a merely conventional relationship to meaning only to fall short of an essential unity with it. Rather than partaking of the missionary and Christian *Aufhebung* of Hegelian philosophy, an 'overcoming' in which sacrifice is eventually turned to the good, the swastika as both a Sanskrit word and a popular Hindu icon is instead an example of both the Indian aesthetic and the primitive symbolic form that Hegel had claimed could only offer a mimesis or ersatz of his Absolute Idea. In Indian art, he argued, no proper union of the concrete and the philosophical Absolute could occur, since all energy was transfixed at the level of an image which was a kind of iconolate heresy, misrepresenting the Absolute in the form of an indefinite visual extension. The autokinetic illusion of the swastika, in which the image may seem to be engaged in an indefinite but inconsequential motion, would also identify it as an example of this heresy.

Tension, anxiety, hybridity, a fruitless striving and a general *Sturm und Drang* are the hallmarks of Hegel's symbolic mode of representation, which perfectly accomplishes its own defeat. The model he applies to Hindu art perhaps more accurately describes a Western cult of self-expression with its roots in the romantic idea of the symbol. Self-expression seeks to contain the subject in the object, and ontology in the image in the form of a representation of the irrepresentable, which, in Hegel's terms, is 'interpreted as if the Idea itself were present in them'.[75] This 'giving of the known the dignity of the unknown' which the German poet and novelist Novalis saw as the defining characteristic of romanticism, indicates the desire for a secular transcendence, the *frisson* of expenditure within the economy of representation. The emphasis in German romantic aesthetics on the energetic struggle of becoming over the classical complacency of being exemplifies this attitude; furthermore, Hegel's views on the ambiguous relationship between the symbol and its meaning suggests the way in which a popular romantic nationalism could construct the symbol *ahistorically*. Since the symbol in this scheme is never either wholly arbitrary nor wholly consonant, its signifying image can occupy or have occupied several sites of meaning over time: 'the symbolic shape contains yet other characteristics of its own utterly independent of that which the symbolic shape signified *once*.'[76] In this way, the image presents itself as the multitude of possible things it may have meant and could mean, rather than the rational and historically situated value of what it actually *does* mean at a given moment, either in a conventional or an Absolute sense. Past and future are conflated in an experience of the sign in the present as a limitless potential: this is the hallmark of the kitsch romantic sublime. This ersatz of infinity is achieved, Hegel argues, in the mimetic quality of Indian art, in which the attempt is made to represent Absolute infinity as an indefinite visual extension: 'the most obvious way in which Hindoo art endeavours to mitigate this distinction [between the naturalistic and the Absolute] is ... by the measureless extension of its images ... the measure-lessness of time durations, or the reduplication of particular determinations.'[77] This is an example of 'the contradiction itself which passes for the true unification' and which mitigates against the possibility of an historical development:

> The Indians have proved themselves incapable of an historical interpretation of persons and events, because an historical treatment requires *sang-froid* in taking up and understanding the past on its own account in its actual shape with its empirical links, grounds, aims, and causes.[78]

Both the India of Hegel and Marx and Hobsbawm's Germany stand accused of 'ahistoricity'. Schliemann's Aryan ancestors are not historically or empirically 'traced', they are ahistorically constructed, like Hobsbawm's German nationalism. The swastika magically appears at Hissarlik unencumbered by a signified meaning and therefore free of history, and links are then forged between this image and the new Germany, a country now unified under Bismarck, and whose attachment to a centuries-old feudalism and aristocracy had been so strong as to circumvent Marx's hopes for a bourgeois-inspired revolution in 1848. At the time of the uprising, Marx commented that 'The German Bourgeoisie had developed ... so slowly, that it saw itself threateningly confronted by the proletariat ... at the very moment' of its threatening confrontation with feudalism and absolutism'.[79] It is worth comparing these words with his vision of a colonised and dialectically perfected India in 1853: 'When a great social revolution shall have mastered the results of the bourgeois epoch ... then only will human progress cease to resemble that hideous pagan idol, who would not drink the nectar but from the skulls of the slain.'[80]

In Marx's terms, both India and Germany fail to achieve the necessary bourgeois 'critical mass' which will propel them into the stream of history. In Germany, the development is perceived as uneven, in India it is seen as completely absent. Aryanism made it possible to accommodate both countries under a single sign of the swastika, a sign which expressed the racial/genetic continuity of a race, rather than the historical/evolutionary *development* of the revolutionary proletariat. In Fichte's *Addresses* of 1807–8, his dialectic of an ancient Teutonic Europe and 'ancient Asia' is synthesised in a vision of the German state as a *perpetuum mobile*, running on the inexhaustible fuel of Aryan race energy:

> Altogether different is the genuine German art of the State ... it seeks from the very beginning, and as the very first and only element, a firm and certain spirit. This is for it the mainspring, whose life proceeds from itself, and which has perpetual motion; the mainspring which will regulate, and continually keep in motion, the life of society.[81]

Fichte's image of the magical and self-generating machine was echoed by Adolf Hitler's declaration that both the principle of race continuity and the principle of 'creative work' towards maintaining the race idea could be discerned in his dynamically slanted swastika, an image which combined India with industry in the mass manufacture of the sign in a way which even Ruskin could not have foreseen.

THE DESTROYERS

In his introduction to the first edition of Schliemann's *Troy and its Remains*, Phillip Smith noted that the hill of Hissarlik 'answers at once to the primitive type of a Greek city, and to the present condition of the primaeval capitals of the East'.[82] In one sense this description is no more than the typical Aryanist reflex with regard to Greek culture that writers such as Martin Bernal have been keen to root out. However, the swastikas of Hissarlik allow us to examine the route from the Indian Vedic myths *via* Troy to Königswalde, in other words a specifically German rather than a generally pro-Greek and anti-Semitic interpretation. If this route is retraced, it becomes clear that Schliemann was rehearsing a narrative which had linked Germany to India for centuries, and that in the 1870s the archaeologist and Germany itself had common cause in their reinvention of this tradition. This Indo-German narrative dates back as far as the twelfth century, when an *Annolied* in praise of the Archbishop of Cologne declared 'they say that in that region [India] there are still people who speak German'.[83] Walter Liefer has noted that this idea persisted throughout the Middle Ages, well before the advent of modern Aryanism. However, it was nineteenth-century politics and philosophy of language which enabled such ideas to assume a new importance and contemporary relevance, and it was Aryanism which mediated between the migrant 'father ancestor' of India and the 'mother ancestor' of German autochthony.[84] It was the *Rigveda* (the 'Vedas' that are mentioned above), the Sanskrit epic poem of around the third century BC in which the tribe of the 'Aryas' is first mentioned, that provided Schliemann and his enlisted 'experts' with the mythological mirror-image of the Homeric poetry that had initially inspired the archaeologist. In the *Rigveda*, the Aryas lay siege to and conquer the forts of another tribe, the forts being interpreted as the defences of an indigenous people conquered by the chariot-riding Aryas, who had, it was supposed, advanced from their mysterious European *Urheimat*.[85] The attempt to make the prosaic facts of excavation fit the poetry of the Vedas was not Schliemann's prerogative: in 1947, Mortimer Wheeler, an acerbic critic of Schliemann's methods, suggested that the Aryas may have been responsible for the sudden disappearance of the Indus valley civilisation.[86] Only Schliemann and his cohorts, however, attempted to link two geographically distant epics to one archaeological site, although Colin Renfrew has suggested similarities between them:

> There is at least one other good example of the production of this kind of heroic poetry after a system collapse: the poetry of Homer. But Homer was writing sufficiently soon afterwards to have had some memory of the pre-collapse Mycenean age ... The *Rigveda* could well stand in the same position in relation to the Indus valley civilisation, except that, perhaps taking shape rather longer after the collapse, it does not really hark back to the golden age before it.[87]

The lynchpin connecting Troy to the Vedas was the swastika: excavated at 'Homeric' Hissarlik, and first named as 'swastika' in the Sanskrit grammar of Pânini on which the language of the Rigveda was based, it appeared to provide the perfect link. It was the 'third city' of Hissarlik, where artefacts bearing swastikas ranging from simple spindle-whorls to eight-sectioned terracotta spheres, were first encountered ('[the swastika] ... was evidently brought to Hissarlik by the people of the Third City, for it never occurs on objects from the first or second city'[88]), that Schliemann saw as the perfect candidate for exalted status as the site of the Trojan war, on account of clear evidence that the entire settlement had been destroyed by fire:

> As we have seen in the preceding pages, the third city of Hissarlik perfectly agrees with the Homeric indications as to the site of Troy ... the third city has, like the Homeric Ilios, been destroyed by the hand of an enemy in a fearful catastrophe, which fell on it so suddenly that the inhabitants had to leave a large part of their treasures behind.[89]

The parallel with the Vedic battles of the Aryas should not be ignored, and nor should the linking metaphor of invasion, destruction and genocide, a theme which Colin Renfrew has identified as that of the 'destroyers':

> Given that the Indus Valley civilisation came to a rather sudden end, which extinguished urbanism in India for a millenium, it is not surprising, in the migrationist climate of the earlier part of this century that scholars should have thought in terms of 'destroyers'.[90]

Half a century before the advent of Nazism, the image of the swastika was being associated with narratives of invasion and the sudden disappearance of an entire population. In his preface to Schliemann's *Ilios*, Rudolf Virchow wrote that at Hissarlik 'Asia and Europe for the first time encountered a war of extermination (*völkerfressendem Kampfe*)'.[91] This discourse was employed against the Nazi terror in the Reverend Norman Walker's pamphlet of 1939, *The Real History of the Swastika*, in which Schliemann's speculations were not only questioned but quite deliberately inverted:

> In the sixth and seventh cities of Troy very few swastikas were found, but in the third, fourth and fifth cities they were found in hundreds. That is to say, the swastika came in with the Hittites, and went out with the coming of the Aryans ... Wherever the Aryans migrated and destroyed the older civilization, the use of the swastika died out – it seems to be specially associated with the pig-tail wearing, hook-nosed and beardless Hittites, the early Elamites, Manchus, Huns and American Indians.[92]

It is interesting to note that Walker's pamphlet, in its attempt to redress the balance against the bias of Germanic prehistory, employed a similar strategy, that of yoking the swastika to a particular race. In challenging Schliemann's Aryan interpretation of the swastika, Walker neglected to challenge the use of the word Aryan as the umbrella racial designation of a language-group, finding it useful to turn the vision of a powerful and all-conquering tribe to his own metaphorical ends. Somewhat more cogent in this regard is another pamphlet, *The Swastika, a Study of Nazi Claims of its Aryan Origin*,[93] published in 1933 by Norman Brown, Professor of Sanskrit at the University of Pennsylvania. Here the word 'Aryan' is put in quotation marks, and although Brown was prepared to admit some links between the term and language and culture, he was adamant that 'in respect of physical stock it affirms practically nothing'.[94] Like Walker, however, Brown was keen to find some way to detach the Aryans from the swastika, asserting that its true home was amongst the pre-Vedic 'Dravidians', a peaceful and 'more advanced' culture destroyed by the invading Aryan hordes. In this way Brown challenged Schliemann's interpretation from the Indian side, just as Walker attempted to do with the swastikas of Hissarlik. Ultimately however, these ownership disputes appear to leave the Aryans (and thus the Nazis) more or less intact, and represent a further example of the academic debate over a context for the image which does nothing to challenge the successful construction of a 'sign field' of immediately recognisable and self-identical swastikas. The Nazis, however, are given short shrift in Brown's pamphlet:

> The present Nazi claims are untenable. Just as their theory of Aryan racial purity is fanciful, so, too, their use of the swastika as an Aryo-

Christian symbol, with aspects of anti-Judaism, anti-pacifism and anti-Marxism, is entirely arbitrary.[95]

Brown's reference to an 'Aryo-Christian' construction of the swastika is a theme which, like that of the 'destroyers', has its roots in the nineteenth century. According to Léon Poliakov,[96] it was Fichte, using an interpretation of the gospel of St John, who first proposed the idea that Jesus of Nazareth was not of Jewish descent, 'thus sweeping aside the greatest obstacle to the quest for an authentically German religion'. An elaboration of this theory as it was applied to the swastika can be found in *The Science of Religions*[97] by Emile Burnouf, honorary director of the French archaeological institute in Athens and one of Schliemann's closest collaborators. Burnouf worked as a cartographer for Schliemann, and is described by Leo Deuel as a polymath of 'outstanding calibre' who was Schliemann's teacher rather than his assistant. Such praise notwithstanding, Burnouf's text constructs a race mythology of the swastika, linking the figure not only to an Aryan thesis (and by extension to Germanic concerns[98]) but also to a specific and violent anti-Semitism.

Burnouf espoused a pseudo-scientific, pseudo-evolutionary model of the growth of religions, in an effort to prove that Christianity was in fact derived from the Aryan 'root-religion' with its origins in the East: 'Christianity as a whole has an Aryan doctrinal tendency.'[99] Judaism, on the other hand, was seen as the aberrant development of a lesser race, whose spiritual, intellectual and cranial inferiority he emphasised in a repellent fashion.[100] By applying this construction to the swastika, Burnouf was led to the conclusion that the figure was the true Aryan cross of Christianity: 'When Jesus was put to death by the Jews, this old Aryan symbol was easily applied to him; and the *swastika*, after successive transformations, became the "hastated cross" of the Christian moderns.'[101] This idea is arrived at by a process of syncretic comparison similar to that through which Schliemann had linked the swastika to the 'Centaurs of the Greeks'. Burnouf began by linking the figure with the Vedic fire god Agni, then by extension to Prometheus, seeing in the bound Prometheus a personification of the crucified Christ. Both schemes ultimately depended on the initial premise that the swastikas found at Hissarlik were identical to the swastikas of the East, despite Max Müller's warning to Schliemann that 'identity of form does as little prove identity of origin in archaeology as identity of sound proves identity of origin in etymology'.[102]

If we return to Schliemann's text linking the swastikas of Königswalde to those uncovered at Troy quoted above (p. 131), a similar privileging of sign recognition across space and time over the immediate relationship of the swastika to its context can be noted, and the distinction between simple identification and a complex reading is clearly drawn. In the same way in which Schliemann identified 'many hundreds' of swastikas amongst the mass of material evidence and variety of marks found at Hissarlik, his textual excavation proceeded by sorting out the symbol 'recognised at first glance' from a heterogeneous mass of apparently irrelevant academic dialogue. What is implied is that there is a right and a wrong way to approach one's ancestors, and that others (the ones who have merely 'discussed' the swastika) have hitherto been blind to the correct method. Not only the swastika itself, *but the way in which it is perceived and comprehended*, must be Aryo-Germanic. The culturally constructed value is again passed off as the true coin of an immediate recognition. As Pierre Bourdieu has said of the aesthetic gaze in general: 'The encounter ... is not "love at first sight" as is generally supposed, and the act of empathy, *Einfühlung* ... implies the implementation of a cognitive acquirement, a cultural code.'[103]

There is an immediate parallel with the Nazi period, insofar as in the 1930s, the burning of books was simply the first step towards imposing a *Gleichschaltung*, a common framework, for the activity of *reading*. Here the Germanic text is created and defined by the removal of all that is declared un-Germanic, and a pure form is that which remains when the impure has been removed from the field of vision. This is the 'double-bind' logic described by Jean-François Lyotard in his refutation of the revisionist historian Faurisson, who had demanded to hear the testament of a deportee who had seen 'with his own eyes' a gas chamber.[104] Lyotard points out that this demand, in which the only possible witness is one who can no longer testify, satisfies the totalitarian logic which 'knows no other reality other than the established one, and ... holds the monopoly on procedures for the establishment of reality'. In 1889, this *Gleichschaltung* was over forty years distant; and yet Schliemann's commentator Zmigrodski's criteria of evidence, and his 'law of the swastika' which establishes the morphology of a symbol of screening out all that this symbol is not, is the ethnographic archetype of this logic. Lyotard's assertion is that Nazism requires nothing from the non-Aryan except that it should cease to exist. Zmigrodski's construction of a 'pure' swastika by subtracting all unwanted elements established the sacred space of Aryan civilisation through the removal of a supposedly primitive Semitic over-growth, a procedure which at once sequestrated the swastika and prepared it for the new role of an image whose function would be racially divisive. At this point Schliemann's and Zmigrodski's uses for the swastika begin to differ: for the archeologist the removal of context allows space for nostalgia, and a 'Broad Aryan' vision of the ancestral home, whereas the librarian's action is more prophetic: the deracinated and thus 'purified' form is redefined as the apotropaic agent of racial hygiene.

ARTEFACT SIGNALS

Shorn of their links to a mythology of race origins, the debates on Indo-European philology still persist in a rarefied and highly specialised form today; however, the academic limelight they once enjoyed has been usurped by a structuralist socio-linguistics and its many posthumous variants, which, by employing the notion of a structured set of differences, appear to reject the idea of a philosophical 'tracing back' of diverse language elements to their common roots. For the greater part of our century, the synchrony of structuralism has satisfied the radical modernist demand for a functionalist language model which could, like a functionalist aesthetics, act unencumbered by the ornaments of history and tradition. It was for this reason that Saussurean structural linguistics became intellectually popular in post-revolutionary Russia, via such figures as Sergei Karcevskij, who had worked with Ferdinand de Saussure in Switzerland, and who returned to Moscow in 1917 to take his part in the 'Formalist' school of Russian linguistics.[105] However, many of the central tenets of Formalism were to be challenged by the publication in 1929 of *Marxism and the Philosophy of Language* under the name of Vladimir Nikolaevich Volosinov.[106] This text not only challenged Formalist theories (which it described as 'abstract objectivism') but dug deeper in positing a methodological link between Saussurean linguistics and Indo-European language theory. It is widely believed that this book was principally the work not of Volosinov but of Mikhail Bakhtin; I intend to concur with that view,[107] and also with the opinion of Graham Pechey, for whom Bakhtin's philosophy was 'a post-structuralism co-inciding with the displacement that brought about structuralism itself'.[108] Bakhtin's critique of the 'abstract objectivist' and hypostasising tendency in both Saussurean and Indo-European linguistics, and of their mutual reliance on the technique of recognising an 'artefact signal'[109] can be seen to relate to the institution of the swastika by Schliemann and others as the visible mark (artefact) which could serve to reify (using the alliance of a 'race' with its 'trace') the concept of a structurally derived proto-Aryan language. For Mikhail Bakhtin, the methods of Indo-European comparative linguistics were the source of Saussure's emphasis on a static structure preceding and governing the communicative act. Despite Saussure's emphasis on synchronic values, his structures are still conceived as the precedents for any kind of dialogue. As Robert Stam has suggested in his conceptual summary of the Bakhtin school, the Russian saw in both Saussurean and Indo-European linguistics 'a kind of linguistic necrophilia, a nostalgia for deceased languages'.[110] Aryanism should also be included in this necrophiliac definition as an ancestor-worship conducted through the medium of the symbol.

I have suggested that the move from Indo-European language theory to an Aryan race is a temporal shift from a synchronic comparison across diverse languages to a diachronically conceived original set of native Aryan speakers, and in this sense, as Max Müller suggested, is as absurd as the notion of a 'brachycephalic grammar'. However, Bakhtin did not allow either philology or structuralism to escape so lightly: he suggested that both must of methodological necessity work with material which is both 'dead' and 'alien' to the actual practice of speech utterances and human dialogue in a living language, and that such an emphasis revealed a hegemonic strategy on the part of a linguistic 'caste' to translate the meaning of 'the word' to the multitude: 'the first linguists and the first philologists were always and everywhere priests.'[111] Once linguistic meaning is perceived as essentially alien to the accidents of dialogue and *parole* ('externally changed and removed from the routine of life'), Bakhtin argued that the responsibility for language and for the generation of meaning is taken away from those who use it for the purpose of intra-personal communication, and placed outside their control. It is important to note that Bakhtin identifies this an essentially 'colonial' strategy:

> The grandiose organising scheme of the alien word, which always either entered upon the scene with alien force of arms and organisation or was found on the scene by the young conqueror nation of an old and once mighty culture captivated, from its grave, so to speak, the ideological consciousness of the newcomer-nation – this role of the alien word led to its coalescence in the depths of the historical consciousness of nations with the idea of authority, the idea of power, the idea of holiness, the idea of truth, and dictated that notions about the word be pre-eminently orientated towards the alien word.[112]

It could be argued that to apply this critique to the 'Aryanisation' of the swastika would be to confuse Bakhtin's linguistic 'word' with a material image. However, in the passage quoted above, we are already in the realm of the reified and alienated 'artefact-signal', the idea of the fixed, secret and monumental sign which represents the border and the limit of a commonly understandable and mutually communicative language. In Thomas Wilson's book on the swastika, the anthropologist quoted a report on the reception of the Christian cross by native Americans: 'this emblem was generally accepted by the savages as the only tangible feature of a new system of belief that was filled with subleties too profound for their comprehension.'[113] In this instance, the symbol is a device heralding the unknown, the unphrasable and the incomprehensible. Aryanism both colonised the Oriental swastika and reconstructed it as an emblem which was later used by Nazism to colonise Occidental space, threatening an invasion of the West under the sign of the East.

Max Müller's witty refutation of the Aryanists provided a much-needed deflation of the myth: yet Bahktin shows how the techniques of Indo-

European philology were already implicated in the myth-making process which was to result in the racist excesses of Michael Zmigrodski and Emil Burnouf. And in his emphasis on the deracination of language elements from the context of their utterance, Bahktin's theories have direct bearing on Schliemann's treatment of the swastika. Wrenched from its stratigraphic context, the swastika became the signal which could be compared with similar signals in a rough imitation of the more complex methods of philological comparison. In this light, Müller's professional/philological censoring of the word 'swastika' simply allowed Schliemann to conduct amateur Indo-European comparisons using the image instead. Edward Said[114] has referred to Müller as one of the philological 'priests': it may be that in this instance we are seeing not so much a concern for the Indian swastika *per se* as an example of the professional pride that wished to keep the brachycephalic brigade and the blundering amateurs out of Indo-European philology. Schliemann's institution of the swastika as the Aryan sign *par excellence* was a caricature of analytical method, but it was a caricature whose material expression in archaeology delineated the essence of an approach in which the 'philologist-linguist tears the monument out of that real domain and views it as if it were a self-sufficient, isolated entity'.[115]

SEEING THE SWASTIKA

Michael Zmigrodski was keen to subsume a diversity of morphological varieties and visual 'expressions' of the swastika under the rubric of a recognisable 'pure' symbol. He believed that careless execution of the sign was sufficient proof that it was universally recognisable to the inhabitants of the third city of Troy:

> I propose that all the figures [of the swastika] are religious symbols and not ornaments, because they are too negligently drawn... proving that it was so familiar to everyone that even the most cursory execution was sufficient to effect a recognition.[116]

Zmigrodski adds 'It is always so with symbols'. Here the notion of a communicable sign is firmly linked to the idea of a uniform set of similar signals, and as with Saussure's *parole* ('we cannot put it [speech] into any category of human facts, for we cannot discover its unity'[117]) the manner in which a language-form is expressed by a particular person in a particular historical context is marginalised. Saussure had spoken of a language which 'governs signs' and under which, presumably, speech assumes the role of an unruly populace. This is in direct opposition to Bahktin's model, in which the normative elements of language are less important than the way in which these elements are rendered meaningful through dialogic utterance.

The example which Zmigrodski used to illustrate his argument was that of a hastily drawn yet instantly recognisable Christian cross, from which he concluded that the inhabitants of Hissarlik worshipped a supreme being in the image of the swastika 'of pure form'. The method of artefact recognition again immediately places the meaning of the sign beyond the reach of ordinary mortals and quotidian realities, and confers visionary status on the one who perceives what others cannot.

An earlier text by Zmigrodski, *Die Mutter bei den Völkern des Arischen Stammes*[118] (The Mother of the People of the Aryan Family), published in Munich in 1886, was more explicitly racist in its treatment of the swastika (Plate 6). Subtitled 'an anthropological-historical sketch' and with its title page adorned with a single left-handed swastika, the publication of this book coincided with the height of 'Aryan mania' in Europe. Again the method of 'artefact recognition' is to the fore, and is on this occasion specifically linked to a concept of miscegenation: referring to the discovery by Schliemann of a swastika on a fragment of pottery at a depth of 16 meters (below the strata containing the many hundreds of swastikas found in the 'burnt city'), Zmigrodski concluded that this 'oldest and purest'[119] occurrence of the swastika, found in a discrete form, was dissimulated through time into shapes which were split or broken in the upper levels, and whose meaning was eventually lost in a decorative scheme where 'the original symbol is simply an ornament'.[120] Zmigrodski then took his argument further, identifying the dissimulated Aryan swastika in Greek fret patterns, and concluding that all Aryan *Volksornamentik* concealed the form of the swastika as its original generative symbol.

Although Zmigrodski's concept of morphological miscegenation was replaced in his later text with the logic of 'familiarity', the common theme of both publications was that of a recognised origin and the recovery, through the weeding out of extraneous visual utterances, of the alien word. It is also significant that in his earlier book, the loss for which the swastika is the fetishised substitute is the loss of 'Die Mutter' of the Aryan race: Tacitus' *Germania* is quoted as 'unmistakable evidence of the Mother epoch'[121] of Aryan autochthony. The *Germania* was one of the key texts of the Aryan myth, and was used by Fichte to represent the German struggle for self- determination against the forces of invasion and miscegenation. Zmigrodski perceived in Tacitus' Roman yoke the forces which would eventually occlude the time of the divine mother: both prostitution and lesbianism are cited as evidence of how far this spiritual 'mother' principle had declined in modern times. The visual analogy for this fall from grace could be seen, he argued, in the hem of the garment of the Virgin Mary, once adorned with a sacred inscription which had become debased into a superficial (*inhaltlos*) ornament.[122]

Zmigrodski claimed that this was also the case with the swastika, emblem of the Aryan *Mutterepoche* which he saw, paradoxically, as representing its own loss of pure symbolic form in the shape of a debased ornamental 'Hälfe der Swastika'. Here representation is divided in two: the arbitrary or meaningless ornamental sign stands for the absence of its meaningful symbolic former self. This echoes, within the domain of a single sign, the 'classical semiology' described by Jacques Derrida,[123] in which the sign maps onto the loss and alienation incurred by the act of representation itself. Homi Bhabha,[124] in his writings on the discourses of colonialism, has argued that the fetishisation of the Oriental (alien or 'other') sign is more than an individual Freudian quirk, and in fact effects a splitting of the 'Western subject' as a social whole, in which the primal absence and substitution which troubles Occidental representation is transferred to an Oriental sign whose sole function must be to contain that absence, and stand as a landmark for that border beyond which our language either cannot, or should not pass: 'the place of otherness is fixed in the West as a subversion of Western metaphysics and is finally appropriated by the West as its limit text, the anti-West.'[125] In Zmigrodski's text, the Oriental term 'swastika', rather than the German *Hakenkreuz* is used as the sign for an image which stands for both the nostalgia of a primal loss and the yearning for a return.

This 'occult of a non-knowledge' through which the unseen is made visible in the form of the swastika places us back with the misrepresented and misrecognised Absolute of Hegel's Oriental symbol: the iconophile heresy which attempts a visual mimesis of the infinite. The occult hybrid of the known and the unknown that formed Zmigrodski's mother image of the swastika is also the Freudian 'scopophiliac' device through which forbidden or repressed desires may be indulged as an image if not as a reality. The Freudian psychoanalyst Karl Abraham, in his essay on scopophilia[126] of 1913, was already drawing parallels between an individual neurotic desire to 'maintain and cultivate uncertainty'[127] and the corresponding monotheistic, logocentric prohibition of all doubt and uncertainty from language. In his essay, Abraham notes that the German word for doubt, *Zweifel*, reveals that all uncertainty is a doubling (*zwei* = two) and this doubling is precisely what a monotheistic faith forbids: 'The prohibition against images [in the Decalogue] immediately follows the commandment to recognise only one god, i.e. the commandment designed to eliminate all hesitation (doubt) between father and mother.'[128] Thus, argued Abraham, the institution of an image or representation immediately introduces the problematic of division: doubt literally 'enters the picture'. But since the neurotic is attempting to obey the law of the father, the forbidden desire to see the mother is replaced by a representation of that desire, through which the act of looking can be indefinitely prolonged: 'his libido is no longer directed to the forbidden (incestuous) aim, no longer to that which one *must not* see, but that which one *cannot* see.' It is in this way that the 'mysterious symbol' is instituted as a scopophiliac device, where a forbidden gaze can be indulged in safety. Here the symbol becomes both the landmark for a forbidden territory and the specular tool for viewing it by proxy.

In his writing on the swastika, Zmigrodski described a prehistoric traject-ory through which the symbolic value of the image, whose origin lies in the *Mutterepoche*, comes under the law of the father with the advent of Greek culture, and whose symbolic value is consequently masked and censored in ornament.[129] His self-appointed task was to reinstitute the swastika as the sign of the absent mother. There is also the larger question of Zmigrodski's emphasis on recognition over meaning, an emphasis which itself prolonged the act of looking (for other *examples* of the swastika) at the expense of the rationalist ideal of final closure and a definitive decoding. Quite often, the late nineteenth and early twentieth-century discourse on the swastika indulges in the former whilst advancing under cover of the latter:

> We have given the remarks of various writers on this symbol . . . and it will be seen that, although they are more or less vague, uncertain, and confused in their description . . . still, with one exception, they all agree that it is a mystic symbol, peculiar to some deity or other, bearing a special signification, and generally believed to have some connection with one of the elements – water.[130]

George Waring's statement demonstrates that the swastika could achieve definition only as the paradoxical sign of uncertainty, whose endless reinterpretation maintained, rather than escaped from, a fetishising of doubt. The fetish, however, is a device whose primary ambivalence of presence and absence is recapitulated in an ambiguous shift between fear and desire. Following Freud in his essay on 'Fetishism' of 1927, Homi Bhabha has pointed out that either affection or hostility can gain the upper hand in the construction of the fetishised object, reflected in a colonialist discourse as either the projection of a desired fantasy or as race hatred.[131] In Zmigrodski's text, and in other examples of a 'extreme Aryan'[132] dis-course on the swastika, we find both a nostalgic evocation of loss (the good and civilised Aryan) and a hostile rejection of an abhorred race (the savage and primitive Semite) bound up in one image which is tem-porally and geographically 'other'. Here the swastika keeps the Aryan within and the Semite without, yet both occupy the same exclusion zone, the alien space bordered by the image itself.

Bhabha has also argued that for the construction of the fetish/stereotype to occur, any contextual meanings appropriate to the chosen Oriental object must be censored and expunged: 'what is denied is any knowledge of cultural otherness as a differential sign, implicated in specific historical and discursive conditions.'[133] This opposition of the stereotypical and static border to a fluid discursive exchange recalls Bahktin's description of how the 'artefact signal' is displaced from its context, the act of alienating an object of discourse which is then, by a *fait accompli*, recognised as alien and 'other' in an abstract, ahistorical way. As I have suggested, Schliemann's physical deracination of the swastika from its stratigraphic context is echoed in the work of his commentators such as Zmigrodski, who carry on the work of displacement where the archaeologist left off. This is not simply a 'misinterpretation' of the swastika: it is the tactical refusal to interpret beyond the level of the recognition and naming of a repeated signal that enables Zmigrodski, in his text of 1891,[134] to identify the swastika as the sign of an unknown god, a 'Deus Ignotus': a clear description of the occult device through which the unseen, as a feared or desired object, can be visualised by proxy in the conjuring-up of a 'symbol'.

It is on this issue of an 'unknown God' that Count Goblet D'Alviella attempted a critique[135] of those authorities who firmly ascribed to the swastika an 'Aryan' origin. D'Alviella, however, did not assert that the whole notion of an original race equipped with a root language had been insufficiently proved, but that the links between the Aryans and the swastika were tenuous. Whilst citing the phonetic evidence of Indo-European language study, and the subsequent assumption of an *Ursprache*, D'Alviella stated that it was yet another leap of faith from that assumption to symbolism, and from the symbol to the theories of R. P. Greg and Ludwig Müller, the former proposing that the swastika had been the symbol of the supreme god the Aryans had worshipped before their diaspora, and Müller overbidding by claiming that this god had in fact been 'the divinity who comprehended all the gods, or, again, the omnipotent God of the universe',[136] thus neatly equipping the root-race with a primal sign for an original deity. D'Alviella dealt firmly with Müller's 'generic sign for divinity', and the reasoning through which a deity of whose name we are ignorant becomes a nameless deity. He was also unsure that our ancestors would have been capable of so abstract a concept, concluding:

> Upon those who wish to make the *gammadion* [swastika] a legacy of the 'primitive' Aryans, it is incumbent to prove that these Aryans practised symbolism; that amongst their symbols the *gammadion* had a place, and that this *gammadion* typified the old *Dieu Pater*, the Heavenly Father of subsequent mythologies.[137]

THE RETURN OF ULYSSES

An alternative to the narrow focus of nineteenth-century Aryanism is to be found in the panoptic vision of Thomas Wilson's *The Swastika, the Earliest Known Symbol and its Migrations*.[138] Despite the startling assurance of his title, Wilson proposed to gather rather than to apply interpretations, staying true to his diffusionist theme by describing his aim as the 'diffusion of knowledge among men'.[139] Judicial language also keeps cropping up throughout his text, supporting his claim to be outside the interpretative fray. Wilson's table of contents, with its classifications of 'swastikas with four arms crossing at other than right angles, the ends bent ogee and to the left' followed by 'swastikas of different kinds on the same object'[140] recalls the minutiae of courtroom evidence, and his careful discrimination of cultural and morphological differences seems opposed to the recognition of the same favoured by Zmigrodski. However, his 'map showing distribution of the swastika' charts a migratory line of identical images supporting both Wilson's diffusionist ethic and his underlying principle of an original 'intention' controlling the diversity of swastika forms in a variety of locations. Wilson could not avoid the lure of the origin presented by the swastika. Unlike the Aryanists, however, he was preoccupied with the diachronic miscegenation of a purpose and a *raison d'être* for the image, not simply the evidence of a pure form:

> The straight line, the circle, the cross, the triangle, are simple forms, easily made, and might have been invented and re-invented in every age of primitive man and in every quarter of the globe . . . But the Swastika was probably the first to be made with a definite intention and a continuous or consecutive meaning, the knowledge of which passed from person to person, from tribe to tribe, from people to people, and from nation to nation, until, with possibly changed meanings, it has finally circled the globe.[141]

This statement placed Wilson on the opposite side of the diffusionist debate from 'evolutionists' such as Adolf Bastian, who had argued a form of psychic parallelism whereby mankind everywhere tended to produce similar forms and ideas. Wilson instead used those same forms and ideas to support the idea of prehistoric migrations from a centre or centres of diffusion.[142] In the same way that the similarity of Egyptian and Central American pyramids was perceived by some as clear evidence of migration from the former to the latter, Wilson at one point attempted to argue that the use of the swastika in American Indian culture might be due to the influence of Buddhism: 'How did this ancient, curious and widespread sign, a recognised symbol of religion of the Orient, find its way to the bottom of one of the mounds of antiquity in the Scioto valley?'[143] His idea of what constituted 'meaning' was consonant with the 'definite intention' he discerned in the morphology of the image: '[the swastika is] an intentional sign, with intentional, though perhaps different, meanings.'[144] Wilson also posed several rhetorical questions that seem to express the frustration of the cryptologist. As well as demanding 'By what people were they made? In what epoch? For what purpose?' Wilson also asked 'Why should we feel ourselves compelled to accept these signs as symbols of a hidden meaning?' Like Hegel's 'symbol' the problem that the swastika presented to the discourse of rationalist anthropology was that of the image as a 'semi-propositional statement',[145] neither wholly arbitrary nor wholly consonant, yet one with the history and appearance of 'having meant', or having meant *once*, in some primal or prehistoric scene. Wilson's swastika is cast in a heroic role, that of the adventurer, a disguised or dissimulated semiotic Ulysses, unrecognisable after having 'circled the globe'.

Wilson was not an Aryanist: judgement is once again reserved, since he wished instead to imply a link between the migration of bronze-age cultures and a supposed migration of the swastika. For all his interest in Buddhism, Wilson was also convinced that we must drop all pretensions to the view that the swastika is or was fundamentally a sacred sign, 'that is, holy and sacred in the light of godliness, piety, or morality'.[146] Along with evidence of the use of the swastika on prehistoric household objects, which he believed implied a secular use as 'amulet' or 'talisman', he criticised those authorities who found sufficient proof in the fact that the swastika was sometimes to be found in conjunction with representations of deities already labelled as 'cosmological' (lunar, solar, etc.), the one interpretation appearing naturally to bear out the other. This definition of meaning applied to the swastika, according to Wilson, thus became the syllogistic interpretation of an interpretation, a method with which he was to take issue: 'In forming the foregoing theories ... the authors have been largely controlled by the alleged fact of the substitution and permutation of the Swastika sign on various objects with recognised symbols of different deities.'[147] He also declared that: 'All pretense of the holy or sacred character of the Swastika should be given up, and it should ... be considered as a charm, amulet, token of good luck or good fortune.'[148]

Wilson's idea of an amulet or talisman pointed the way beyond his own philosophical quandary, through which the visually uninterpretable is something which seems to be controlled by some missing *verbal* encoding or programming. It could be argued that Wilson was an anthropologist who had fallen into a primitive trap, his gaze fixed and held by the specular device of the swastika. Alfred Gell, in an essay on the 'technology of enchantment' has referred to the design volutes on the canoe prow-boards of the Trobriand Islands as weapons of war designed to 'dazzle the beholder and weaken his grip on himself'.[149] Certainly Wilson's compulsive vision of swastikas on the carpets of the National Museum might be regarded as an instance of such a hypnotic effect. But Gell goes further:

> The canoe board is a potent psychological weapon, but not as a direct result of the visual effects it produces. Its efficacy is to be attributed to the fact that these disturbances, mild in themselves, are interpreted as evidence of the magical power emanating from the board.[150]

Wilson consciously sought to avoid the visually hypnotic effect of the swastika by denying that it appeared to move, but he could not avoid the lure of the talisman. The talisman is a figure which includes both an object and its representation, a sign whose power is written on its surface rather than being 'written elsewhere'.[151] Wilson's 'intention' theory and his identification of the image as 'amulet' recognised this power, but stopped short of the realisation that the swastika was not formed and set in motion by words, but had instead moved *through* a series of coded interpretations, both in his own text and in a succession of global contexts, acting as the vehicle of meanings rather than their equivalent image. It is clearly not the meaning, but the image, that migrates. Wilson's swastika map shows the 'heroic' swastika slipping through successive interpretative nets, propelled by its own secret purpose and intention. In my introduction, I suggested that any resemblance between Wilson's map and the trajectory of Nazi conquest is no accident, since Hitler's use of the image was as a landmark for the successive conquest of *space*, using the mythology of an Aryan conquest over time, and his aim was the application of the swastika to a totality of forms and surfaces. And as with the talisman, the alternately promising and threatening message of the Nazi swastika was understood by a reading from symbol to symbol and from surface to surface, rather than from surface to depth, withholding and delaying the symbolic referent whilst offering it as the promise of the past to be accomplished in the future. The colonising trajectory of Nazism was potentially as global as the network shown in Wilson's map; but no matter how far the sign field could have extended, the arrival of the Aryan referent promised by the Aryan symbol would have been indefinitely delayed.

Thomas Wilson could not work beyond the paradigm comparing symbols to words, because of his unsolved paradox of a single intention and multiple meanings. However, it is precisely this paradigm which has been placed in doubt by anthropologists in the second half of the twentieth century, followed inevitably by critiques of those critiques. Dan Sperber's polemical and idiosyncratic brand of post-structuralism has given short shrift to cryptology and structuralism alike. Cryptology is described as content to examine an element in isolation, divorced both from cultural context and a relationship to other symbols in that culture, and semiology, though 'culture-specific', as positing a decodable set of meanings as the basis of symbolic activity. In his *Rethinking Symbolism*, Sperber's claim, the basic message of which was elaborated in later texts, was that symbols can function *as symbols* without a hidden or unconscious other meaning to refer to. 'Symbolism' as here defined is a universal cognitive phenomenon, whose essence and application is radically different from a language employing words as a currency of representation.[152]

Sperber's critique also suggests how in an emphatically rationalist society, an irrational image will be interpreted as 'archaic', not because the irrational is somehow logically or sub-cortically 'pre-rational' but because in a society which sees itself as evolving through making more and more sense of the world, irrationality can appear in no other light. In his essay 'Is Symbolic Thought Pre-Rational?'[153] Sperber argues that the opposite is in fact the case, and that rationality precedes symbolic processing, which is a 'fail-safe' system for material that will not submit to a rational explanation. His argument is summed up in his description of 'three principles' of symbolism:

> When some information challenges the basic assumptions of a cognitive system, it will be symbolically processed, whatever the degree of intellectual alertness.
> When the degree of intellectual alertness is very low, most information processed tends to overload the rational device and thus to trigger a symbolic evocation.
> Mastery of rational, culturally adapted schemata will proportionately limit the occasions on which symbolic interpretations must necessarily occur.[154]

Sperber's text does not give much space to the rhetorical and coercive possibilities his model suggests, and which I have described as heralding, delimiting and directing the visual movement towards 'making sense' of a visual or textual landscape. However, Sperber's 'third principle' of symbolism provides a clue as to how the swastika was given a cognitively prehistoric status in the nineteenth century, as an image resisting a rationalist closure, and therefore as one which was constantly being processed according to a 'symbolic' method out of line with a rationalist orthodoxy. It could be argued that the swastika was defined as a symbol because the only cognitive schemata that yielded results with it was the symbolic. Returning to the definition of the swastika as the 'sign of non-signability', we can see that here the image comes to represent the symbolic realm or the symbolic process *per se*, as a meta-symbol or 'symbol of symbolism', a status which Aryanism reflected by naming the image as the 'symbol of symbols', set apart from all others and representable only by itself. In the modern era, the era of infinite translatability and exchange, this particular role can only be seen as remedial, reactionary or nostalgic.

This same argument has also been applied to the sociology of memory: 'the history of memory is one of its steady devaluation as a source of knowledge.'[155] Memory as the constant, 'phatic'[156] and intra-personal activity of reshaping and re-membering the material of tradition is replaced in the modern era by static and external mnemonic systems such as photography and text. In the Aryan myth, the anti-modernist, anti-rationalist values of symbolism and an ancestral and orally transmitted memory are appealed to through the swastika, as the emblem of an Aryan speech. This raises the question of how an image can be effectively bound to an ideology of the phonetic when it so obviously resists being dissolved or obliterated in printed text. Suzanne Küchler and Walter Melion[157] have suggested ways in which a visual, as well as an oral, phatic memory can be socially established, and how the activity of inscribing or representing can be seen to be equivalent to the activity of rehearsing or remembering:

> The hand, when it inscribes an image on a material surface, is precipitating memory, shaping it and consolidating it. The image documents this complex interplay between recollection and handiwork.[158]

This particular variety of externalisation differs from photography and the printed text, since it constitutes a recognisable social signature, not the operation of a disembodied technology. I have already referred to the status conferred on the swastika as 'Aryan handwriting' and it is this construction which maintains the sense of a meaning visually written onto the image through its repetition. The swastika then becomes an expression of a Aryo-Germanic 'attitude', the frozen gesture which acts as a cultural mirror to those who use it and identify with it, inviting the completion of meaning not within the sign as content but outside of the sign in the body, as the pseudo-awakening of race identity. The complete visualisation of the phatic principle, through which memory itself becomes the thing which is remembered, occurs in Nazism, which constructed its sign field as the simulacrum of race memory, a constant rehearsal of the gesture which is both attractive (the mirror) and to the 'non-Aryan' represents a repulsive and coercive threat.

Once more, the relevant question becomes not 'what does this symbol mean?' but 'what does this message achieve by being symbolically constituted?' In Aryanism and, ultimately in Nazism, the visual image of the swastika was constructed and put to use, in which case it is worth asking 'why the swastika?' On the other hand, in Thomas Wilson's exhaustive taxonomies we see a textual deracination of the image without any subsequent use for the motif other than as the object of an indefinite reinterpretation. A fascination with the talisman has Wilson seeing swastikas everywhere by the end of his book, but this repeated visual signal is not enough. The rationalist anthropologist could not be content with *seeing* the unseen like Zmigrodski and Blavatsky; his Cartesian text attempts to separate a knowledge of the swastika from that which is visually known, and therefore tries to *name* the unseen.

SYMBOL AND ORNAMENT

It is this transformation of a perceived 'symbolic use' into a presumed 'symbolic essence' that forms the unacknowledged stimulus for much discussion of the swastika in the nineteenth century. The concept of symbols as being dependent on, rather than the agents of, a unit of meaning frustrated most efforts at a reasoned discussion of the swastika. It seemed puzzling that the swastika could be used as a symbol in two disparate places without there being an identity of meaning to support the identity of the image. It is also significant that the only alternative to the 'meaningful symbol' view of the swastika was the contrasting absolute of the 'meaningless ornament'. As soon as the idea of meaning was disposed of, the symbol was also eclipsed, to be replaced by the notion of the swastika as mere form. The 'ornamentalist' faction of this either/or debate is well represented in Andrew Lang's *Custom and Myth* of 1910:

> The svastika, as it is called . . . is found everywhere . . . as a natural bit of ornament. The allegorising fancy of the Indians gave it a mystic meaning, and the learned have built I know not what worlds of religious theories on the pre-Christian cross, which is probably a hasty bit of decorative work with no religious meaning at all.[159]

Lang's indignant reaction to the accumulated interpretations of the swastika is understandable. But it is based on precisely the same understanding of what constitutes a symbol as those authorities with whom he demurs. In this instance, the swastika fails the 'meaning test' that others apply and reapply because of the symbolic history of the image. For Lang, instead, this same symbolic history is an example of how 'the art of savages' has misconstrued nonsense as sense, and ornament as symbol. Thomas Wilson made this opposition of ornament and symbol synchronic rather than universal, which allowed him to hold both views simultaneously: 'however many meanings it may have had . . . it was always ornamental as well.'[160] However, the split between the 'meaning function' of the symbol and the insignificance of the ornament is retained. Augustus Pugin, however, was prepared to describe the swastika as 'a mystical ornament'. Citing the authority of one Augustini Antonii Georgi, Pugin declared that the swastika was the symbol of a god crucified for the human race: 'From these accounts it would appear that the fylfot [swastika] is a mystical ornament, not only adopted among Christians in primitive times, but used, as if prophetically, for centuries before the coming of our Lord.'[161] Georgi's text, which was published by the Sacred Congregation for the Propagation of the Faith in 1762, was more concerned with rooting out Manichaean heresies than with promoting mystical doctrine. However, it provides an example of a parallel between the Eastern swastika and the Christian cross which extends further back than the date Martin Bernal has identified as the beginning of the Aryanist discourse.[162]

The terms of the 'ornament or symbol?' discussion also bore upon the issue of the diffusion and migration of the swastika. Goodyear, in his *Grammar of the Lotus*, claimed that the swastika had 'originally' been a fragment of the Egyptian meander, whereas Sir George Birdwood held the contrary view, arguing that the swastika as symbol had preceded its ornamental applications.[163] In a typically Aryanist fashion, R. P. Greg wished to exclude both the ornamental and the symbolic swastika from Judaism:

'Both the Greek fret and the fylfot [swastika] appear to have been unknown to the Semitic nations as an ornament or as a symbol... It is, I believe, generally admitted that the fylfot is of early Aryan origin.'[164] Donald A. Mackenzie was a steadfast supporter of the 'symbolic' faction, echoing Wilson when he argued for an original, true and 'fundamental' meaning for the swastika, which had become distorted through migration and a species of symbolic miscegenation: 'Although in some areas a symbol may have acquired new meanings, or vague secondary meanings, certain far-carried symbols, as is shown in this volume, have retained much of their original significance in different parts of the world.'[165] In view of the absence of this much-sought-after value, Mackenzie like others sought safety in numbers, as if the dead weight of interpretations constituted some kind of surrogate meaning: 'no symbol has of recent years aroused more interest among students of antiquities in both hemispheres.'[166] What this to and fro debate reveals is how the symbolic genre was becoming ornamentalised as a supplement and the ornamental was correspondingly taking on a 'purely symbolic' value. In fact, the phrase 'purely symbolic' provides a key to both operations. Sperber identifies symbolic language as a means of communication in excess of ordinary speech and which essentially speaks 'only of itself'. However, normally the job of the symbol is not to draw attention to itself but to the message which it adorns, acting as the beguiling ornamental nonsense on the well-founded and coherent wall of language and sense.

Raymond Firth has discussed the recognition of significant excess with reference to the public rhetoric of the 'symbolic gesture' which, he claimed, we recognise as symbolic because it seems surplus to the purely functional.[167] Lighting a cigar with a ten-pound note is a symbolic gesture: buying a cigar with a ten-pound note brings us back to the quotidian realities of representation and exchange which are the prerogative of language. The arresting image of the burning currency first of all shows us that we are in the presence of a symbolic, extra-linguistic or extraordinary phenomenon: then encoded 'contents' or an intended meaning behind the act may or may not become apparent. Symbolic communication also has the advantage of speed over decoding, which requires time for deliberation: a 'symbolic significance' can be instantly recognised more quickly than a message can be interpreted and read.

The Aryanisation of the swastika in the nineteenth century was the most 'purely symbolic' gesture of all, since its tendency was to expunge and censor all those factors which were foreign to the 'pure form' of the image and thus to a pure manifestation of the symbolic phenomenon. If the symbol had become supplementary to a textual meaning, it also then followed that meaning was an element foreign to the symbol *qua* symbol. As language strove for a pure and unadorned functionality in the modern era, so the symbol achieved its own self-determination as that which language was *not*, and their alienation from each other suggests that they could only work together as mutual opposites or sites of contestation, despite being constituted within the same methodological framework. Just as ornament becomes increasingly distinct and visible when set against the sign of pure functionality, so the symbol is 'set apart' and achieves its fullest definition when cast adrift from language. As the image of the swastika was deracinated, reconstructed and refined by Aryanism into the *symbol* of the swastika, a morphological hygiene undertaken in the name of race purity prepared the way for an uninterrupted symbolic field, and also for the totalitarian dream of a power divorced from reason and a depth psychology, from an explanation and a *raison d'être*.

The shift from Aryanism to Nazism is also accompanied by a narrowing of the symbolic focus of the swastika, and an attempt to relocate the deracinated sign in a specifically Germanic context. After 1933, the Nazi *Gleichschaltung* set about habituating the citizens of Germany to their new 'national symbol' using a synchronic field of signs, but up to that point self-identity still had to be archaeologically inferred along a vertical axis rather than visually presented as a totalising field. However, minor changes in the archaeological 'placement' of the swastika chart a progress from diachrony to synchrony. One of these reorientations can be seen in Otto Grabowski's *Das Geheimnis der Hakenkreuzes und die Wiege des Indoger-manentums* (The Secret of Swastikas and the Cradle of the Indo-Germanic Race), published in Berlin in 1921, just one year after the swastika made its first appearance in Munich as the emblem of the National Socialist German Worker's Party.[168] Grabowski, whilst allowing that the distinctive form of the swastika might inspire every race, argued that the Germans had a genuine right (*echten erben*) to use it, since they were closer to the source of its Indo-Germanic origin. With reference to Schliemann's Trojan swastikas (which were at that time on display in the Berlin museum), but arguing against the archaeologist's predilection for an Asiatic explanation, Grabowski once more shifted the axis of the Aryan question towards autochthony and a Germanic homeland for the Aryan race. The importance of this emphasis after World War I is obvious: in his conclusion, Grabowski writes of the winter of the German people, soon to be replaced by a 'morning, which approaches under the light of the swastika'.[169] He begins his text with a discourse on origin and archaeological genesis, and ends with the swastika as a herald of revelation and rebirth. The colonised sign was now set to become a *colonising* sign, in an unprecedented shift of power from the margins to the centre.

2

ORNAMENT

But what, in ordinary daily life, appears to be a playful scribble of lines, assumes a different complexion when considered as the artistic expression of a whole race.

(Wilhelm Worringer, *Form in Gothic*, 1927)

As a German, I wish to lodge a complaint against everything that has been abandoned by other peoples only to be proclaimed thereafter as German.

(Adolf Loos, *Spoken into the Void*, 1931)

A visit to the Nuremberg Zeppelin field as it exists today supplies evidence of a healthy disrespect for the few remaining monuments of National Socialist architecture. On Sundays, Turkish *Gastarbeiter* and their families picnic in the shade of trees flanking Hitler's 'Great Road', the grand thoroughfare which was intended to link the ancient Nuremberg, the 'City of Imperial Diets' with his modern 'City of the Rallies'. Tennis is played against the walls of the Zeppelin tribune, and teenagers tryst on the steps. However, this reclaiming of Nazi architecture for leisure activity is frustrated by the neo-Nazi swastika graffiti which must constantly be removed from the tribune towers and entranceways. This is also the case at the Olympic stadium in Berlin, where the bronze swastikas which have been partially erased from the ceremonial bell reappear in graffiti on the lavatory walls, contesting with the countering phrase 'Nazi raus' (Plate 18).

Nazi architecture can be rehabilitated and used for other purposes; the Nazi swastika cannot, and it remains in neo-Nazi iconography as a portable monument to the regime. And as I mentioned in my introduction, both the racist sign of the swastika and the perimeter of the concentration camps define spaces which cannot be reappropriated and reused. The Nazi swastika was the visual perimeter, the linked chain of imagery, with which Hitler sought to encircle first Germany, then the whole of Europe. Yet this mnemonic of power concealed a different loading of memories and desires that had become attached to the swastika when it was chosen as the DAP (Deutsches Arbeiter Partei) emblem in 1919. The following section traces the genealogy of those desires which were obliterated in the totalitarian form of the swastika, first as they were represented in the debates of National Socialist ideology, and then in a more general sense through a philosophy of ornament in the modern era.

EXPRESSIONISM AND THE 'RACE SPIRIT'

During the time of Hitler's *soi-disant* National Socialist 'revolution', a period beginning with his taking office as chancellor on 30 January 1933 and ending in the Röhm purge of 30 June 1934, there was heated debate amongst National Socialist ideologues about the relative merits of Expressionist or *völkisch* art as a means to convey the spirit of the movement.[1] The principal adversaries in this debate were Josef Goebbels, who had expressed equivocal support for the principle of 'expression', and Alfred Rosenberg, then head of the Kampfbund für Deutsche Kultur, who had attacked it. For Rosenberg, all art that deviated from the established canon of objective naturalism expressed the deracination of the Germans from their blood and native soil. 'The German peasant', he declared, 'is the original source of life'[2] a statement which affirmed both his belief in the unconscious visual expression of the *Volkgeist* and his rejection of what he saw as the self-conscious urban intellectualism and subjectivist tendencies of the avant-garde.

It was Goebbels' position, as the head of the 'Ministry For Popular Enlightenment and Propaganda', whose remit overlapped with that of the Kampfbund, that caused the clash with Rosenberg, rather than any fervent wish on Goebbels' part to promote Expressionism. However, Goebbels' speech at the opening of the Reichskulturkammer on 15 November 1933, in which he provided tacit support for the idea of a National Socialist avant-garde, gave a fresh impetus to the anti-Rosenberg faction and resulted in the establishment of the National Socialistischer Deutsche Studentbund by a group of young Berlin Expressionists. Expressionism received further support from Professor Alois Schardt,[3] who attempted to bridge the ideological divide by suggesting that it was objective naturalism, and not subjectivism that was un-Germanic, and that the Expressionists were the true heirs of the Gothic. In this, and in his belief that the grounding principle of German art was its quality of *Unendlichkeitsgefühl* (endlessness), Schardt echoed the theories espoused by Wilhelm Worringer, whose race-romantic ideas of the Gothic will be examined in depth later in this section.

However, perhaps the most significant aspect of this debate was the manner in which it was concluded. On 5 September 1934, Hitler made a speech in which he condemned both the 'danger to the German Nation' represented by avant-gardism and the 'romantic illusion' of Rosenberg's *Volkgeist*.[4] Hitler's silencing of both parties represented more than the application of the principle of divide and rule; his action reaffirmed that the guiding principle of National Socialism was the 'Führer principle', which united the positions of both the Rosenberg and Goebbels factions by the totalitarian logic through which the will of the many was seen to be expressed in the will of the one. This denied both the individual 'expressive' subject and the unconscious *Volkgeist* any autonomous power of expression, since both were seen to be subsumed in the person of the *Führer*. In Leni Riefenstahl's film *Triumph of the Will*, Rudolf Hess declares to the massed ranks of party members that: 'Hitler is Germany, Germany is Hitler.' When Hitler is absent in Riefenstahl's film, his place is taken by the swastika, which, like the image of the *Führer*, becomes a switching station for personal and national identities.

Each Nazi swastika 'symbolised' its ornamental field of signs, and thus visually re-enacted and illustrated the *Führer* principle, in which the German people were constantly encouraged to acknowledge the interpenetration of the many by the one. Yet this visual rehearsal of the cult of individual and collective 'personality' concealed and repressed the abolition of personal opinion. Donald Kuspit, discussing the 'Entarte Kunst' (Degenerate Art) exhibition of 1937, has suggested that Hitler 'had a vested interest in repression' and a corresponding wish to exalt clear and unified images over those requiring debate and textual exegesis, and which therefore introduced the possibility of uncertainty.[5] Hitler's own words on this exhibition reveal a wish to erect a barrier between image and text: 'Works of art that cannot be understood but need a swollen set of instructions to prove their right to exist ... will no longer openly reach the German nation.'[6] When 'art' becomes propaganda, then image and text are not required to explain each other, but instead to participate in a mutual objectification. A swastika on a banner and the legend 'Deutschland Erwache' beneath it are not there to account for their coexistence but instead to constitute a rhetorical non-statement as an objective fact. The self-supporting 'swastika system' was paradigmatic of the manner in which image and text, gesture and sign exist in an apparently dialogic relationship which in fact substitutes the rhetoric of statement/response for the communicative act.

This cancelling out of values was reflected in the annexation by the Nazi swastika of the roles of German symbol and Germanic ornament.[7] The self-identical image appeared as a framed and foregrounded sign and as a decorative motif which implied a previous era and an unconscious, unawakened race energy. The gold-plated and laurel-wreathed swastika which once crowned Albert Speer's Zeppelin tribune represented the apotheosis and fulfilment of the swastikas which are still present, but sublimated in the decorative scheme of the tribune's interior. Ornament as the unconscious graphology of the *Volkgeist* was thus 'completed' in the self-conscious presence of the Nazi symbol, and the sign of a (Gothic, mediaeval) past is linked to the rhetoric of a glorious future, thus avoiding the displacement of tradition implied by an Enlightenment concept of progress. The Tribune swastikas expressed in microcosm Hitler's aim of uniting the medieval Nuremberg with the 'modern' National Socialist city, giving equal weight to a glorious past and a glorious future, and thereby defining the present as a moment of transition from one to the other.

GESTURE AND CHARACTER

I have shown how the construction of the swastika as a symbol of the Aryan race in the nineteenth century was informed by discourses of the symbol which ran against the grain of tendencies towards rationalism and rational explanations, and the same is also true of certain discourses surrounding ornament in the twentieth century. Yet in the same way in which the symbol was defined in opposition to a functionalist/structuralist concept of language, twentieth-century ornament could only appear under the sign of industrial and architectural modernity, in which construction and decoration were separated from each other. In what follows I have contrasted the Austrian architect Adolf Loos' warnings against the false-hood and anachronism of ornament in the modern era with the writings of his German contemporary Wilhelm Worringer, who in his *Formprobleme in der Gotik* (Form in Gothic) of 1912 evoked the vision of an ornamental form which stood outside the idea of progress or historical development, and which expressed the unchanging character of a Germanic racial will. The morphology of Worringer's Germanic ornament is thus necessarily autokinetic, repetitive and circular rather than logical/linear, and in his emphasis on the morbid qualities and 'fruitless striving' of this race roman-tic energy, Worringer seemed to be aware of the writing, or Germanic handwriting, on the wall.

In her study of expressionism and expressionist theory in Wilhelmine Germany, Helen Boorman cites Wilhelm Worringer as one critic respons-ible for packaging Expressionism as 'an authentically German, *geistliche* Kultur' during this period.[8] She has suggested that the cult of individual autonomy in German Expressionism was both facilitated and funded by new democratic freedoms, and paradoxically aligned with the anti-demo-cratic, aristocratic and militaristic tendencies of *Kulturpolitik*:

> The promotion of Expressionism as a serious art was, it seems, at one crucial level a strategy for popularising without trivialising a culture which could be seen as vital in contemporary terms as military discourses.[9]

Boorman quotes Douglas Kellner's opinion that expressionism 'retools bourgeois ideologies of subjectivity'.[10] It is also the case that Nazism in its turn retooled expressionism: not the 'aesthetic' (positional, debatable) expressionism of the Deutsche Studentbund, but a militant expressionist politics of individual and national autonomy, and a theory of representation which had its origins in romantic theories of the symbol. Boorman's view that Expressionism mediated between the discourses of a personal and a national self-representation suggests how both these positions could become united in the sign of race and the sign of the swastika, in which a racist ideology achieves the difficult feat of 'popularising without trivialising' an expression of autonomy. The introduction by the Nazis of race as the dominant issue effected an illusory solution of the tensions between democracy and aristocracy in German culture, since once Nazism became a mass movement, every party member could become a member of an Aryan aristocracy.[11] The radical autonomy and cultivated difference of the expressionist aesthetic had offered the newly-created and newly-moneyed German *haute-bourgeoisie* a chance to align itself with a mannerist and aristocratic idiom in painting. In order to be recognisably German, democracy had to pay homage to anti-democratic values. Nazism was to take this trajectory one step further (and one class lower) in the form of a fully-fledged ideology of race and the armorial emblem of the swastika. The swastika and its assertion of Germanic difference offered the German *petit-bourgeois* the chance to become members of an aristocracy of the masses. Hermann Glaser has identified *petit-bourgeois* 'Spiesser' culture as the ideal audience for National Socialist propaganda: from this populist base the gap between individual and collective autonomy could be closed by bypassing the democratic tradition within which the concepts of individual and nation had initially been developed.[12] Democracy could then be declared a foreign and un-Germanic import, a logic which Hitler developed in the turgid rhetoric of *Mein Kampf*:

> A philosophy of life which endeavours to reject the democratic mass idea and give this earth to the best people – that is, the highest humanity – must logically obey the same aristocratic principle within this people . . . Thus, it builds, not upon the idea of the majority, but upon the idea of personality.[13]

That the reunification of Germany has intensified the need to rebuild the bridges between democracy and Prussianism was emphasised in September 1993 by General Werner von Scheven, commander of the Bundeswehr in East Germany:

> There have been two traditions in our country. One, the military tradition, was profoundly anti-democratic. The other, the democratic tradition, was always directed towards freedom. We in today's Bundeswehr believe we have finally brought the military and democratic traditions together.[14]

What has made this alliance so difficult to bring about has been the aristocratic discourse which defined the Germanic negatively as that which is opposed to the non-Germanic. Democracy, on the other hand, is necessarily a non-exclusive, trans-national and 'translatable' notion. In 1912, Wilhelm Worringer had side-stepped the question of historical beginnings and the question of style and gone out of his way to define the Gothic as a morphology of difference, and difference as the distinguishing mark of the Germanic. Worringer saw the Gothic as an ahistoric racial phenomenon 'irreconcilably opposed to the classical' and as an energy which adopted or 'assumed' various forms rather than as an art-historical style established on the basis of formal criteria. His rejection of a classical aesthetic in the name of a Germanic anti-aesthetic may seem at odds with Nazi enthusiasm for overblown neo-classical architecture. However, the swastika demonstrates the divide between the signs of imperial power (borrowed at third hand from Italian fascism), and the sign of race, the self-representation and identifying mark which distinguished Nazism from its precursor in Italy.

The study of expressionist modes of representation as nationalist or political propaganda reveals the fallacies behind the ontology of knowledge in the 'self-knowingness' of race. The attempt to close the gap between individual and mass using the theories of collective *Erlebnis* and a common will confined the physical body within a repertoire of 'expressive' signs and postures, of which the most grotesque was the sign of the swastika. Worringer, in his attempt to bridge the gap between the nationalism of the Bismarckian era and the emergence of a bourgeois *Personlichkeitsrechte* (right of personality) in the early twentieth century, presages this atrophy in his definition of the Gothic and Germanic ornament as a ghostly, morbid imitation of life. What the expressive gesture of race ornament revealed it also concealed, since the concept of a Germanic ornament linked *Volk* continuity to a craft tradition in an unholy alliance of values whose rhetorical expression denied their redundancy and superfluity in the modern era. In a more general sense, all ornament in the twentieth century, in concealing the gap between the mark of the hand and the mark of the machine, functions as the mere *sign* of life.

ANTI-ORNAMENT

Adolf Loos, in his famous polemic 'Ornament und Verbrechen' (Ornament and Crime) of 1908, declared that the greatness of the modern age was that 'it is incapable of producing new ornament', a position which he had first worked out in articles published in the *Neue Freie Presse* a decade earlier.[15] As an insight into the future, this argument appears self-evident, since a century of mass production, mass consumption and mass culture has nullified the ontological grounding of ornamental art. If, as Hans Georg Gadamer[16] has suggested, ornament is the icing on the ontological cake, an 'accompanying effect' which re-presents the being of what it adorns, then the self-conscious ornament of mass manufacture achieves precisely the opposite effect. It draws attention to itself as the sign of a supplement without inner substance, an effect without an ontological cause. The 'being' of the adorned object here referred to by Gadamer should not be confused with the object as utility or materiality, since in this scheme, ornament is not excess material but something *in excess of* materiality and utility which can reveal the ontological truth within gross matter. However, when ornament becomes something applied as an afterthought to the mass-manufactured object, then the necessary links which Gadamer perceives between the ornamental sign, the physical object and the ontological truth of that object are broken. The sign itself as ornament, trademark and commodifying stamp then assumes the quality of being, and the physical object is subsumed in a discourse of production and utility. The hysterical ornamentation of Victoriana, an accompaniment which has lost an anchoring in the manufactured object, is an example of this phenomenon. In Victoriana, ornament as the sign of aristocratic, cultural and historical 'depth' is freely applied to every available utilitarian surface. In the modern era, the links between ornament and group identity, and ornament and a craft tradition were rendered superfluous and meaningless in a broad cultural sense, surviving in the West only as sub-cultural representations of a difference antagonistic to mass cultural hegemony. This last point Adolf Loos had already grasped in 1908, when he pointed out that the primitive urge towards ornament now most frequently assailed people in the lavatory.[17] Henceforth, he argued, ornament should ideally disappear from the activities of labour and architectural construction, to appear only under the sign of base sexuality, obscenity and the postures of sub-cultural rebellion.

What Loos had also realised was how quickly this fallen state of ornament had been reintegrated into European visual culture as an idealised symbol of its former role, since many mass-produced artefacts still carried the sign of ornament which inevitably evoked an earlier time through its aspect of cultural/historical 'sedimentation'. The 'style' of the ornament was immaterial: applied ornament itself was the generic signifier of memory. Writing on the 'modernity' of art nouveau ornament in 1898, Loos declared:

> These things are modern; that is, they are in the style of the year 1898. But how do they relate to the objects that are currently being passed off as modern? With a heavy heart we must answer that these objects have nothing to do with our time. They are full of references to abstract things, full of symbols and memories. They are medieval.[18]

This use of ornament as symbol and nostalgic camouflage is contemporaneous with the advent of modern production techniques and in fact precedes the development of a modernist *aesthetic* appropriate to those techniques: however, it is also a quintessentially 'postmodern' device. This definition may seem paradoxical, but in this instance the prefix 'post' functions in a cosmetic or supplementary sense, and the modern denotes a means of production rather than an aesthetic law. Loos directed his polemic against this marriage of modern production and nostalgic consumption in *Ornament and Crime*, supplanting it with his vision of a future Zion, a holy city of gleaming white concrete. However, his intellectual modernism did not simply contrast the purity of structure with the redundancy of ornament, but advocated instead a proportionality in design which looked back to a classical tradition in architecture. In fact, to draw the simple antithesis of 'modern' structure and 'traditional' decoration ignores Loos' message that the crime is perpetrated not by ornament but by its mass-produced simulacrum. As Aldo Rossi has pointed out:

> The difference between Loos and the 'modernist' architects is so profound that there is no communication between them; it is not a question of decoration or function, of the classical style or the new styles, but of the defense of the city of man against any utopia that is a slave to power.[19]

The 'decorated sheds' built by the architect Robert Venturi in the sixties, in which an ornamental gloss was applied to modernist concrete façades, affirmed architectural modernism in this hypostasised and normative role by using a language of fixed signs for both the modern and the ornamental.[20] This rhetorical façadism has led Brandon Taylor to suggest that Nazism, with its conflation of traditionalist, classical and modernist signs, might be seen as an example of postmodernism *avant la lettre*, 'a heavily militarised form of modernism itself'.[21]

This is one solution to the problem of defining a Nazi aesthetic, but to focus on the juxtaposition of opposites tends to obscure the way in which Nazism used the signs of both past and future in the service of a rhetoric of race progress. This phenomenon is most clearly seen in the Nazi swastika, whose modernist dynamic slant quite literally balanced the image on a fulcrum between the myths of a past and a future race. An autokinetic 'forward' and rightward turning motion is fixed within a dynamic square, setting up an unresolved tension between stasis and movement, thus isolating in a symbolic form the *possibility* of a return. The first Nazi swastikas have been described by Ernst Nolte as a 'symbol of salvation and hope',[22] a definition for which he provides no further explanation. Nolte's own preferred and contentious 'phenomenological' method of reading fascism might suggest in this instance that 'salvation' meant the deliverance from present circumstances and 'hope' was the illusion of a return of the Aryan past in the near future *via* the Nazi movement. In this sense the early swastika, accompanied by the text 'Deutschland Erwache', became the fixed sign through which Germany would be 'mobilised': nostalgic metaphors of awakening blended effortlessly into the language of war. Post-1933, however, the potential energy of the sign was realised as a totalitarian sign field of identical images, and the grandiose ideas of Aryanism were replaced by the low church of the *Führer* cult, whose adherents were the ever-increasing number of party members.

Significantly, the rhetoric of the past and the rhetoric of the future, rather than functioning as opposing elements, can both be seen as a reaction to anxiety and disorientation in the present tense. The swastika offered the paradoxical solution of a 'return to the future' and a fictitious path through the uneven political terrain of post-1918 Germany. This logic also applies in general to the ornamental gesture in the modern era, which appears as a reactionary or nostalgic image or sign: reactionary in the deepest sense not to some supposed counter-aesthetic of modernism but against its own deracination and redundancy. Ornament as an over-determined 'accompaniment' draws attention to itself, a role-reversal which conceals the absence of its ontological grounding element. Loos' description of primitive graffiti on the modern lavatory wall is one example of this rhetoric, the classical flourishes on a postmodern concrete façade are another, and the Nazi swastika is a third. The effect of the emphatic gesture is to conceal the emptiness and futility of its appeal. As was the case within Nazism itself, the central struggle of the swastika was not directed against its ostensible counter-signs (the Star of David, the Hammer and Sickle) but against its own paucity of meaning and occultation of absence. In the seventy-four years since the design of the party emblem, the swastika has occupied positions on both the architectural façade and the lavatory wall, in both cases apparently serving as a violent challenge to the values of Enlightenment modernism. This 'primitive' ornament, however, can now only be seen as a parody or reactionary grotesque, grotesque because the violent political expression and military/industrial 'modernisation' of nostalgia only served to widen the distance between Aryo-Germanic fantasies and what was being done in their name.

THE LAVATORIAL GROTESQUE

That the Nazi swastika should be seen as a reactionary sign is entirely correct, although not in the sense of a romanticism reactionary to rationality, but in the same way as Hegel's symbol, which struggles instead against the inevitable failure of its declared aims. On the other hand, the sledgehammer tactics of Lukács' *The Destruction of Reason*, which, as the title suggests, implied that Nazism was another example of the 'modern irrationalism ... [which] arose and became operative in perpetual conflict with materialism and the dialectical method'[23] represents an ideologically over-determined simplification. Lukács instituted the paradox of a programmatic and consciously oppositional 'irrationality' and evoked an eternal fight to the death between fascism and communism. It could also be argued that the variety of romantic irrationality which bore fruit in Nazism was rather a type of arationality whose agenda was already a manifest impossibility, and whose 'destruction' was self-accomplished and pro-grammed in from the start. The lack of substance and meaning which Lukács detected in Germanic 'irrationalism' was not opposed to some concrete reality of the 'crucial class struggle' but instead fixed and hyposta-sised a moment of loss, and constitutes, like Hegel's symbol, a *mimesis* or illustration of its own internal 'struggle'. If the early swastika, as Nolte claims, fixed German minds on the theme of 'salvation and hope' then it also reified and confirmed the feelings of national despair on which such vain hope grew. A presage of this emblem is Zmigrodski's 'anti-Semitic' swastika, which ostensibly stood for the struggle of one race against another, but was in reality the landmark for a prehistoric *Mutterepoche* so remote that the longing for it could only remain perpetually unsatisfied.

Similarly, the modern ornament is not anti-functional but anti-ornament, a parody of tradition and not its standard-bearer or successor. Its form therefore, is that of the architectural grotesque, which must be seen not as the deviation from a canon of visual beauty but as a figure which, as the architect Peter Eisenmann has suggested, represents an impossible relation-ship: 'No longer does the object need to look ugly or terrifying to provoke an uncertainty; it is now the distance between object and subject – the impossibility of possession which provokes this anxiety.'[24] In the Nazi swastika, the binding threads of folk ornament were distorted into the modern abstraction and lowest common denominator of 'race', the wasted labour contained in industrialised ornamental forms[25] was represented as an effortless or magical 'creative work', and Loos' notion of primitive sexual desire was transformed into the auto-erotic space and indefinite time of the spectacle. The critic Matthias Winzen has suggested that the heroic public statuary of sculptors such as Arno Brecker, who worked for the Nazi regime, possessed a quality of suppressed and unfulfillable homo-erotic desire which recruited 'the viewer's physical body as living raw material for military action'.[26] The dynamic yet 'endless' form of the Nazi swastika, as well as its links with a romantic concept of interminable struggle, fulfil a similar role of transforming auto-eroticism into military aggression. In this regard it is worth noting the qualities of visual 'requi-sition' and 'unnatural satisfaction' that Worringer attributes to the endless and self-generative character of Gothic ornament. In the Nazi swastika, the cultural trajectory which Loos plotted is carried to its logical con-clusion: modern ornament becomes purely aesthetic, existing only in the image state, and is thus transformed into symbol, a 'purely symbolic' (and so redundant) gesture. This erotic/organic ersatz in the form of an image also explains why the Nazi swastika continues to function as effective pornography, a lineage which can again be traced back to Zmigrodski's scopophiliac substitution of the fetishised swastika for the absent mother.

71

Of course, the Nazi sign is not regarded as an aesthetic or idealised image, rather the moral order of civilisation and barbarity that Loos used when he contrasted modern man with the tattooed savage is recapitulated in the mixture of right-thinking revulsion and prurient fascination that the sign of the swastika now provokes. The modern ornament of the swastika once again becomes an obscene scrawl on the toilet wall, the fascist obscenity that Julia Kristeva has defined as breaching the rationalist limits set by language, but which must logically result in a defensive rationality circumscribing itself still further.[27] Yet a further obscenity of swastika graffiti lies in the way in which it underlines the violence and violation perpetrated by the Nazi sign. For Adolf Loos, any attempt to construct a modern ornament would not be a purposeful crime directed against an emergent modernism but a violation of ornament itself: in other words, a form of tomb-robbery in which an exhumed 'tradition' becomes grist to the mill of mass consumption.[28] The process of deracination that Adolf Loos saw as unstoppable, and his appeal for a corresponding honesty of attitude towards ornament, was reversed in Adolf Hitler's sign. As soon as war was declared against the un-Germanic, the Germanic itself is simultaneously declared null and void, and the rhetoric of ornament reveals that ornament is a lie. Hitler's silencing of the Rosenberg vs Goebbels debate represented at once the negation and completion of the nationalist nostalgia implicit in both *völkisch* thought and 'aesthetic' Expressionism, a negation that had begun with his initial politicising of the romantic nationalist swastika in 1919.

The object of nostalgia is by definition unattainable, and the politicisation and militarisation of nostalgia can only constitute parody and self-mockery. The comparison I propose to draw between the Nazi swastika and the 'revolving wheel' motif described by Wilhelm Worringer is intentionally parodic, but it is a parody which is intended to illustrate the form of the grotesque, the figure which embodies Eisenmann's 'impossibility of possession'. Worringer himself identified the grotesque as the intangible 'form within form' of the Gothic: 'Behind the visible appearance of a thing lurks its caricature, behind the lifelessness of a thing an uncanny, ghostly life, and so all actual things become grotesque.'[29] It is also appropriate that this styleless style should be used to illuminate the similar *Formprobleme* posed by the hybrid nature of Nazi 'aesthetics'. This cannot be accomplished art-historically by comparing, for example, the style of a Gothic cathedral with that of Albert Speer's cathedral of searchlights, but through an assessment of the character ascribed to a Germanic racial 'will', which constitutes above all an emphasis on an exaggeration of *differences* between the Germanic form and those of other races. Worringer wrote of an 'elementary Aryan grammar of line' which developed into a 'specifically Germanic idiom'.[30] Adolf Loos threw light on this issue in a foreword to the 1931 edition of his essays. On this occasion Loos' polemic was directed against the German 'Gothic' or Fraktur script, and the practice of capitalising nouns. Arguing against the way in which enforced habit is dressed up as custom, and the formal repetition of a sign is substituted for a living tradition, Loos wrote:

> Besides having a German god, we also have a German script. And both are false... Jacob Grimm says, 'it is unfortunate that this tasteless and depraved script [Fraktur] is identified as 'German' as if every fashionable abuse of ours ought to be stamped innately 'German' and freely commended'.[31]

For Loos, Fraktur was an example of a foreign import which had been hallowed by time into one of the 'sacred artefacts of Germanness'. He also detected a tendency for the German to define itself by adopting as its own those forms which had been rejected or abandoned by other cultures. The Gothic script formed a line of defence between the German and the non-German, and its idiosyncratic form signified 'Germanness' only because it proclaimed its radical difference from other scripts. As Loos showed, morphological details and the question of style became less important than the rhetorical expression of a singular and exceptional character, which had the effect of alienating form from meaning. He declared that both the Gothic typeface and the capital noun had the same paralysing effect:

> The rigid... practice of capitalising nouns has as its consequence the return of language to a barbaric state. This derives from the abyss that opens up in the German mind between the written and the spoken word. It is impossible to utter a capital letter.[32]

The printed Fraktur typeface became the public expression of a national 'character' which Loos also saw as policing private communication. The capitalised noun ensures that even personal handwriting takes on a collectivised, nationalistic aspect: 'when a German takes pen in hand, he can no longer write as he thinks, as he speaks.' Those who write do not simply write in German, they *write Germany*. Discourses on the Aryan swastika in the nineteenth century showed that the image, like Fraktur, had begun to constitute a defensible Germanic space, a 'pure form' recognisably set apart from others. Fraktur has now fallen into desuetude, but the swastika is still being used as the typographic supplement and authenticating stamp of 'Germanness' on a text.

Wilhelm Worringer's *Formprobleme* displayed a range of *völkisch*, proto-expressionist and romantic nationalist reflexes which were linked to the idea of the Gothic as a latent, secret force, a powerful but underground tradition. In embarking on a close reading of this by now generally ignored and politically dubious book, I have traced the literary tradition of the romanticised Gothic of which it is a part. Nicholas Goodrick-Clarke, in his survey of the links between Austrian and German occultism and

Nazism, has shown how a version of the Gothic tradition which had developed in the secret rites of freemasonry became one of the cultic forms of nationalism in early twentieth-century Germany:

> craft traditions became the allegories and symbols of a deistic and fraternal doctrine . . . It was in Germany, where the growth of deviant masonic rites was greatest owing to the profusion of mystical and theosophical sects, that Freemasonry became confused with a Templar heritage.[33]

The 'deviant' nature of the twentieth-century Gothic was revealed in Worringer's ambivalent morphology. As Paul Frankl has noted, Worringer 'shows no interest in ribs, and indeed, hardly any at all in "morphological" details' and is instead preoccupied with style as racial volition: 'the thesis in question cannot be Gothic in the narrower historical sense but rather a secret, latent Gothic in the psychological sense.'[34] This was the occultation of the Gothic, a graphological 'seeing of the unseen' and the textual description of a trans-historical inner form within an historically constituted architectural style. Using Worringer's graphological reading of the Gothic with reference to Nazism, I will work in the opposite direction: from the secret tradition and the romantic longing to its realisation in Nazism and beyond as an architectural and lavatorial grotesque.

AUTOKINESIS AND AUTONOMY

Hermann Weyl once described how whilst delivering a lecture on symmetry in Vienna in 1937, he spoke of the swastika; discussing its nature as a form which presents rotational without bilateral symmetry, and its use (in the form of the three-armed swastika or *triskelion*) in Greek art in conjunction with the Medusa's head.[35] Weyl recalled that when he pointed out how during the Nazi period the swastika had become a symbol far more terrifying than the Medusa's head, 'a pandemonium of applause and booing broke loose in the audience'. He concluded this anecdote with the observation that 'it seems that the magic power ascribed to these patterns lies in their startling incomplete symmetry – rotations without reflections'.

It is significant that the examples Weyl used to illustrate his lecture were the *triskelion* and 'swastika-like wheel' patterns on the staircase of the *Stefansdom* in Vienna. According to the Viennese occultist Guido von List, the *triskelion*, swastika and other Aryan signs could be recognised in the design of the late Gothic tracery and rose windows, and, like Weyl, Guido von List saw the visual autokinesis of the swastika as the source of its power: 'only there, uniquely and alone, understand the thrice-high-holy secret of constant generation, constant life, the uninterrupted recurrence.'[36] And in 1912, Wilhelm Worringer had described the same 'startling incomplete symmetry' in Gothic ornament as productive of an impression of violent movement that was non-classical and essentially Aryo-Germanic:

> In the North, there are a number of ornamental motives [sic] which have an undoubted centric character, but here too we note a decisive difference if we compare similar Classical ornament. For example, instead of the regular and invariably geometrical star or rosette or similar restful forms, in the North we find the revolving wheel (*drehende rad*), the turbine or so-called sun wheel, all designs which express violent movement (*eine heftige Bewegung*). Moreover, the movement is peripheral and not radial. It is a movement which cannot be arrested or checked.[37]

Steven Heller has claimed that 'the swastika [is] also referred to as a sun wheel',[38] whereas in his *Book of Signs*, the typographer Rudolf Koch shows the sun wheel as a cross within a circle, which is then broken to form the swastika.[39] Given that Worringer's emphasis is on a turbiniform (spiralling or spinning) movement, which he then compares with a 'so-called sun wheel' (*sogennante sonnenrad*) he was clearly describing a set of forms possessing 'swastikal' symmetry. It is also crucial to note that for Worringer, Gothic motifs were not named symbols, but graphological 'expressions'. In *Formprobleme der Gotik*, Worringer constructed an entire Aryan race psychology using the linked ideas of autokinesis and repetition. Whilst it is clear that spinning motifs are not the exclusive property of Gothic ornament, a straightforward refutation of Worringer's claim that autokinetic forms are, in their 'violent movement', expressive of the Germanic soul was countered by his emphasis on the way in which such motifs are employed. He perceived a difference in method between classical and northern ornament, and claimed that the same motif would be employed in radically different ways. According to Worringer, the emphasis of northern ornament is on repetition, and that of the south on the homogenisation of repetition in balanced mirror symmetry.

Worringer's graphology of style, which set out the conditions of recognition for a Germanic aesthetic, bore a methodological similarity to Zmigrodski's identification of the 'pure' Aryan swastika. This similarity existed in spite of the fact that Worringer's divination of the character of the Germanic soul admitted to a morbid anxiety which is repressed in Zmigrodski's nostalgic evocation of the *Mutterepoche*. Both authors constructed an Aryan morphology which was distinct, self-generative and 'active underground ... even where, obstructed by more powerful external conditions and hindered in its free expression, it assumes a foreign disguise'.[40] The ahistoric and disruptive unconscious race energy that was Worringer's 'Gothic' allowed him to simultaneously free his discourse from the bondage of art-historical facts and construct a psychology of style that implied the possibility of recollection, resurgence and renewal: 'It must at once be said that the psychological conception of the Gothic style, as it will be revealed by our investigation, in no way coincides with the historical Gothic.'[41] There is an entire phenomenology of style in Worringer's writing, which is not necessarily the style of the Gothic cathedral. Nonetheless, this romanticised and Germanic concept of form caught the public imagination, and proved to be in tune with the *Zeitgeist* of Germany in the early twentieth century. According to his translator, Herbert Read, Worringer 'gave the Germans what they had longed for – an aesthetic and historical justification for a type of art distinct from classicism, independent of Paris and the Mediterranean tradition'.[42] Again, the requirement is for a semiotic of distinction, and Worringer made this plain: his Gothic is 'strength of expression' opposed to a classical 'Beauty of expression'. Expressive rhetoric has not simply replaced aesthetics, since Worringer defined it as an anti-aesthetic: 'the so-called beauty of Gothic is a modern misunderstanding.'[43]

Whilst *Formprobleme der Gotik* described the 'underground' Gothic as an invisible energy which constitutes form, Worringer persisted in describing this energy using morphological criteria. Visible ornamental form traces the figures of this invisible inner geometry. Whereas for Zmigrodski the debased ornamental form of the swastika concealed its higher symbolic aspect, Worringer's graphology proposed that this same marginality of ornament, like a specimen of handwriting, offered the possibility of an unhindered revelation. He declared that 'it is of the essence of ornament that in its products the artistic volition of a people finds its purest and most unobscured expression'.[44] Worringer claimed that when the Germanic strain was absent, as in the English Gothic for example, then ornament did indeed become 'arbitrary decoration' and lost its expressive value.

In the double repetition of the revolving wheel, which repeats its own form within itself and then is itself repeated, the morbid, oppressive, feverish and exalted qualities of the northern psyche were, Worringer claimed, made manifest. This ornament could in fact be described as *fractal*: in Worringer's own words, 'a world which repeats in miniature, but with the same means, the expression of the whole'. Worringer wrote of 'that will to form ... which is as strongly and unmistakably expressed in the smallest crinkle of Gothic drapery as in the great Gothic cathedrals'.[45] As well as reading from the ornamental surface to the invisible and latent psychological depth, Worringer also saw significance in the way in which his Gothic transfixed and held the viewer's gaze on its surface. In this second reading, the race handwriting of the Gothic is endlessly reproduced as the expression of an inescapable and implacable will:

> The expression of Northern ornament does not directly depend upon us; we are met rather with a vitality which appears to be independent of us, which challenges us, forcing upon us an activity to which we

submit only against our will. In short, the Northern line does not get its life from any impress which we willingly give it, but appears to have an *expression of its own*, which is stronger than our life.[46]

Here visual autokinesis is linked to semiotic autonomy: the revolving wheel not only appears to have independent motion, but that self-willed movement has the hypnotic effect of imposing its secret design on us. We do not 'decode' the image and give it a meaning which we had already possessed: instead, the uncanny vitality which Worringer attributed to the Gothic is a force which itself takes possession of the mind. The image is not tied to a fixed or consonant meaning, nor even to a free associative range or 'band' of different meanings; instead, the phantasmagoric image itself becomes the fixed point and the focus of our gaze. Worringer wrote of the outright deception perpetrated by Gothic ornament, which 'requisitions' our vision in the service of its autonomous and unnatural motion. In Guy Debord's situationist text *Society of the Spectacle*, a similar hypnotic power is ascribed to the autonomous image. For Debord, as soon as lived reality becomes a spectacular and commodified representation, it constitutes a magnet for the collective gaze:

> The specialization of images of the world is completed in the world of the autonomous image, where the liar has lied to himself . . . the spectacle presents itself simultaneously as all of society, as part of society, and as an instrument of unification. As a part of society it is specifically the sector which concentrates all gazing and all consciousness.[47]

Debord's spectacle is also 'the autonomous movement of the non-living'.[48] We are held at the level of the purely visual, transfixed by the form of an image which appears supernatural only because it has become divorced from reality. What Worringer's 'eternal' Gothic described was the spectacular form of ornament in the twentieth century, whose only function is to create a mirage of times past and to camouflage its means of its production.

THE COMPULSION TO TEST

E. H. Gombrich has compared Wilhelm Worringer's opinions on the Gothic to those of Oswald Spengler, and referred to his 'vulgarised and sensationalised' writing which made the idea of 'Gothic man' popular currency.[49] Whether or not one agrees with this assessment, there is no doubt that Worringer's theories proved to be in tune with certain tendencies in early twentieth-century German romanticism. In 1908, the same year that Adolf Loos wrote 'Ornament and Crime', Worringer achieved unprecedented success with the publication of his doctoral dissertation *Abstraktion und Einfühlung* (*Abstraction and Empathy*) which, as he reveals in the foreword to the 1948 edition 'has probably run into more editions than any doctorate thesis'. There is a certain symmetry between the reasons Worringer gave for the success of *Abstraction and Empathy* and the subject of his book, which is particularly concerned with the idea of decorative style as the litmus test for the psyche of a period or culture. He also employed the idea of a *Zeitgeist* to explain the popularity of the book, describing himself as 'the medium of the necessities of the period'.[50] His assessments of psychological states as revealed in ornament are based on the idea of differing propensities amongst various cultures and races for the two basic values of Abstraction and Empathy. Worringer defined the former as anti-material and transcendental, the latter as relating to a recognition by an organism of the organic, and the subsequent ability to 'lose oneself' in empathy with this likeness. He describes northern European ornament in general, and the Gothic style in particular, as a hybrid of Abstraction and Empathy, in which heightened expression and 'livingness' is lent to abstract and unliving form:

> It is not the life of an organism that we see before us, but that of a mechanism. No organic harmony surrounds the feeling of reverence toward the world, but an ever growing and self-intensifying restless striving without deliverance sweeps the inwardly inharmonious psyche away with it . . . into a fervent excelsior.[51]

The implied autokinesis in the symmetry of the 'revolving wheel' provided Worringer with a concrete example of the 'animation of the inorganic' that he defined as the essential quality of the Gothic. The swastika provides one example of such an autokinetic 'trick' or deception in which a stationary object is apparently in motion. Gombrich discusses this quality of the swastika in *The Sense of Order*, and ascribes it to the phenomenon of 'visual redundancy' described by Gestalt theory. We look, claims Gombrich, for order and pattern in our visual environment; where one kind of order is not present, we will search for others. In the swastika what is first of all noticed is the lack of mirror symmetry, which is the most 'predictable' variety of symmetry in our experience. He then describes how we perform an 'imaginary rotation' on the figure of the swastika, in an attempt to establish whether each of the four arms is identical to the others: this is proved, but the search never stops, and in this way the illusion of perpetual motion is established: 'we follow, I believe, not with the eyes but with the mind.' In view of Worringer's dialectic of Abstraction and Empathy, it is noteworthy that Gombrich equates the absence of mirror symmetry in the swastika with the recognition of an organic type of order: we will 'empathise' with mirror symmetry in images and objects because it is the symmetry of our own bodies. When we encounter the hybrid of rotational symmetry and bilateral asymmetry that is present in the swastika, however, a different reaction occurs:

Hence, perhaps, the compulsion to test by mental rotation these puzzling forms which are both alike and different. Rotational symmetry represents an order which is visually less easy to grasp. I hope it is a pardonable exaggeration to say that it is not the motif which is unbalanced but that it upsets the balance of our mind. Random shapes do not produce this effect, it arises from the clash between our sense of order and a visible regularity which eludes the basic laws of simplicity, the first for which we test our environment.[52]

Gombrich is dismissive of Worringer and what he regards as his 'marketplace' Gothic: yet in the passage quoted above, a very similar phenomenology is applied to the swastika as a hybrid form which is 'both alike and different'. Implied in this description is the idea that the swastika is not 'animated' in the same way that we are, and that its autokinesis is somehow unnatural. Compare Gombrich's 'compulsion to test' and 'upsets the balance of our mind' with Worringer:

It is impossible to mistake the restless life contained in this tangle of lines. This unrest, this seeking, has no organic life that draws us gently into its movement; but there is life there, a tormenting, urgent life that compels us joylessly to follow its movements. Thus on an inorganic fundament there is heightened movement, heightened expression . . . The inner need for life and empathy of these inharmonious peoples did not take the nearest-at-hand path to the organic . . . it needed rather the intensification of a resistance, it needed that uncanny pathos which attaches to the animation of the inorganic.[53]

In this instance, Worringer did not refer to the revolving wheel but to Gothic interlaced strapwork ornament. And in discussing the swastika, Gombrich does not refer to the Gothic. But their descriptions of the effects of hybrid, unnatural and yet animated forms bear many points of similarity. There is compulsion rather than affirmation, and an 'inhuman' order and dynamism. Gombrich, like Max Müller before him, notes the 'puzzling' aspect of the swastika and similar motifs, Worringer suggested that northern man may have actively sought the difficulties and the 'resistance' to Empathy that hybrid forms present. Gombrich, however, would not claim that a preference for such motifs could be racially contingent. But having established the idea that the swastika unbalances the mind, it would not be going too much further to say that an unbalanced mind might be able to share an unnatural 'empathy' with it. Worringer described Gothic man experiencing 'the same logical frenzy, the same methodical madness'[54] that Gombrich sees in the endless mental chase around the form of the swastika.

One obvious weakness of such a thesis is that it is at the mercy of absolutes, of declaring that in all circumstances, from Buddhism to Nazism, the form of the swastika will be regarded with unease and distress by onlookers. This is manifestly not the case: Gombrich, in his discussion of the idea of 'the logic of situations' as applied to ornamental style, has warned that we should be wary of seeing the choice of styles or motifs as the necessary condition of some embracing *Zeitgeist*, but that attention should instead be paid to which aspects of form, whether that be asymmetry, clarity or flatness, are the subject of emphasis in particular instances, and which therefore promote a particular position or confirm cognitive patterns and habits of thought.[55]

Thomas Wilson's view that the swastika was distinct from 'more easily made' forms confirms Gombrich's distinction between the uncanny or disturbing order of the swastika and 'random shapes'. Despite this similarity, Wilson, unlike Gombrich, denied that the swastika appeared to move, and his refutation of its autokinesis was underlined by the horizontally placed image which appeared as a heraldic device on the first page of his book, and which emphasised the more stable 'cross' and 'square' aspect of the swastika rather than the wheel or the vortex. Wilson had rejected Count Goblet D'Alviella's assertion that the swastika is an ideal representation of the *perpetuum mobile* and all that 'moves of itself':

> An objection is made to the theory or hypothesis presented by Count Goblet D'Alviella, that it is not the cross part of the Swastika that represents the sun, but its bent arms, which show the revolving motion ... the author is more in accord with Dr Brinton and others that the Swastika is derived from the cross and not from the wheel, that the best arms do not represent rotary or gyratory motion, and that it had no association with, or relation to, the circle.[56]

This debate might appear as pointless as the search for a *perpetuum mobile*, but it does indicate that the 'wheel or square?' aspect of the swastika's hybrid form is a riddle that might be visually 'solved' by placing emphasis on one aspect or the other. In the Nazi design, as I have already mentioned, the swastika is placed in a dynamic square which situates it at a point of transition between these two poles, lending it a transfixed (and perceptually transfixing) quality which coerces and paralyses the gaze more effectively than the spiralling or wheel-like motion which Worringer describes. Roland Barthes has likened the spiral to a poetic phrase, 'a return in difference, not a repetition in identity'.[57] The endless 'displacement' of meaning to which Barthes refers also characterises the poetic ambition of romanticism, but in Worringer's text, we see romanticism decaying into atrophy: his 'revolving wheel' still has a morbid half-life, but his emphasis on identical repetition replaces an organism with a mechanism. In Nazism, the atrophy is complete: in its swastika, the image of an arrested motion and a stillborn romanticism was offered as the emblem of 'national awakening'.

its corresponding Indian symbol. We find it twice on a large piece of ornamented leather contained in the celebrated Corneto treasure preserved in the Royal Museum at Berlin; also on ancient pottery found at Königsberg in the Neumark, and preserved in the Märkisches Museum in Berlin, and on a bowl from Yucatan in the Berlin Ethnological Museum. We also see it on coins of Gaza, as well as on an Iberian coin of Asido;[1] also on the drums of the Lapland priests.[2] It is just such a troublesome puzzle as the Nile-key or *crux ansata*, that symbol which, as a hieroglyph, is read *ankh* ("the living one"), which very frequently occurs in the inscriptions in the Nile valley, and which we see of exactly the same form on a sepulchre of Northern Asia Minor.[3]

The 卍 is a sort of cross, whose four arms are bent at a right angle; it resembles four conjoined Greek Gammas.

Burnouf thinks that "the 卐 and 卍 represent the two pieces of wood which were laid crosswise upon one another before the sacrificial altars, in order to produce the sacred fire (*Agni*), and the ends of which were bent round at right angles, and fastened by means of four nails 卍, so that this wooden scaffolding might not be moved. At the point where the two pieces of wood were joined, there was a small hole, in which a third piece of wood, in the form of a lance (called *Pramantha*), was rotated by means of a cord made of cow-hair and hemp, till the fire was generated by friction. Then the fire (*Agni*) was put on the altar close by, where the priest poured the holy *Sôma*, the juice of the tree of life, over it, and made, by means of purified butter, wood and straw, a large fire."[4]

Burnouf further maintains that the mother of the holy fire was *Mâyâ*, who represents the productive force.[5] If his views are correct, they would go far to explain the presence of the 卍 on the vulva of the idol No. 226. They would also show that the four points which we so frequently see under the arms of the 卍 or 卐 indicate the wooden nails with which this primitive fire-machine was fixed firmly on the ground; and, finally, they would explain why we so frequently see the 卍 or the 卐 in company with the symbol of lightning or burning altars. The other cross too, which has also four points, ✛, and which occurs innumerable times on the whorls of the three upper pre-historic cities of Hissarlik, might also claim the honour of representing the two pieces of wood for producing the holy fire by friction. Burnouf asserts that "in remote antiquity the Greeks for a long time generated fire by friction, and that the two lower pieces of wood, that lay at right angles across one another, were called σταυρός, which word is either derived from the root *stri*, which signifies lying upon the earth, and is then identical with the Latin *sternere*, or it is derived from the Sanskrit word *stávara*, which means

---

[1] Zobel, *de Zangronis*, 1863, Pl. 1 and 3, and p. 397.

[2] Rochholz, *Altdeutsches Bürgerleben*, p. 184.

[3] Guillaume and Perrot, *Exploration archéo-* *logique de la Galatie et de la Bithynie*, Atlas, Pl. ix.

[4] See Émile Burnouf, *La Science des Religions*, p. 256.

[5] Émile Burnouf, *op. cit.*

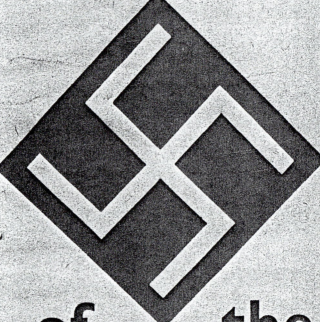

2 Cover of the pamphlet *Real History of the Swastika* by Norman Walker, London, 1939.

3 Outlining the text. Girls' hockey team Edmonton, Alberta, *circa* 1916.

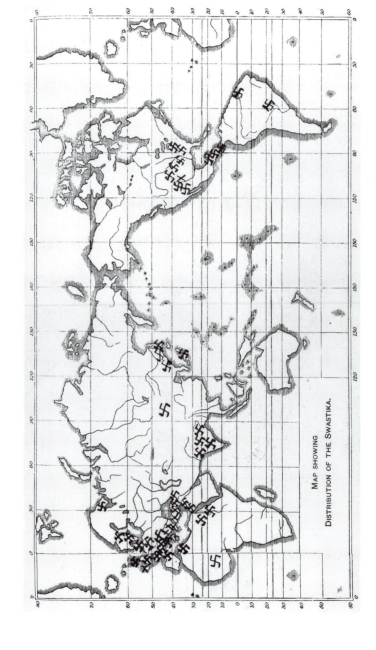

MAP SHOWING
DISTRIBUTION OF THE SWASTIKA.

4 'Map showing distribution of the swastika.' Thomas Wilson, *The Swastika, the Earliest Known Symbol and its Migrations*, Washington, 1896.

5 Regimenting the race: Berlin policemen practise for the 9th Indoor Sports Festival, held on 17 March 1934 in the Berlin *Sportspalast*.

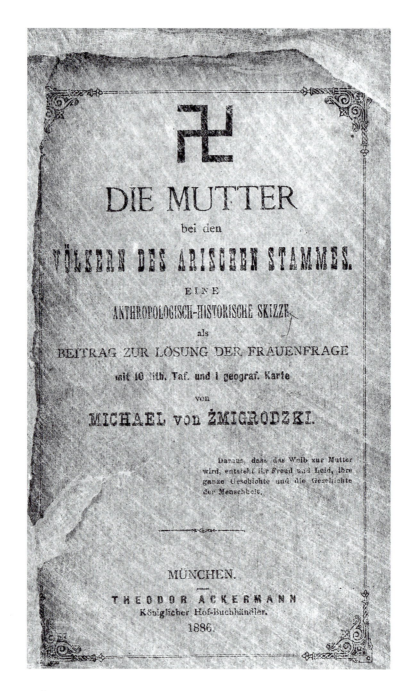

DIE MUTTER

bei den

VÖLKERN DES ARISCHEN STAMMES.

EINE

ANTHROPOLOGISCH-HISTORISCHE SKIZZE

als

BEITRAG ZUR LÖSUNG DER FRAUENFRAGE

mit 10 lith. Taf. und 1 geograf. Karte

von

MICHAEL von ŻMIGRODZKI.

Daraus, dass das Weib zur Mutter
wird, entsteht ihr Freud und Leid, ihre
ganze Geschichte und die Geschichte
der Menschheit.

MÜNCHEN.

THEODOR ACKERMANN

Königlicher Hof-Buchhändler.

1886.

6 Fetishisation and scopophilia: Michael Zmigrodski, *The Mother of the People of the Aryan Family*, Munich, 1886.

7   The *bricoleur* of myths: Heinrich Schliemann as a Russian merchant, aged 40.

8   The construction site: Troy in 1989.

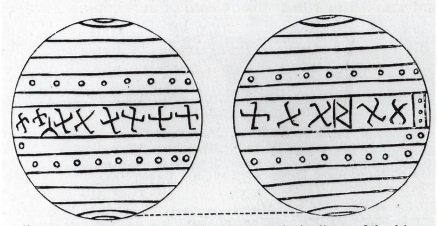

Nos. 245, 246. Terra-cotta Ball, representing apparently the climates of the globe.
(Actual size. Depth, 26 ft.)

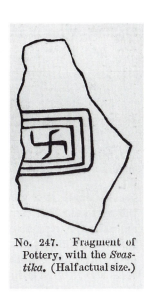

No. 247. Fragment of Pottery, with the *Svastika*. (Half actual size.)

9 Symbol or 'writing'? 'Terra-cotta Ball, representing apparently the climates of the globe' and 'Fragment of Pottery, with the *Svastika*'. H. Schliemann, *Ilios*, London, 1880, figs 245, 246 and 247.

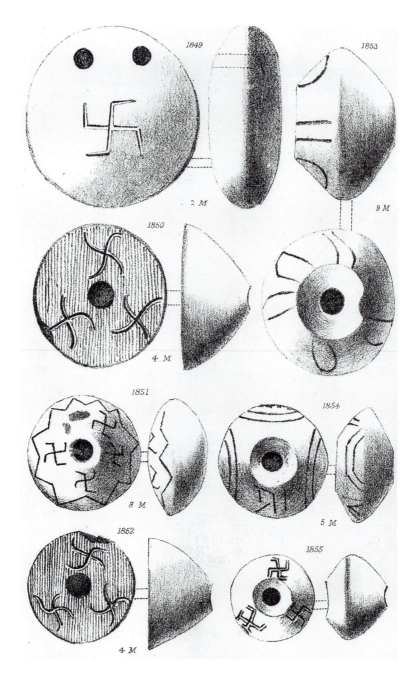

10 'Specimens of whorls, etc. dug up at Troy.' H. Schliemann, *Ilios*, London, 1880, figs 1849–55.

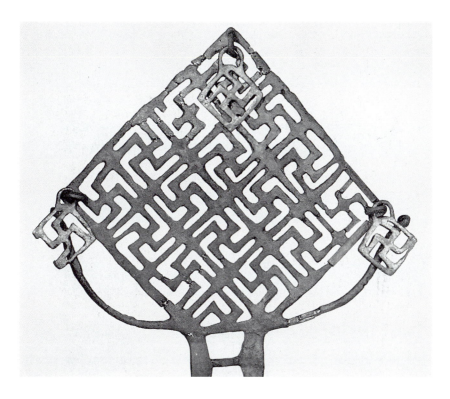

11 Hittite ritual standard with swastikas. Bronze, height 34cm. From Alaça Hüyük, Grave B, 2300–2100BC.

12   Karatay Medrese portal, Konya 1251.

13   Versions of the swastika from the *Pedagogical Sketchbook* of Paul Klee.

14 The Day of German Art, 15 October 1933. Wulf Bley, *Das Jahr 1*, Berlin, 1934.

15 'Saarbrücken was a single sea of flags.' Wulf Bley, *Das Jahr 2*, Berlin, 1935.

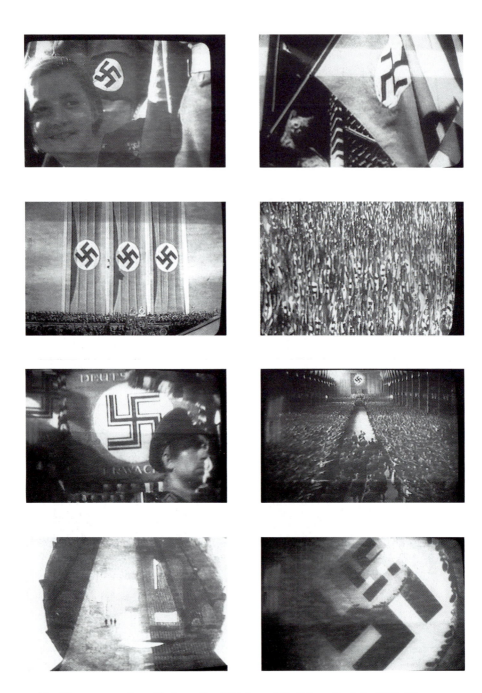

16 Phantasmagoria: stills from Leni Riefenstahl's *Triumph of the Will* (Germany 1935).

17 'The first of May then brings the entire German people together.' Wulf Bley, *Das Jahr 1*, Berlin, 1934.

18   Site of conflict: swastika graffiti in Berlin, 1993.

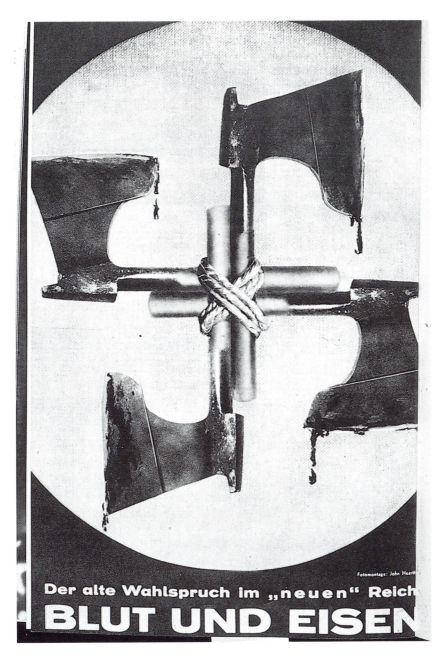

Der alte Wahlspruch im „neuen" Reich

BLUT UND EISEN

Fotomontage: John Heartf

19   *The Old Slogan in the 'New' Reich: Blood and Iron.* John Heartfield, *AIZ*, 8
March 1934.

20 'Thus the German people can once again celebrate a truly German Christmas.'
Wulf Bley, *Das Jahr 1*, Berlin, 1934.

GOTHIC MAN

Whether it was Worringer's intention to popularise his ideas is debatable, but the basis of his argument, if not its dialectic of Abstraction and Empathy, had been academic and literary currency for over a century. What Worringer had done was to apply the old idea of a causal link between the Germanic race and the Gothic to the more recent ideas of Theodor Lipps and Alois Riegl. From Lipps came the idea of 'empathy' as a phenomenological reaction to style, and from Riegl the *Kunstwollen*, or 'will to art'.[58] Worringer moved the emphasis of Riegl's theory away from the aesthetic expression of individual will, towards the notion of style as the unconscious graph of the collective or racial will. Worringer's hybrid theory united elements from Riegl's thought with those of Gottfried Semper, whom Riegl's ideas had in fact been developed to challenge: 'Semper believed that artistic activity is determined, like the mechanics of heavenly bodies. Riegl recognised the element of free will. Artistic *volition* means no *compulsion* (*Kunstwollen* is not *Kunstmüssen*.)'[59] Worringer's new emphasis united the determinism of Semper's 'technological causation' of styles with Riegl's 'willing organism' in a theory of *racially determined* will that drew from the long history of German thought on the subject of 'Gothic man'. As early as 1502, in Jacob Whimpheling's *Epitome Rerum Germanicum*, references can be found to the Gothic architecture of Strasbourg cathedral as a symbol of Germanic excellence. But it is Goethe's essay on Strasbourg Cathedral, written in 1772,[60] that initiated a debate that was to transform 'the Gothic' into a concept independent of art-historical facts. Goethe's youthful enthusiasm for the Gothic excited contemporary comment and had lasting effects: Herder used the essay in his collection *Von deutscher Art und Kunst* of 1773, and considered what aspect of the Gothic answered to 'a nordic urge and is an exception to the rule of greater beauty, or is even perhaps a greater plan for a new kind of beauty'.[61] Here we see the clash between Classical and romantic aesthetics that Worringer was to recapitulate: Herder saw the Gothic as an aberrant yet powerful manifestation of the 'nordic urge'. Goethe, however, was later to have second thoughts:

> I, too, was once interested in these matters, and likewise practised a kind of idolatry with Strasbourg Cathedral ... To me, the strangest part of all of this is the German patriotism that would like to represent this obviously Saracenic plant as having sprung from its soil.[62]

In 1820, Christian Ludwig Steiglitz contrasted the 'plastic' virtues of Greek art with the 'romantic' appeal of the Gothic: 'the one appeals to reason (*Verstand*) the other 'excites, with the mysterious meaning, the emotions (*Gemüt*).'[63] This dialectic had been discussed by Schopenhauer a year earlier, but despite his own overwhelming emphasis on 'will' it is significant that he regarded the romantic phenomenological 'affect' of the Gothic as being based in its nationalistic 'effect': 'Our pleasure in Gothic works is quite certainly based in a large part on associations of ideas and on historical memories, thus on an emotion foreign to art.'[64] Here the same distinction between expression and aesthetics that Worringer was later to employ, was used in a critique which revealed that the true issue at stake in the nationalist Gothic was a problem not of form but of identity. In view of what Worringer was to say about 'requisition', it is significant that Schopenhauer referred to 'fiction and delusion' in the Gothic idea, which he traced to a misplaced nationalist feeling applied to irrational and ambiguous forms:

> Everyone will easily be able to realise how from the fundamental idea ... of Gothic architecture here indicated there results the mysterious and hyperphysical character it is acknowledged to have. It arises chiefly ... because of the fact that here the purely rational has been replaced ... by the arbitrary. So much that is really purposeless ... arouses the supposition of unknown ... purposes, that is, the mysterious appearance.[65]

What Schopenhauer is discussing here is the psychological conception of a fictional idea of visual style rather than style itself. But such criticism did not arrest the progress of 'Gothic man': 'Gothic had become the symbol of an attitude towards life, and its rebirth was to be the symbol of the recognition of this *Weltanschauung*.'[66] The fictions founded in the apprehension of mystery expressed the nationalistic emotional investment that had been placed in them: Schlegel likened the Gothic to the trees under which the ancient Germans had worshipped, Schelling saw in it the symbol of the infinite and an essentially Oriental extravagance and excess. In this way an ahistoric and 'Indo-European' heritage for 'Gothic Culture' was established, a heritage which Hippolyte Taine had identified as the agent of strange side-effects at the time the Gothic Cathedrals were built: 'by its universality it testifies to the great moral crisis, at once morbid and sublime, which during the entire middle ages exalted and deranged the human spirit.'[67] Here, some forty years before Worringer, is the idea of 'morbid differentiation' and the dead brought to an exalted life. Paul Frankl draws particular attention to this divorce of the Gothic idea from its ostensible subject in Worringer's writing. Techniques of description and analysis applied to styles, Frankl argues, are subsumed in Worringer's ideas of 'uncanniness, ghostliness, spectralness, unnaturalness ... such is the deepest meaning of the Nordic or Germanic spirit'.[68]

And just as Worringer was indebted to other German writers for his ideas, others were to borrow from him. The idea of the Gothic as a 'secret, latent' force is taken to absurd heights in *Der Geist der Gotik* (The Spirit of Gothic) by Karl Scheffler (1917), who felt free to abandon the mere 'academic' or art-historical concept of the Gothic. His substitute was a free-floating phenomenology of forms expressive of 'will': thus we are able to have 'the Gothic' in Negro, Eskimo and South American art forms. Scheffler also treated chronology with the same respect he had for geographic boundaries: 'the American quality of Roman architecture is a manifestation of the Gothic spirit because it is an expression of a violent will.'[69] It is easy to ridicule Scheffler's prose whilst ignoring the popular appeal of his ideas; as Frankl points out, such authors 'have an appallingly large public':

> [Scheffler] . . . is concerned . . . with the myth of eternal and secret Gothic. The book should be regarded as an expression of the 'feuilletonistic age' indeed as indicative of what the half-educated public around 1917 wanted to hear about Gothic; at the same time it is characteristic . . . of the nationalistic trend that postulated a Nordic or Germanic or German 'racial' admixture as the necessary condition of Gothic.[70]

Scheffler went further than Worringer in proposing the complete abandonment of the term 'Gothic' as being too narrow and time-bound a concept to describe the potency of the ageless force which gives rise to its forms: 'From the point of view of stylistic history, the new will look all the less Gothic the more Gothic [is its] innermost nature.'[71] Oswald Spengler also included a phenomenonology of the Gothic in his *Der Untergang des Abendlandes* (*The Decline of the West*), first published in 1926. Like Worringer, Spengler's first concern was the inner morphology which dictates things and events, the cyclic geometry which can be read off from a multitude of phenomena: 'there is found nothing, however small, that does not embody in itself the entire sum of fundamental tendencies.'[72] Unlike Worringer, however, he stressed that ornament operated at one remove from the spirit of a race, whose purest expression was in spontaneous and ephemeral phenomena such as songs, parade marches and dances. Ornament for Spengler was a public *langue*, whose fixed signs did not carry the same expressive power as a racial *parole*. However, the Gothic, as a form which was morphologically defined as becoming, as movement rather than fixity, provided a bridge between form-language and expressive speech. Gothic ornament was the rhetoric of ornament. Spengler used many of the stock romantic metaphors and images of the Gothic in his description, referring to forest groves and the Nordic world-ash, to Vikings and to Faust. But at the centre of his argument was a phenomenology of will, and anthropomorphism:

> This first person towers up in Gothic architecture; the spire is an "I" the flying buttress is an "I" and therefore the *entire Faustian ethic*, from Thomas Aquinas to Kant, is an *excelsior*.[73]

Here morphological syntax precedes semantics: how the form is expressed is more important than which forms are used; but the Gothic for Spengler is form *as* expression: 'a distinctly characterised form of "people" '.[74] When he wrote that the Gothic 'transcends the possibilities of the Apollonian' he iterated the theme of an anti-aesthetic. Towards the end of *Decline of the West*, however, there is a passage which suggests that this supposedly unconscious, innate and pre-ordained recognition of the form within form is in fact a culturally acquired and cognitively rehearsed judgement of taste: 'strategic and business flair, the collector's eye for precious things, and the subtle insight of the judge of men – and generally all that which one has and does not learn . . . which as "form" directs the course of events.'[75] Yet the 'Gothic' as identified by Spengler and Worringer stands or falls by its inevitability, its fatedness, its lack of contrivance and conscious aesthetic design. The dominant sign of 'race' despite the efforts of both these authors to employ this word in a qualified sense,[76] requires that history, chronology and *habitus* should be taboo. The Gothic is unconsciously willed or it is nothing, and Spengler does not acknowledge the literary/historical genealogy of the romantic nationalism of which he is the successor. This same preference for an ahistoric explanation emerges in Nazism, even in criticism of the regime. In 1930 Karl Radek[77] defined the Nazis as 'a party without a history' that had appeared like a volcanic island in German political life; the same phenomenology of 'manifestation' attaches to the swastika, which is quintessentially 'Gothic' in its apparently prehistoric or ahistoric assertion of the will of the collective 'I'.

ROMANTIC RHETORIC

If Paul Frankl is correct in seeing Goethe's essay of 1772 as the germ of a discourse that accorded a symbolic nationalist value to the Gothic, a discourse which reached its limits in the writings of Worringer, Scheffler and Spengler, then it is also possible to see in Goethe's theories of the symbol the mirror image of this process, in which representation is accorded an aesthetic value. In the romantic tradition, as I have already suggested, ornament becomes a symbol of national identity and the symbol is aestheticised and removed from the labour of representation. Both strategies represent a means of achieving autonomy and self-determination, in both the collective (ornamental) and the individual (symbolic) sense. Consequently both appear as the visible consequences or result of their meanings, rather than conventional signs with no ontological relationship to what they represent. In the Nazi swastika, both these discourses converge in the form of a 'National Symbol' of the party and its leader, a symbol which is the ornamental flourish, the stamp of Germanic authenticity, on the text 'Deutschland Erwache'. However, again it is important to distinguish between some supposed 'Path to Hitler' and a 'Path for

Hitler', and to focus on the radical shift of values which occurred in a heavily politicised romanticism in the context of the twentieth century. It is also important to ask what crisis in romanticism resulted in such an explicit politicisation. As Ernest A. Menze has commented: 'Hitler's rise to power did not initiate the crisis; it made it apparent.'[78]

Hans Georg Gadamer has identified romanticism itself as responsible for an abstract contrast between myth and reason, which had become an impassable gulf by the twentieth century. The romantic desire for autonomy above all transforms a system of differences into a conflict of opposites, leading inevitably to the cult of the individual and the nation. In order to understand the way that the romantic nationalist swastika signified, it is important to note how Gadamer sees this contrast between romantic myth and enlightened reason as restaged in the opposition between the symbol and allegory:

> The symbol, as what can be expressed inexhaustibly, because it is indefinite, is opposed to allegory, understood as standing in a more exact relation to meaning and exhausted by it ... the very indefiniteness of its meaning is what gave the victory to the word and the concept of the symbolic, when the rationalist aesthetic of the age of enlightenment succumbed to the critical philosophy and the aesthetics of genius.[79]

What began as a relation between the two figures or devices of allegory and symbol had become an absolute contrast and contest of values, each expressing an entire philosophy. The idea of the symbol becomes individualised to the point of anthropomorphism, and allegory becomes increasingly identified as disembodied rhetoric. Gadamer notes that in the eighteenth century, the modes of poetry and rhetoric could coexist, but that a romantic emphasis on individual expression resulted in the poetic/ symbolic becoming something set apart. He traces the origins of this schism to the correspondence between Schiller and Goethe.[80] Where Kant had spoken of the 'merely symbolic', implying the idea of an ersatz or substitute, Goethe wrote of the 'properly symbolic' which embodied the idea, whereas allegories 'employed' their signifiers at one remove to illustrate or exemplify the idea: 'Allegories employ the particular as an example of the general, symbols embody the general in the particular.'[81] The contrast here is between the lived experience, the individual *Erlebnis* obtainable in the symbol and the dead codes of allegory and rhetoric. However, this could also be interpreted as the generalisation of a type of personal experience thenceforward labelled as symbolic, an idea not without rhetorical and dogmatic possibilities of its own. This becomes evident when we realise that Goethe does not simply eulogise a single and personal 'pregnant moment' but a generic faculty or type of experience: 'Everything that takes place is a symbol, and, in fully representing itself, it points toward everything else ... the true relationship expresses at the same time the meaning.'[82] The symbol as substitute is here replaced by the symbol as substance. As a self-sustaining entity, it gains autonomy from the slavish role of 'standing for' a meaning, and appropriates meaning to itself. The signifier of the Goethean symbol asserts itself without the controlling 'other' of meaning present in the encoded *allos*, the 'speaking otherwise' of allegory. This quality was also stressed by Schelling, who referred to the German translation of the word 'symbol' as *Sinnbild*, or 'meaning image' 'as concrete, resembling only itself, like an image, and yet as universal and full of meaning as a concept'.[83] This individual communion with the symbol and the national consciousness represented by Strasbourg cathedral are the poles that Worringer's discourse was later to unite, but in a way which subsumed an individual 'self-willed' autonomy into the inescapable movement of a collective will.

The aestheticisation of the symbol which takes place when it is freed from the labour of representation and the formalities of rhetoric carries the seeds of its future incarnation in a new, 'expressive' rhetorical form. A potential for the collectivisation of the personal *Erlebnis* of the symbol is present in Goethe, and resurfaces in Carl Gustav Jung's notion of the 'archetypes'. Jung's points of reference were German idealist philosophy and Goethe, and an emphasis on the idea of invisible spirit animating material presence (hence his interest in alchemy). The archetypes were for Jung the 'ideas that have always existed'[84] which also links them to the 'ahistoric' element in romanticism. These were the predilections that enabled him to express hope for 'a New Enlightenment, in which rejuvenating symbols arise, carrying us forward into a epoch more wonderful than we can imagine'.[85]

The links between Jungianism and Nazism should not be over-stressed: Jung's model of the archetype was fundamentally egalitarian, reminiscent of Adolf Bastian's *Elementargedanken* (elementary ideas) which manifested themselves in *Volksgedanken* (ethnic ideas). Yet both Jungianism and Nazism shared a common concern with the prehistoric or ancient as an 'ahistoric' unchangeable value. Race theorists such as the Comte de Gobineau had identified an entropic force in history, and named Judaism as the source of the malaise. For Jung, decline was caused by an ever-increasing materialism and lack of spirituality. However, whilst he claimed that the archetypes could put us in touch with the unchanging fundamentals of our humanity, Jung was wont to confuse the image and the content value of archetypes, sometimes defining them as 'the unconscious images of the instincts themselves' and on other occasions denying their substance even as images: 'the archetype as such is a hypothetical and irrepresentable model.'[86] What was not at issue, however, was the status of the archetype as ancestral memory: 'All those factors ... that were essential to our near and remote ancestors will also be essential to us, for they are embedded in our inherited organic system.'[87] This recalls Schliemann's references to 'remote ancestors', and the buried, unrecognised but potent value that the archaeologist had seen in the swastikas of Königswalde. In March 1936, Jung discussed the 'German faith' outlined by Wilhelm Hauer's *Deutsche Gottschau: Grundzüge eines Deutschen Glaubens*, in which Hauer had proposed a new 'Indo-Germanic' religion to replace Christianity. J. P. Stern has claimed that Jung took Hauer's claims seriously, regarding them as 'the psychic *donnée* of contemporary Germany'.[88] Rather than interpreting National Socialist culture (as Jung did) as a manifestation of the Wotan archetype, it is more fruitful to concentrate on the ways in which it politicised romanticism, shifting the sign of autonomy from personal to collective experience. Alfred Bauemler, one of the more partisan academic philosophers of the Third Reich, made his distinction plain in an essay on 'Nietzsche and National Socialism', in which he exalted the values of romanticism over those of the Enlightenment:

> [in the Enlightenment] ... Man was viewed as a wholly individual entity, cut off from all original orders and relations, a fictitious person responsible only to himself. In contrast, Romanticism saw man again in the light of his natural and historical ties. Romanticism opened our eyes to the night, the past, our ancestors, to the mythos and the Volk.[89]

Here individual autonomy is construed as alienation, and a Goethean wish for the unity of the particular and the general is used to reunite the deracinated individual with the racial group.

That Jung's theories were recognised as essentially Germanic and opposed to the Jewish, materialist and 'Marxist' psychoanalysis of Freud was made evident in the polemics of the psychotherapist and Nazi propagandist Kurt Gauger. For Gauger, 'Freudian psychology incorporates all the advantages and dangers of the Jewish spirit, Jungian psychology all those of the Germanic soul'.[90] Jung's predilection for the potent force of ahistoric and racially contingent energies is clear even in his later writing, where he describes the swastika as a representation of the archetype that held the German people in its sway:

> There is no lunacy people under the domination of an archetype will not fall prey to. If thirty years ago, anyone had dared to predict ... that instead of the Christian cross, an archaic swastika would lure on millions of warriors ready for death – why, that man would have been hooted at as a mystical fool.[91]

Leaving aside what Terry Smith has referred to in another context as the 'we wuz brainwashed'[92] apologetics of this statement, Jung's central theme is that our age has witnessed a move from the privacy of a shared but unspoken 'collective unconscious' into a primitive and regressive era of 'collective representations' in the conscious realm. In fact, he found the strident voices and 'high-flown language' of contemporary archetypes rather embarrassing: 'Archetypes speak the language of rhetoric, even of bombast.'[93]

Jung's view was shared by Jolande Jacobi, for whom the swastika was an 'authentic symbol' which had fallen victim to Nazism, an archetype displaced from the depths of the collective unconscious to become a token of the mass.[94] Like Wilhelm Reich, Jacobi was concerned with the 'content' of the swastika, which she saw as abused or perverted in the Nazi image, while the neo-Freudian Reich argued that it was repressed or concealed. In Jacobi's view, the swastika had fallen from grace by the exhibitionist simulation of its essential content: the internally implicit had become the externally imposed. It is with the public broadcast of a shared but unspoken secret that Jacobi appears to take issue, and she draws a clear distinction between the authentic archetype and its 'pale copy', the collective sign which had been employed to manipulate and deceive: 'When the content of a symbol is exhausted, when the secret contained within it is ... made entirely accessible to consciousness and rationalized ... all that remains behind is the husk of the symbol, which forms part of the collective consciousness.' Jacobi regarded the action of the mass emblem as 'quasi-archetypal', its propaganda value drawing on stolen energy. However, another way of reading her 'implicit' sign is as a *potentially* meaningful image whose explicit and public form negates this potential energy and reveals it as an imaginative projection. This is how the Nazi swastika both completes and ends romanticism, insofar as it abolishes the distance between the fullness of the sign and the emptiness of quotidian reality that had been carefully cultivated as the space for romantic yearning. 'Content' in the abstract is a chimera; a vague 'meaningfulness' which is discerned in the image simply signifies the wish for another order of meaning.

This notion of a secret and secreted content for the swastika also occurs in theosophical and occult texts. In her *Relation of the Seen and the Unseen*, Madame Blavatsky had said that 'few world symbols are more pregnant with real occult meaning than the swastika' which had, she claimed, 'seven keys' to its inner meaning.[95] These keys appear to have been mislaid, but the alluring title of Blavatsky's text made the nature of the seduction quite explicit. Once the unseen content was itself 'seen' by naming (conjuring up) 'the symbol', then the individual *frisson* or sensation of meaningfulness could become a more generalised 'sensationalism'. This precisely defines the appeal of populist Theosophy and occultism in Austria and Germany during the early years of the twentieth century. Nicholas Goodrick-Clarke has said in this regard that: 'fantasies can achieve a causal status once they have been institutionalized in beliefs, values and social groups',[96] but the Nazi party under Hitler was to reject Theosophy and its leftward-turning swastika as being too esoteric. In Nazism the symbol was made a figure of rhetoric again, as it had been before romanticism: such esotericism may account for Jung's embarrassment at the archetype's proletarian accent, and its noisy bombast.

Wilhelm Worringer's own attempt to develop a theory of ahistoric and archetypal forms negotiated the rocky shores of romanticism with some degree of difficulty. Whilst expounding the idea of 'the will to form' as applied to race, Worringer distanced himself from the 'race romanticism' of writers such as Houston Stewart Chamberlain. Towards the end of *Formprobleme in der Gotik* Worringer rejected the idea of 'race in the narrow sense of racial purity' in favour of the idea that the stylistic force of the Gothic succeeded in establishing itself *'in spite of* racial differences in the ordinary sense'. Yet in the same passage he states that the 'Germanic strain is probably the *conditio sine qua non* of the Gothic'.[97] Implied in this partial qualification is a paradox that celebrated the Gothic as spectacle, whilst warning that this same potency might exert a deleterious effect on those exposed to its morbid exaltation. Worringer did not abandon what he saw as the necessary connection between the Germanic race and the Gothic style, but he did comment that wherever this element was present, it introduced 'among self-confident peoples that germ of sensuous uncertainty and spiritual distractedness'.[98] Gothic had become not so much a style as a force, a hybrid which disrupted the naturally ordered dialectic of Abstraction and Empathy:

> Gothic was the name we gave to that great phenomenon irreconcilably opposed to the classical, a phenomenon not bound to any single period of style, but revealing itself continuously through all the centuries in ever new disguises: a phenomenon not belonging to any age but rather in its deepest foundations an ageless racial phenomenon, deeply rooted in the innermost constitution of Northern man.[99]

The etymology of the word 'archetype' as an innate or inherited 'first pattern' links Worringer to Jung, as does Jung's prevarication on the issue of whether the archetype was itself a form or simply a way of conceptualising phenomena. Worringer's 'Gothic' was also sometimes employed as the sign of a latent race energy and, less frequently, as a term of classification. It is this distinction that separates the 'Gothic' from the 'English Gothic' in his texts.

WORLD DOMINATION

In *Abstraction and Empathy* Worringer had contrasted 'the symbolic value of the motif' with the demands of the 'will to form'.[100] In this instance the word 'symbol' did not refer to the romantic tradition but was instead used to indicate a rationally understood and encoded message. What Worringer had in fact done was to contrast a linguistic definition of the symbol with a romantic one ('will to form'), in which the symbol is freed from the task of representation to become the autonomous signifier of a national/racial selfhood. It is significant that Worringer used this distinction in the context of debates surrounding the recurrence of the same motif in different cultural contexts. If the motif was regarded as isomorphic with a symbolic (definite) meaning, Worringer argued, then 'the world domination of certain motifs would be inexplicable'. The 'world domination' of the swastika which Thomas Wilson had mapped out in 1894 had provided the anthropologist with a similar conundrum, but both Wilson's and Worringer's definitions of the symbol as a single locus of meaning tended to obscure the relationship of motif to overall field which their own cartographic vision had created.

The issue of 'the constraints of signification' placed by a single meaning on the decorative motif has also been addressed by Gombrich. He implies that patterning tends to work against signification, describing how repetition will camouflage the symbolic meaning of the motif, and stating that we 'have purchased this order at the expense of meaning'.[101] However, what the ornamentalised sign loses in depth of meaning it gains in rhetorical emphasis. Gombrich does not address the question of whether all decorative schemes tend to negate 'meaning' in the same way, and whether the repetition of a figurative motif (which constitutes a semiotic law unto itself) would have the same effect as the repetition of an abstract one whose individual geometric order could be easily adapted to suit the requirements of an overall grid. In Worringer's *Formprobleme*, this issue of the antagonistic relationship of motif to overall field finds a solution in the fractal ornament of the revolving wheel, in which the morphology of the part 'symbolises' the morphology of the whole whilst still functioning as an integral part of the scheme. This preserved the romantic fusion of subject and object, and saved the signifying image from the ignoble fate of an ersatz or mere representation. One form of servitude, however, was then replaced by another in which both part and whole traced the inner geometry of race energy, which they unconsciously and helplessly 'express'. Both Worringer and Gombrich rely on the isomorphic or 'one-to-one' model of the symbol, and the corresponding notion that to understand symbolism is to decode a language. Worringer did not describe the 'revolving wheel' as a symbol, since it lacked the isomorphism or correspondence that was necessary to fulfil his definition. He instead describes it as a 'northern ornament': northern because it possessed the requisite aspect of violent, mechanical movement through which the Aryo-Germanic soul could be recognised. Rather than seeing in the image a reference to or representation of something else, 'Gothic man' could instead *refer to* the racial mirror of the ornament, and see himself reflected.

All ornament must be seen to signify: the true issue at stake will be in what way it signifies and to whom. The Nazi swastika, as the frozen image of a dynamic motion, lay somewhere between the static typographic Germanism of Fraktur and the ornamental race signature of the nationalist Gothic, a morphology of relentless progress. Yet both Gothic script and Gothic ornament signified within the scheme of radical autonomy and the assertion of difference that was the legacy of romanticism. They were not 'German' in form, but in expression and rhetorical force; form was placed in the service of a semiotic of excess, whose collectivised representation became confrontational and aggressive. The swastika was 'expressive' in a rhetorically Germanic sense which depended on the Nazis' own version of romanticism transfigured and transfixed for the collective gaze. It is this configuring theme of race romanticism which dispenses with the 'ornament or symbol?' question as an *a priori* of discussion, since both were interpenetrative tropes of the same pseudo-aristocratic and nationalist project.

Taken out of context, Walter Benjamin's often-quoted assessment that Nazism was 'an aestheticisation of political life'[102] tends to confuse the role of the aesthetic with that of the visual. Instead, the phrase 'visualisation of politics' might usefully separate the 'distancing' semiotics of art from those of political design. And the nature of the political message dictated the morphology of symbolic forms: an aggressive nationalism adapted signs that, as Brandon Taylor has suggested, were imbued with the values of 'the harsh, the expressive and the coercive'.[103] Yet this negatively aesthetic and aggressive morphology was immediately recognised as the essence of all that was authentically German. In 1912, Worringer wrote that when confronted with the Gothic, 'we have an impression that we are being coerced by some alien, imperious will'.[104]

Arising directly from this definition is the question of whether the use of the swastika as the signifier of difference and an anti-aesthetic could be included in the total history of uses of this image, and whether such an inclusion, if possible, would be defensible as cultural anthropology. Can a cultural context for coercive form constitute the basis for a cross-cultural comparison? To effectively define cultural use, it is not sufficient simply to ask 'why this motif?'; it is necessary to look at the problem from the other side, and ask 'which features or aspects of this motif work within or against the context in which it is placed?' The migration or otherwise of 'meanings' is irrelevant to everyone except the encyclopaedist. A more interesting question is why some forms are retained and others never adopted in a particular context. Adolf Loos' suggestion in 1931 that 'everything that has been abandoned by other peoples' is 'proclaimed thereafter as German'[105] implies that a particular form of colonisation, rather than a gradual assimilation was at work. Neglected or anachronistic forms are employed because they have a distinct and recognisable character; they are both 'foreign' and alien to their context, yet on that same basis are recognisable as truly German. This paradoxical logic, which worked well with the swastika, caused difficulties for the Nazi regime when it attempted to employ Fraktur as the universal script of National Socialism. Fraktur could not be easily read; its hallowed and Germanic distinctness was revealed as useless in a modern semiotic environment and its disuetude entirely justified. The swastika worked better because it did not require a supplementary reading, it needed only a universal recognition. An effective communication circuit was thus completed: everyone in Europe could recognise the swastika, but it was simultaneously recognised as a signifier of the German. In the swastika, the degree zero of rhetoric, form as pure 'expression' could signify on both levels simultaneously, appearing as an unequivocal challenge to and declaration of war on the 'un-Germanic'.

This conflation of a universal and a nationalist/racist message is one reason why the Nazi swastika cannot be rehabilitated in a European context, since its signifying form and its 'meaning' have become interchangeable: there is no space between a signifier and its signified into which a new meaning could be inserted. If the image cannot be reassigned, could it be replaced within the global diaspora of similar signifying forms? The paradoxical status of the Germanic swastika, which was adopted only in order that it could signify something distinct, pure and 'set apart', would seem to suggest that orthodox models of cross-cultural comparison are inapplicable. Throughout this book, however, I am proposing that in the case of a form 'like unto itself' the ideas of context and comparison should be used literally: that is, context (from *contexere*, to weave together) should be used to indicate a patterned or ornamental scheme, and comparison should consist of the relationship of motifs within this scheme. For the swastika, the largest of these schemes is the world map drawn by Thomas Wilson; yet the example of Nazism, a local race politics with global ambitions, indicates how the particular relates to the general in a way which Wilson overlooked. Diffusionism, an idea which fed on metaphors of expansionism, colonisation and war, provided a precedent for the Nazi *Blitzkrieg*.

The fact that Fraktur was unreadable and the swastika could command immediate recognition also suggests how diffusion and 'migration' are facilitated. In the swastika, the typographic or graphological 'symbolic' element exists in its own right; in Fraktur, the symbolic (Germanic) and the linguistic (German) elements are inextricably linked. But as Loos had pointed out, the Germanic element of the equation was not linked to the language in any essential way, and constituted a detachable, portable and therefore transmissible element that was adopted at some point in the past. Dan Sperber has argued that this is the reason why 'symbols' can migrate, and languages tend to stay within well-defined limits:

> The fact that a datum participates in the symbolism of one culture does not prevent its symbolic processing in a second culture ... In the case of language, the set of data is defined by a state of the

language at a given time and place, and no fact foreign to this state will be processed. But the corresponding notion of a state of symbolism for a given culture at a given moment does not imply any strict criteria of inclusion or exclusion.[106]

Here the structural consistency of language is contrasted with the symbol, which is either a heterogeneous 'landmark' which draws together particular elements of the existing context into a recognisable cultural pattern, or a floating value around which new cultural paradigms can form. Although Sperber's ideas do not rule out the possibility of independent invention, they show how migration might occur, insofar as the symbol in this model is not supplementary to a particular language, but to established language *per se*. This might provide a partial answer to the question that Thomas Wilson had posed when he asked 'whether it was by migration and contact or independent invention' that the swastika had come to be globally dispersed. By separating the creation of the swastika and its cultural institution as symbol into two distinct acts, it is possible to explain what might have befallen the mysterious 'original meaning'. Images or objects, once employed as symbols or used in ritual, can be used elsewhere for the same purpose without their attached meanings being employed as well, but they must be reinstituted as symbols in each new situation. The swastikas which Schliemann found at Troy and the swastikas of the Nazi party rallies are united by the fact that Schliemann is at the beginning and Hitler is at the end of a single process in which a 'found image' has begun to function *symbolically* within a particular culture. This cultural invention of the symbol is the act of 'setting apart' an image from existing texts, and the construction of a new set of texts around it. This suggests that rather than invariably reading symbols as the 'products' of a cultural context, they may also be seen as deliberately sited 'non-texts' (Sperber's 'nonsense') to be read against, rather than with the grain. This is not meant to imply that cultural context is irrelevant, because the nature of the context dictates the nature of its subversion: new myths are spun from existing material, using symbols which facilitate both the unpicking and the rebinding of textual threads. The power of the symbol 'in its own right' is to imply the possibility of such a transformation. In the case of the Nazi swastika, the already unstable context was Weimar Germany, and the objectification and 'enlargement' of the nostalgic and reactionary fantasies that the Aryan swastika had come to represent occurred in a situation in which these fragmentary texts could be effectively politicised. In this instance, the symbol acts as foreign or irritant matter to the existing context, and becomes the nodal point around which other discourses can reify and establish themselves.

CONTEXT AND NON-TEXT

'Context' has become one of the shibboleths of recent anthropology and archaeology. Marxist notions of economy and structuralist ideas of a system of differences are applied on a micro-level to place material symbols within their 'context'. Ian Hodder has suggested that without context, archaeology becomes mere antiquarianism, and claims that:

> An object out of context is not readable; and a symbol painted on a cave wall when there are no deposits in the cave, when there are no deposits in the region that contain other depictions of the symbol on other objects, and when there are no graves containing the symbol, is scarcely more readable.[107]

The symbol 'out of context' *is* readable; here it is 'read' as a contradiction in terms, the collision of context and non-context. The image on the wall can stand either as the barrier to an interpretation within the existing context, or as the gateway to an alternative interpretation and the possibility of an entirely different context within which it would make perfect sense. As a 'barrier' the image would tend to emphasise rather than invalidate the self-consistency of the established context, yet as 'gateway' the symbol in the cave could also be seen as the sign at the birth of a new regime of meaning and a refutation of the old. On the other hand, like Loos' grafitti on the toilet wall, such a sign might also constitute an empty and redundant gesture of defiance around which no new structures could form: but the lack of a sociological background or history for the author of the gesture does not make the sign any less readable *against* its immediate surroundings. A consideration of how material symbols as a 'figure' are enmeshed in their contextual 'ground' must be augmented by recognising the possibility that they are placed in tension with it.

The cross-cultural study of the swastika which follows is based neither on the self-defeating practice of comparing one meaning to another, nor on the idea that the image simply *reflects* a structured set of relationships, but instead examines the tensions that are set up between one structure and another: between a self-identical 'swastika structure' and one in which the symbolic motif is sublimated within a system of differences. It is intended to constitute a visual and scalar, rather than an absolute, basis for a distinction between the modes of 'symbol' and 'ornament' and to suggest that in order to develop a visual construction of the symbolic marker, it is necessary to heighten the disjunction between locality and field.

Henrietta Moore, in her study of Ricoeur's hermeneutic philosophy as applied to material culture, has proposed a model for placing the material figure within its contextual ground:

> We could take, for example, the problem of decorative designs on a pot. On the 'first' level we have the individual motif (word), on

a 'second' level we can identify design sequences (sentences) and on a 'third' level we should consider the decorated pot as a whole (text).[108]

In this instance, a linguistic metaphor is used to imply that signification can only occur within a structuring system in which all the parts stand in a coherent relationship to the whole. Moore has also noted that in the model she outlines above, any 'polysemic' vagueness of meaning in the motif is screened out by its being included in the 'sentence' of the design sequence, so that it is limited to a single ('monosemic') meaning. The polysemy of the individual unit in isolation corresponds to Ian Hodder's symbol in the cave, which can only be understood as *potentially* meaningful, insofar as it suggests alternative 'sentences' and ultimately alternative texts.

Yet within this model, there also remains the possibility of employing the motif in such a way as to suppress the existing structure of meaning, without thereby instituting an alternative monosemy or reinstituting a previous polysemy. This would occur were we to isolate the motif from the syntactical system of the 'sentence' and replace it with simple repetition or multiplication. Such a substitution would have the effect of replacing both the 'polysemic' overflow of the disembodied motif and the 'monosemic' limitations of the design sequence with a system in which meaning would exist in the relationship of the individual motif to a multiplied field of similar motifs, an interrelationship which would consequently be vying with the larger field or area represented by the object/text. Rather than functioning as a landmark, each individual symbol then configures an alternative 'landscape' of signs. In this instance the polysemic or 'poetic' symbol has been rhetoricised, and its potential for alternative meaning can be used as a method of simultaneously controlling the space of the object and subduing existing 'readings'. The symbol as the imaginative catalyst for a new context has been transformed into a totalising framework for the control of the existing one. This is the model I am proposing for the Nazi swastika, one in which Nolte's symbol of 'salvation and hope' becomes a totalitarian sign field. The following examples propose that the swastika as it occurs in the micro-environment of an ornamental scheme can be employed as a model for the institution of the symbol as a method of asserting control over social space.

The first two examples are related geographically but not temporally, the second two belong to the same time and the same culture but were produced for entirely different reasons. Plate 11 shows a Hattian (pre-Hittite) 'ritual standard' made around 2300–2100BC, with swastikas arranged in a scheme of squares.[109] It is in the collection of the Museum of Anatolian Civilisations, Ankara, and is one of the many funerary objects excavated from the graves of Alaca Hüyuk in northern Turkey. Plate 12 shows the carved stone doorway of the Karatay Medrese (Islamic school) in Konya, about fifty miles distant from the graves of Alaca Hüyuk, and completed around 1252.[110] Chronologically distant, yet geographically close, the bronze ornament and the carved doorway exhibit roughly the same scheme of swastikas 'turning' alternately to the left and the right. However, they differ fundamentally in their approaches to the motif: in the Hattian ornament the swastika is 'rhetorical', in the Seljuk doorway 'syntactical'. In the Hattian device, the structural hierarchy of the 'decorated object' is displaced, since the object is simply a vehicle or frame for the repetition of the motif. This repetition of the symbol in the funeral object (further emphasised by the discrete swastikas dangling from the corners) becomes in the Karatay façade a process of dissolution through interconnection and interrelationship. In this doorway we can see, for example, either a pattern composed of swastikas or one made up of 'stepped' rhomboids. The 'word' of the individual swastika motif is still present, but subsumed in the dynamics of pattern: it is not singled out for attention, but instead has a role to play in the total geometric scheme. In Islamic art, the lack of a system of symbolism based on the one-to-one relationship between signifier and signified has puzzled some art historians, and has been attributed to a reluctance to adopt a Christian style of iconography.[111] Other authorities, however, view in a more positive light the Islamic emphasis on the symbolism of the whole decorative scheme rather than the isolated motif. Titus Burckhardt refers to a process of 'levelling out', in which ancient symbols are adopted and transformed:

> It levels them out in a certain sense, and thereby eliminates any magical qualities they may have possessed . . . Islam assimilates these archaic elements and reduces them to their most abstract and generalised formations . . . in return, it endows them with a fresh intellectual lucidity, one might say – with spiritual elegance.[112]

The swastika was one such 'archaic element' absorbed by Islam in its progress and conquests, although the appearance of the swastika in early Islamic pattern is primarily ascribed to Graeco-Roman and Byzantine influence, suggesting that a certain amount of 'levelling out' had already taken place.

There is a parallel here with the distinction that Worringer drew between the treatment of the individual motif in Gothic and Classical ornament. When he discusses the 'revolving wheel' in *Formprobleme der Gotik*, Worringer had already established a contrast between the overall symmetry of Classical ornament and the repetition of asymmetrical motifs in northern styles. Where the repetition of a motif occurs in Classical ornament, Worringer argued, it is resolved into harmony within a greater scheme of balanced mirror symmetry:

> It is true that the repetition of a single motif plays its part in Classical

ornament also: but . . . is of an entirely different nature. In Classical ornament, there is a general inclination towards repetition of the selected motive [sic] the opposite way round, as in a mirror, thereby avoiding the appearance of endless progression produced by repetition . . . By this repetition in reverse order . . . the hurrying, mechanical activity is, as it were, bridled . . . On the other hand, in Northern ornament repetition does not bear this restful character of addition, but has, so to speak, the character of multiplication.[113]

Worringer located the wheel motif in the northern tradition despite its element of symmetry, claiming that the difference between radial symmetry in the antique and rotational symmetry in the north was similar to that which exists between the balanced repetition of a motif and its mechanical or 'simple' repetition. For Worringer the 'rotation without reflection' of this form embodied the principle of simple repetition that governs all northern ornament in microcosm: 'in the one case there is quiet, measured, organic movement, in the other, the uninterrupted, accelerating, mechanical movement.'[114] In Henrietta Moore's terms, the 'word' of the self-signifying motif here constructs not a meaningful sentence but a repetitious *sequence*, which imposes its own order on the architectural and environmental text. Every architectural surface and every gaze is controlled by the imposition of an identical design.

The third example I have chosen is a sheet of drawings from the *Pedagogical Sketchbook* of the artist Paul Klee (Plate 13).[115] A single swastika had in fact been used as part of the emblem of the first Bauhaus at Weimar, but in this analysis of 'dynamics based on the square and the triangle, in part related to the circle', Klee developed the image of the swastika as a visual 'theme' with fifteen variations. He begins with the horizontally grounded four-armed swastika, and proceeds to an image resembling the Nazi 'slanted' variety (Klee noted that this is the 'best position of the swastika from the dynamic point of view').[116] The direction of apparent rotation is then reversed, and in drawing number ten the three-armed *triskelion* makes an appearance, and is explored along similar lines. For a full critical understanding of these images, it is not sufficient simply to refer to Klee's description, and say that in this sheet of drawings he sees the swastika as a 'form' and not as a symbol. What requires elucidation is the way that this approach to form differs from the 'abstract and generalised formations' of Islamic pattern that Titus Burckhardt has described. Referring again to Henrietta Moore's model, we can see in Paul Klee's drawings a visual equivalent to the polysemic 'overflow' of the individual motif. Freed from both the limitations placed on it in the syntax of the design 'sentence' and the repetition of the identical in rhetoric, the swastika is shown in fifteen ludic transformations.

In contrast to the images of play, *différance* and transformation in Klee's sketchbook, my fourth example is of the swastika as it was used in the Nazi spectacle. Plate 14 is a photograph of the 'Day of German Art' in Munich on 15 October 1933. The original caption read: 'On the Day of German Art, streets everywhere are full of happy and ceremonial decorative flags (*Fahnenschmuckes*).'[117] The use of the word 'decorative' in connection with the Nazi emblem here implies something given, the natural or logical supplement of object and context. It is such an interpretation that allows for an eventual structuralist reading in the reverse direction, from the motif to the context which 'produced' it.

I am suggesting a more critical look at the relationship between this photograph and its accompanying text. The words 'happy', 'ceremonial' and 'decorative' are there to sugar the pill of the totalitarian *Gleichschaltung* of 1933, and to naturalise the imposition of a geometry of the swastika on the geometry of the streets. I would again argue that this 'decoration', this rhetoric of ornament, is here being used to screen out the existing ontology of object, context and environment and suppress any other texts which might have supplemented them. The functionality of objects and the nego-tiability of spaces remains unaffected: even under Nazism, a pot is a pot. But the contextual meaning of the object is disturbed by the overstamping of the Germanic swastika. Henceforth all objects must question their ident-ity relative to this overall scheme: Germanic art, Germanic cars, Germanic clothes. The supplementary and connotative roles of ornament and symbol are brought together in one image which functions as a single commod-ifying stamp:

> it was repeated constantly in an astonishing variety of forms: the swastika as flag, bunting, armband as expected but also as altar cloth, silver paperweight, fan decoration, cover of sheet music for the Horst Wessell song, on goblets, cutlery, children's swapcards and books, a toy to be assembled in the kindergarten, embroidered pillows, toys, mantelpiece and wall decorations, wallpaper and decals – these are just some of the uses of the swastika.[118]

The image reinforcement achieved by the kindergarten toy is at work in another photograph from the annual *Das Jahr*, bearing the caption 'Saar-brücken was a single sea of flags'.[119] It shows a group of young children giving the Hitler salute beneath a canopy of hundreds of swastikas printed on flags and bunting (Plate 15). This photograph shows the completion of the circuit between the image of the swastika and an appropriately Ger-manic response to it, a circuit which was being constructed as far back as 1871. The 'over-stamping' of the swastika is as much a mental as a physical phenomenon, but the response is here being instituted as a physical reflex. The swastika that was transforming architecture and objects into Germanic commodities also appears in the form of the body. The recognition of the image is coupled with a set of learned acknowledgements and gestures which, far from acting as a 'context' for the swastika, simply redouble the image's own self-reflexivity. The swastika as the visual rehearsal of the interpenetration of *Führer* and *Volk* is the key element in a set of collectively rehearsed gestural representations and their spoken equivalent ('Heil Hitler') which all form part of the same circuit.

MIMETIC CODES

The repetition of the swastika to form a field of images was not simply a way to reinforce the potency of the image, since the 'motif' of the swastika should be recognised instead as one part of a strategy of gestural repetition and self-signification. The swastika is the key symbol which represents whilst 'expressing' this set of signs and gestures. In her essay 'Fascinating Fascism',[120] Susan Sontag claims that this strategy required the 'multiplication or replication of things ... Its choreography alternates between ceaseless motion and a congealed, static, "virile" posing'. Sontag sees this excessive yet regular, grandiose yet geometric spectacle as an end in itself, extending to all citizens of the Nazi state: 'the masses are made to take form, to be design.' To return to Gombrich's description of the way in which order and meaning in ornament are mutually exclusive, the Nazis may have 'purchased this order at the expense of meaning' but the system of differences within which meaning operates is replaced by what Terry Smith has describes as a 'State of Seeing' in which the citizens of Germany see themselves constantly reflected as the *Volk*.[121] Like Worringer's 'Northern ornament' the indefinitely reproduced Nazi swastika was a part in which the 'expression' of the whole could be recognised, the gesture of race identity in which others are reflected. For Worringer, the coercive aspect of the northern ornament lay in its ability to involve the spectator in mimesis: the repetition of movement in his revolving wheel 'compels us joylessly to follow its movements'.[122] This phenomenon links the kindergarten toy in the form of a swastika with the children of Saarbrücken, whom we see in the photograph in the process of *acquiring* a set of images, gestures and responses which are paradoxically construed as innate, given and racially determined. This type of reinforcement has been described by Ilse McKee in her eye-witness description of a National Socialist gymnastic display:

> While the bands played ['an uncanny sound, hollow and threatening'] the gymnasts marched in. The boys, who were dressed in black P.T. kit, formed themselves into the shape of a giant swastika on the arena floor; then the girls, in white P.T. kit, formed a circle around the swastika of boys. Next the gymnasts started to perform, accompanied by appropriate music blaring from the various loudspeakers, and all

the while they kept their formation as a gigantic black swastika in a white circle.[123]

This demonstrates another aspect of the process of counterfeiting the encultured gesture as a Germanic racial 'nature', a naturalisation which is underlined by reinforcing existing gender roles within this embracing scheme. Contemporary advertising employs gender images in a similar fashion, presenting them as the natural or innate value to which stereotyped images of male and female roles supposedly conform. Kate Linker, writing on the work of the artist Barbara Kruger,[124] has suggested that Kruger's photomontages expose the relationships between the body and its image stereotypes, relationships which result in images or poses becoming 'written onto the body'. This inscription is effected through imitations which are then themselves imitated. In this way all social space and every body becomes an advertising screen for a culture which has become 'second nature': the constant rehearsal of the gesture results in a transformation of reality, and imposes the form of the image on that of the physical object. Power is not contained and centralised in the form of the symbolic image, but in the way in which the image suppresses other systems of relationships and contextual meanings. As McKee's 'human swastika' shows, some existing systems, such as the roles assigned to male and female, are accommodated within the new patterns of power, and others are profoundly altered, yet theories of race allow the new order to appear as something expressed rather than enforced. Jean Baudrillard, in his essay 'Symbolic Exchange and Death'[125] has distinguished between the 'commodity law' and 'centralist injunction' of totalitarianism, which imposes a form of general equivalence, and the decentralised power of the simulation, which appeals and does not directly command. This is an over-generalisation on the basis of the already abstract term 'totalitarianism'. Baudrillard's simulation is also his 'genetic code' in which the response is programmed into the structure of the sign. In Nazism, the sign of race functions through the swastika as the image in which, as in Baudrillard's model of the simulation, 'mandatory passivity evolves into models constructed directly from the "active responses" of the subject'.[126] In this regard, Alfred Rosenberg's *Mythos des 20. Jahrhunderts* (The Mythos of the Twentieth Century) is illuminating: 'This message is addressed to no-one who does not already possess it as his own life or at least as a yearning of his heart.'[127] Rosenberg's statement, which echoes Hitler's preface to *Mein Kampf*, reveals how an ideology of race dissimulates command and control as the fulfilment of and appeal to a pre-existing desire. The distinction between 'mandatory passivity' and 'active response' is blurred in the swastika, which is recognised rather than read.

The dances, parades and sporting events which Oswald Spengler saw as the visible expression of an organic racial will indicate a desire on Spengler's part to show that present conformity is in fact the expression of an organic and ahistoric form. 'Race', like gender, provides a pseudo-ontological justification for stereotypical behaviour, which may then appear to be natural rather than something artificially imposed. Spengler's discourse places the body somewhere between the immaterial energy of race and the atrophied language of ornamentation, which had, he claimed, duration but no organic life. A compromise is effected in his concept of the Gothic, a form which is pure expression, a frozen gesture rather than a coded ornamental language. This conflation of the metaphysical, the ontological and the representational in both Spengler and Worringer provides the justification for an ornament which is written into the body like a genetic code, and which will be responded to, like the swastika, with an acknowledging and reflecting gesture. The Gothic style becomes Worringer's 'Gothic man', an abstract category and the sign of an involuntary group conformity to an invisible morphological law.

THE MASS ORNAMENT

Between 1926 and 1928 Spengler was writing enthusiastically about 'inspired mass units' and in June 1927 the German critic Siegfried Kracauer contributed an essay on 'The Mass Ornament' to the literary section of the *Frankfurter Zeitung*.[128] There was a fascination in Weimar culture with synchronised displays of every type from sporting events to night-club revues, but Kracauer and Spengler's interpretations of group morphology diverge in many respects. Uniting them, however, is a concern with the 'form within form' which results in Kracauer describing the Tiller Girls, an American dance troupe who performed Busby Berkeley-style routines, as 'swallowed up by the physical nature of the event'. This is a similar assessment, from a very different theoretical standpoint, to Spengler's description of 'bands that feel themselves in the common wave-beat of their being'.[129]

Andrew McNamara has perceived a 'myopic determinism' in Kracauer's notion of the body as 'swallowed up' by the mass ornament, and his extension of this idea to the group displays of the Nazi rallies.[130] Whilst the links which Kracauer sees between the high kicks of the Tiller Girls and the rhythms of Fordist production may be over-determined, I would also argue that in his distinction between the 'folk ornament' which emerges from within the community and the constructed, modern mass ornament 'which seems to hover in mid-air', Kracauer identified an aporia or fissure in which the Nazi sign of 'race' could be inserted:

The bearers of the ornaments are the masses. This is not the same as the people, for wherever the people form patterns, these patterns do not hover in mid-air but emerge from the community. A current of organic life flows from these groups, whose shared identity connects them with their ornaments.[131]

Kracauer then proceeds to contrast the ontological fullness of the folk ornament with the deracinated and alienated quality of the mass ornament of modern sports stadiums and cabarets, which rather than being organically grounded 'is an end in itself'. The mass ornament foreshadows Guy Debord's 'spectacle', as a phantasmagoric and purely visual phenomenon which is formed both in and for the collective gaze. Folk ornament is produced *from* the body; the regimented geometry of the mass ornament imposes itself *on* the body and suppresses its autonomous system of gestures and codes. Kracauer claims that the Tiller Girls form 'a closed ornament, whose life components have been drained of their substance'.[132] This recalls Gramsci's statement that industrial methods of production have eroded the 'animality' of man:

> an uninterrupted, often painful and bloody process of subjugating natural (i.e. animal and primitive) instincts to new, more complex and rigid norms and habits of order, exactitude and precision which can make possible the increasingly complex forms of collective life which are the necessary consequence of industrial development. This struggle is imposed from the outside, and the results to date . . . have not yet become 'second nature.'[133]

Hitler's Nazism, unlike its fascist precursor in Gramsci's Italy, advanced under the banner of race, a sign which functioned to make the imposition of a 'rigid norm' in every sphere of life appear as the return to some pre-industrial and organic Aryan paradise. The swastika was the sign in which a modern mass was encouraged to see itself as an ancient community, a *Volksgemeinschaft*. A representational gesture towards the folk ornament was reproduced in the form of a symbol which was displayed in parades, rallies and in the mass medium of the propaganda film. At the parade inaugurating the Day of German Art in Munich in 1939, which was filmed for national release, German citizens dressed in 'folk' and medieval costume carried ornamental swastika banners, and heraldic swastikas emblazoned on the shields of knights. As Hitler watched the parade, the military/industrial complex of the Nazi *Blitzkrieg* was already poised to invade Poland. This constructed display of *völkisch* spontaneity coheres with Walter Benjamin's assessment of Nazism as an intensification of the power of capital and industry masquerading as communal expression:

> Fascism saw its salvation ('Heil') in allowing masses to obtain self-expression (certainly not to attain their rights). The masses have a right to change the relations of ownership; fascism seeks to give them a means of *self-expression within the preservation of these relations*.[134]

The granting of supposedly inherited 'rights' to an expression of national selfhood is used to conceal both existing injustices and the forfeiting of any claim to civil rights and personal freedoms.

Kracauer defined the mass ornament as 'ambivalent' insofar as its suppression of organic nature turned nature into an abstract and potentially threatening value. The imposition of a controlling grid on modern communal existence set up a polarisation and oscillation between the absolutes of a 'for its own sake' rigidity and an equally blind and unreasoning energy:

> Nature can no longer covert itself into patterns which are powerful as symbols, as was possible during the times of primitive peoples and religious cults... So in the end nature is all that remains, nature which resists even the statement and the formulation of its own meaning. In the mass ornament we see the rational, empty form of the cult stripped of any express meaning.[135]

For Kracauer, the romantic desire for transcendence led through the regimented identity of the mass ornament, but this resulted in a stasis that prohibited the possibility of any real change of state. The spectacle is born: 'abstract signs.... portray life itself'.[136] The deracination of ornament from folk or artisan production and its realisation as a purely visual and immaterial phenomenon replaces ontology with ersatz.

Kracauer also claimed that: 'nobody would notice the pattern if the crowd of spectators, who have an aesthetic relationship to it and do not represent anyone, were not sitting in front of it.'[137] The form of his mass ornament illustrates the gulf that mechanical production had opened up between ornament and the human body, since individuals no longer constructed ornament; instead they were constructed by it into mass formations: individual action is subordinated to a vision of order. The swastika, however, was the sign which crucially distinguished the Tiller Girls from the Nuremberg rallies, insofar as it represented the promise of a bridge between an alienated mass audience and the mythical homogeneous *Volk*, in the form of an image which linked together the physical (performing) and visible (observed) body, in the form of a *recognised* gesture. The difference between a disinterested and a *völkisch* spectatorship is that which exists between seeing oneself as part of a mass, in which the act of vision does not imply any further level of relationship, and seeing oneself as oneself, in which case vision is returned as an ontological connection, a recognition. This is similar to Gadamer's definition of the symbol as that which presents in the form of an image that which is already present as an ontological reality. Yet in the case of the swastika as both ornament and symbol, we have an ontological rhetoric whose gestural and expressive force conceals its lack of substance. To the spectating eye, the Nuremberg rallies are just another modern sports event or military display whose mass ornaments 'hover in mid air', but the swastika provides these displays with a symbol, a self-presentation which seeks to justify the presence of the mass as the self-presence of a race.

In his unpublished essay on 'Mass and Propaganda', written in exile in Paris in 1936,[138] Kracauer developed a variation on the theme which he had explored a decade earlier. His discussion of Nazism, as McNamara implies, does seem to suggest a logical progression from the Tiller Girls to Hitler in which Nazism, and not consumerism, would constitute the true apotheosis of mass production: 'All mythical powers which the masses are capable of developing are exploited for the purpose of underscoring the significance of the masses as a mass. To many it then appears that they were elevated in the masses above themselves.'[139] In this scenario racism is the wild card, since its reactionary tendencies would tend to impede rather than to assist in the formation of such a 'mass religion'. The 'mass religion' thesis is supported by Karsten Witte, who in his commentary on Kracauer suggests that Nazism turned the passive visual consumption of ornamental figures into a situation in which the masses experienced 'their own triumph of the will'.[140] The notion that Nazism was capitalism *in extremis* is a cliché, but reading Kracauer's 1927 text against his later work suggests a different interpretation. The overwhelming emphasis placed by Nazism on race was the one element that could transform the disinterested spectators of 1927 into the Nazified masses who 'see *themselves* [author's italics] everywhere . . . are always aware of themselves in . . . an ornament or an effective image'[141] in Kracauer's later essay. Such a transition from alienation to self-knowledge is not possible without an 'effective image' such as the swastika, which appears to mediate between mass culture and the ground of being, between ornament and the body. Without its swastika, Nazism does indeed become equivalent to the Tiller Girls, a fact which Mel Brooks has used in good effect in parodies such as the fictional revue 'Springtime for Hitler' in his film *The Producers* (USA 1968). The ironic intent of the Mel Brooks' film is to reconstruct Nazism as a phenomenon for disinterested and ironic spectatorship, a cabaret in which the repertoire of Nazi signs and gestures becomes a robotic farce; but racism is still the skeleton at this visual feast. This is why I have suggested that the swastika is the only image which remains of Nazism *qua* Nazism, the one sign which distinguishes farce from terror.

KINO SWASTIKA

The polar opposite of Mel Brooks' Broadway revue Nazism is to be found in *Triumph des Willens* (Triumph of the Will), Leni Riefenstahl's film of the 1934 National Socialist *Reichspartei* congress at Nuremberg,[142] in which the two leading actors are Hitler and the swastika. Both of these filmic signifiers alternately assume the role of the dominant screen icon, and around them the concept of the mass transformed into a *Volk* is visually constructed (Plate 16). *Triumph of the Will* opens with a shot of Hitler's plane, its tailfin adorned with an image of the swastika as it descends towards Nuremberg, and ends with massed ranks of soldiers marching into a swastika which fills the entire screen.[143] Throughout the film, the image of the swastika is used to establish a sense of national autonomy and self-celebration, subsuming all existing codings within this scheme. Women, children, soldiers, animals and architecture are all over-stamped by the identifying typography of the swastika, the filmic 'Frakturisation' of a familiar and universally accessible visual language. This is rather different than simply 'foregrounding the signifier', since here a signifying system is being included within a self-signifying one, rather as in Ilse McKee's 'human swastika', the gender difference girl/boy is included within the form of the swastika, which contains and suppresses differences within a totalitarian culture of Germanic self-identity.

Significantly, the estrangement effect described by Loos which divides the 'German' from the 'human' still obstructs a Brooksian 'de-Nazified' reading of *Triumph of the Will* as kitsch or mass media *schmaltz*. However, this same *Verfremdungseffekt* through which a quotidian decoding of filmic language is typographically elevated by the imposition of a sign field, may account for the fact that after its release, *Triumph of the Will* failed to achieve mass appeal within Germany itself.[144] 'Frakturisation' via the swastika meant that communicative language was simultaneously ennobled and obscured. However, this made the sign field of the swastika itself more, not less, readable outside the country as the assertion of a self-justifying and confrontational 'Germanness'.

Triumph of the Will is the film which Kracauer saw as effecting the transfiguration of reality into a National Socialist 'swastika world', a judgement partly based on the mistaken assumption that the rally was staged for the benefit of the film.[145] In Kracauer's book *From Caligari to Hitler*, Riefenstahl's film is placed at the end of a line of development stretching back to Wiene's *Cabinet of Dr Caligari* (Germany, 1919), a film which Kracauer claimed crystallised the mood of morbid introspection characteristic of the Weimar years, a mood leading eventually to the complete estrangement from reality as inaugurated by Hitler. Kracauer's comparison of the hypnotist Caligari with Hitler is typical of the assertions which, as D. N. Rodowick has suggested, have led to this book being 'often and unfairly maligned'.[146] The book and its often profound insights are perhaps best read as a case study in cognition and perception, rather than in the spirit of its sub-title, *A Psychological History of the German Film*. The motifs which Kracauer employs have a lineage of their own, and his analysis of *Caligari* as a Gothic, morbid and deranged world bears striking similarities to the morphological tropes employed by Wilhelm Worringer:

Significantly, most fair scenes of *Caligari* open with a small iris-in exhibiting an organ grinder whose arm constantly rotates, and, behind him, the top of a merry go-round which never ceases its circular movement. The circle here becomes a symbol of chaos. While freedom resembles a river, chaos resembles a whirlpool. Forgetful of self, one may plunge into chaos; one cannot move on in it.[147]

The Gothic urgency and hypnotic qualities of Worringer's 'revolving wheel' are revived in the form of a motif of chaotic and meaningless motion. Kracauer identified this motif in several films of the Weimar period, noting gradual changes in successive films until the hypnotic wheel of *Caligari* has been transformed into 'repeated close-ups of waving swastika banners, which serve the additional purpose of hypnotising audiences'.[148] The swastika, claims Kracauer, is used in film for its 'stimulative power' welded to 'total mobilisation'.[149]

Rather than simply adding the lineage 'Worringer to Caligari' onto the one established 'From Caligari to Hitler' it is worth noting how Kracauer's analysis of the revolving wheel motif evolves from an insignificant, individual and introspective signifier of doubt and chaos into the oppressive uniformity of identical swastikas occupying the entire field of vision in Riefenstahl's film. Kracauer notes this progress from question to assertion in the films of a single director, Fritz Lang, who was asked to make a Nazi propaganda film by Goebbels after he and Hitler had seen Lang's *Metropolis* (Germany 1926). Kracauer argues that the primitive ornaments 'rich in meaning' which adorn Lang's *Niebelungen* (Germany 1924) had become an 'all-devouring decorative scheme' in *Metropolis*, whose only purpose is to demonstrate control over bodies and the spaces they occupy.[150] Similarly, in Walter Ruttmann's *Berlin, Symphony of a Great City* (Germany 1927), the chaotic and hypnotic motifs of *Caligari* are present in the form of a rotating spiral seen in a shop window, but, claims Kracauer, 'what once denoted chaos is now simply part of the record – a fact amongst facts'.[151] Chaos is recast in the form of order, and doubt as certainty, but the prevailing conditions have not altered: instead, representations have replaced reality.

Kracauer's analysis of 'Propaganda and the Nazi War Film' in *Caligari* offered a model for the Nazi colonisation of the visual field which made sense of his more speculative analyses of the progress from chaos to totalitarian order. Quoting Hans Speier's essay on 'Magical Geography',[152] Kracauer suggests that Nazi film motifs and cinematography conspire to demonstrate cartographically a total victory over spaces and surfaces. This is the colonisation of space undertaken by the swastika as the symbol of the new regime, and the corrosion of materiality and ontology which it initiates is manifest in Riefenstahl's film. *Triumph of the Will* is a film in which we follow the progress of the swastika in its journey back into itself, having swallowed up a culture in the process: 'movement around and above a field implies control of that field.'[153] Here Thomas Wilson's notion of a 'continuous and consecutive' meaning for the swastika is realised, since the Nazi swastika now represents its temporal *continuity* as a self-identical emblem of race 'progress' and spatiallly embodies its own *consecutiveness* as a visual environment.

Kracauer also identified the separation of image from text, and the subsequent rule of image over text, as 'an important and extensively used device' in Nazi film:

> The use of visuals in connection with verbal statements is determined by the fact that many propaganda ideas are expressed through pictures alone. The pictures do not confine themselves to illustrating a commentary, but, on the contrary, tend to assume an independent life which ... sometimes pursues a course of its own ... The Nazis knew ... that the contrapuntal relation of image to verbal statement is likely to increase the weight of the image.[154]

This contrapuntal relationship is most clearly seen in the swastika, the free-floating Germanic typography which could be applied to any visual or material text. But in order to function effectively in this role, the swastika had to operate within its own self-identical system, one which confirmed its status as the emblem of race purity whilst achieving autonomy from and suppression of the system of textual differences at work within the wider culture. The logic of autonomy inherent in the German romantic concept of the symbol is pushed to its very limits in the Nazi swastika, since oblique expression had replaced direct representation. But the morbid romanticism of Worringer and *Caligari* has been transformed in a situation where the autonomy of alienated introspection is replaced by autonomy as violent self-assertion. However, the divorce of image from text meant that the 'swastika system' instituted not revolution but inertia. Within this system, texts and contexts could be suppressed, books could be burnt, *Triumph of the Will* could overstamp a cinematic Germany with the swastika. But the possibility of writing a new text around the swastika had been a nostalgic fantasy in 1886: all that remained was to transform anxiety and wish fulfilment into anti-Semitic antagonism, and romantic autonomy into the rhetoric of race. The obscene grotesque of the Nazi swastika was and still remains a violent but hopeless gesture. The image can be reinscribed, as it has been on post boxes in London, toilet walls in Berlin and war graves in Holland, but this self-presence of an image at the expense of its context remains the only possible way in which the Nazi swastika can be read.

3

SWASTIKA

The fact that the logo exists . . . is itself a form of communication.
(Wally Olins, *Corporate Identity: Making
Business Strategies Visible Through Design*, 1989)

In his report to the fourth communications conference of the Art Directors'
Club of New York in 1958, Dr Felix Marti-Ibanez spoke on the subject
'Symbology and Medicine'. In an extended comparison of corporeal disease
with symbolic phenomena, Dr Ibanez described the swastika as a symbol
that had been 'stricken with a mortal infection' by Nazism:

> a paranoid schizophrenic Viennese house painter succeeded, using all
> the resources of modern propaganda, including mass hypnosis and –
> why should we not say so – collective symbolism, in dominating
> almost all Europe on his way to mastering the whole world. The
> swastika, which had been a symbol of well-being and enlightenment,
> then became a symbol of chaos, sadism, oppression and tyranny.
> Infection of its original meaning condemned this symbol to fall victim
> to a chronic infection, which will take centuries to heal.[1]

Leaving aside the mistaken description of Hitler as a 'house painter', it is
worth noting how the metaphors that Dr Ibanez employed reveal as much
about a subjectivist model of symbolism and its relationship to corporate
identity programmes as they do about the history of the swastika. The
intimate link established in his address between the image of the swastika
and its 'original meaning' typified the essentialist and anthropomorphic
discourse on corporate symbolism developed by designers and advertisers
in the post-war era. Dr Ibanez' naming of the swastika as a sign for
the universal and sublime ('well-being and enlightenment') also parodies the
romantic idea of the symbol. His anthropomorphic model of the swastika
echoes the romantic concept that the symbolic 'event-image' is the self-
expression of its content, and his 'chronic infection' sets in when the visual
image has been divorced from the state of nature represented by its 'original
meaning'.

This romantic and subjectivist theme has been maintained in current writing on corporate design. According to the corporate identity designer Wally Olins, the symbol or logo should embody the universal and timeless, rather than signify the ephemeral qualities of the product or the floating and quantitative values of commercial exchange: 'The symbol designer should . . . introduce concepts that both represent the particular organisation and are directly accessible to people through the visual representation of universal human values.'[2] Olins argues that the combined effects of an increasingly competitive commercial environment and changing labour patterns are now producing a situation in which brand identity is eclipsed by corporate identity. Increased competition, he claims, is making products more and more similar, and as a result companies must now differentiate *themselves* from each other to attract both potential employees and customers. This necessitates a symbolic reunification of image and identity, of symbol and meaning, that had previously been prevented by the 'soulless' aspect of the manufactured object. The logo or logotype is now seen as the point of origin for rhetorical statements on corporate goals and missions as much as a guarantee of the reproducibility and quality of manufactured goods.

This shift towards the universal and the ahistoric in corporate design has a history all of its own. The 'trademark', a sign which once indicated a distinct grouping of manufactured objects, was eventually superseded by the logo or 'corporate identity' in which emphasis was placed on the continuity of the company as an origin or source guaranteeing the reproduction of an identical type or quality of goods. More recently, corporate design discourse has travelled away from the productivist idea, in which the logo functioned as a manufacturing archetype or 'gene', and has substituted psychoanalytic metaphors for the corporeal images of sickness and infection employed in Dr Ibanez' address. In this discourse, the 'corporation' as a producing and issuing body becomes an organising and intuitive mind. Designers now speak of the 'corporate psyche' and 'corporate personality' which the logo is intended to articulate and reveal, and insofar as the logo as a psychological self-image 'gives the company away' it represents a different relationship to the consumer than that established by the commodity which must be bought and sold.

The following section of this book develops a comparison of the Nazi swastika and the corporate logo, a comparison predicated on a common 'trans-economic' ambition to supersede both the commercial and the communicative act of exchange. As the emblems of this supersedence, both swastika and logo have followed similar paths in the twentieth century, but to a radically different purpose, since what the logo now establishes as a 'free gift' and supplement to commodity laws of value, the Nazi swastika instituted as an injunction and a law in its own right, in the form of a 'national awakening' in which the individual subject was returned to himself as a member of the Aryan aristocracy. It might also be argued that the logo is an aristocratic sign; not because it seeks to elevate its products above others, but because it establishes a lineage of identity and quality of which the manufactured object is merely an example. In the Nazi swastika, however, the object is superfluous, and a lineage is established not only without recourse to exchange, but in the attempt to transcend it. The appeal to 'race' through the swastika was at once eternal and non-negotiable, established by communal and supposedly pre-existing rights of 'blood', not by the rights of private ownership. This transcendence was of course dependent on what it avowed to transcend, and the race distinction of the swastika was no less ephemeral than the contingent human groups established by commodity signs. However, what both the Nazi swastika and the logo have in common is their phantasmagoric ability to conjure up the image of a frozen time, a time beyond, before or outside the quotidian. In the swastika, this is currently expressed negatively in the form of a signal which refuses to disappear, a mnemonic which we could well do without. In the logo, it has been the guarantee of satisfaction, of a governing and controlling source. More recently, corporate design has begun to focus on the future tense, since the era of the corporate merger has eroded the status of the logo as a 'genetic' guarantee of similar object forms. The discourse of the logo is now about objectives, missions and goals, rather than traditions and continuities.

SWASTIKA AND LOGO

A comparison between swastika and logo can only be sustained at the point at which 'product marketing' is separated from 'corporate marketing', a point at which the company as a 'psyche' purports to establish a self-conscious identity and a certain distance from its manufactured products. Logos have become signs of the first person, signs in which a visual address and a corresponding recognition by the viewer takes precedence over the communication of information or the sale of a product. As Wally Olins has pointed out, 'the fact that the logo exists at all is itself a form of communication'.[3] In stating this precedent, this 'existence for itself', the logo appears as the 'human' or 'natural' point of origin for the dehumanised or denatured commodity. The logo suggests that commodities are produced magically, *ex nihilo*, which may explain the historical cult of mystery and opacity in the design of these images.[4] By revealing the company as the *source* of production, the logo simultaneously conceals the economic *conditions* of production. The logic of the logo's 'free gift' is that no strings are attached, and all signs of labour (which always carries its price) have been erased. It is a 'purely symbolic' gesture, and its lack of necessity immediately refers us to a world where things are magically begotten, not physically made.

However, the more recent 'psychologising' of the logo has attached this mute image of origin and primal innocence to a discourse of sophisticated self-awareness. The free space which was at one time simply indicated or suggested by the discreet presence of the logo in the corner of an advertisement now fills the entire surface in the paradigmatic and notorious example of the Benetton campaign, a myth told in advertising hoardings which manages to be both commercially innocent and worldly-wise. The self-revelatory 'flash' of the logo is here obscured and overwhelmed by a confessional baring of the corporate soul. Here the first person is not simply represented, it has become the starting point of a psychoanalytic discourse in which companies 'give of themselves', rather than turning the more familiar trick of mythologising their products.

That subjective signs have only a provisional autonomy, and that the 'corporate image' which the logo represents is merely an epiphenomenon of exchange, lessens neither the rhetorical force nor the appeal of these symbols. In the modern era, the nostalgic notion of a *ding an sich* of the object 'as such' outside commodity laws has been replaced by the image *qua* image of the symbol, of which the corporate logo is a contemporary form. The optimistic fiction of the logo is that the subject need not continually defend her/himself against being bought and sold. In fact, the logo seems to reassure us that subjectivity and a human essence still exist somewhere beyond production and consumption: 'The logo – unlike almost all the other incentives to communication to which man is exposed – does not demand anything in return from its viewer, not even attention. It reaches out to him.'[5]

Between 1921 and 1933 the Nazi swastika proclaimed this appeal to commonly held rather than economically differentiated values as a policy in its own right. The fact that the organic community promised by such 'commonly held' values could only be established within a discourse of race revealed the false basis for such an appeal, and disclosed the proximity of the Nazi swastika to a commodity type of distinction. The swastika made German nobodies into Aryo-Germanic somebodies in much the same way as the commodity sign continues to set standards for judgements of value, class and gender.[6] However, part of the appeal of the swastika lay in its ability to cut across social stratification by commodity and wealth with its single division of race, whilst at the same time leaving those distinctions intact, distinctions which a Marxist form of the state would immediately have erased. In the Nazi state, Jewish property could be confiscated, but the notion of property itself was not disturbed.[7] Like the logo, the promise of the swastika was trans-economic, not post-economic, just as the promise of the romantic symbol had been to make the ordinary extraordinary without thereby cancelling out quotidian space with its elevation of 'experience' to a higher power.

Designers and design historians have lately become aware that the visual image of the logo can easily become a crude device which tries and fails to conjure up a 'false consciousness' of economic and productive realities. However, rather than abandoning the aesthetics of the logo altogether and thus presenting productivist ethics in the raw state, corporate image programmes have instead begun to actualise as a set of goals what the logo once represented, statically, as a simple declaration of identity. As occurred in the nineteenth-century institution of the swastika as an Aryan symbol, in the logo we can perceive the shift from the symbol of a set of (productive) practices to the institution of a set of practices which will 'produce' the corporate mission or goal embodied in the symbol. In tracing the history of this development in the form of the logo, the writer Rose de Neve has remarked that in a contemporary context, the terms 'corporate identity' (the company logo) and 'corporate image' (how the company is perceived) represent a puzzling transposition of values. She argues that the word 'identity' suggests an essence or ontology:

> Identity ... has nothing to do with a designed logotype and the attached 'bug' [logo] – that is with a visible object – so much as with a condition or state of being and the awareness of that state. 'Corporate image' might have been a better way to describe a visual signifier.[8]

De Neve suggests that the reason that the corporate logo is not referred to as an image is because the word 'image' has connotations of falsehood or unreality. Her argument implies a cosmeticising of the cosmetic, but a more radical way to look at this issue is to suggest that the transposition has not been cosmetic but actual, and that the visual image has in fact taken on the ontological qualities which were once seen as proper to identity.

This transformation of image into identity has been a gradual process, and the mediating role of the manufactured object different at every stage. At one time a sign or signature on the object stood simply as a maker's mark, and the 'trademark' was a device through which faulty or sub-standard goods could be traced back to the work of a particular craftsman. The split between the object and its maker, between 'brand identity' and 'corporate identity' begins when several products are issued by a single manufacturer: the trademark then refers to the maker not via the materiality of the object but through an abstract set of values or some psychological trait such as 'decency' or 'integrity'. The phantom image takes one step further away from the manufactured object with the advent of the professional trademark design company, a division of labour which follows the split between designing and making in Fordist methods of production. After World War II, Rose de Neve identifies a crisis in corporate image, which had become a universal abstract token applied 'after the fact' by designers to companies which were now themselves split into several corporate divisions. She suggests that the answer to this crisis of identity has been on the one hand the division of product marketing from corporate marketing, and also a foregrounding of the logo as a unifying and 'express-ive' image: 'The major difference between "then" [the 1960s] and "now" is that the new corporate identity begins with the need to delineate the fundamental nature of the corporation – *to formulate a statement for the corporate mission* [my italics].'⁹ Here the corporate image, instead of being something which is applied to the company as an afterthought or cosmetic illusion, takes on a strange ontology of its own, as a projected 'state of being' towards which the company is supposedly moving. The shift in values is then complete: the trademark which was once a postscript, signature or maker's mark applied 'after the fact' to the object has grown in stature to become an image which *precedes* both the manufactured object and the company itself. The alienating gap between identity and image has been removed by collapsing the former into the latter, in the form of a visual symbol which is then given the paradoxical title 'corporate identity'.

This trajectory of the corporate image as something 'moving towards' a state of being rather than representing a ready-made object had already been completed by the Nazi swastika in 1920. The total conversion of the swastika into a sign of race and the final abandonment of associated 'meanings' and explanations of the sign accomplished the same insinuation of an ontological value into a representative one. Hitler's description in 1925 of the swastika as representing the 'mission of the struggle for the victory of the Aryan man' also emphasised the goal and the mission which the symbol supposedly embodied. The referent of the swastika was now placed in the future, in a notional Aryan body and a race consciousness: the *image* of the swastika would be completed by a race *identity*. The interim solution was to continue the 'tradition of the symbol' spatially and synchronically as its own self-identical referent, since the Aryan had failed to make an appearance. However, the years after 1933 saw the attempt to realise the Nazi racial 'mission' which culminated in the Wannsee confer-ence and the Holocaust.¹⁰ The fact that in 1993 the racist swastika still requires a visual iteration and that its 'mission' could never have been accomplished, shows that Nazism was following the obscene logic of its self-representation. Only in the name of swastika, the sign of race, could Nazism identify and distinguish itself.

COMMODITY AND GIFT

In the 1920s, the Nazi party and its swastika could have been seen as yet another example of reactionary nostalgia and a 'false consciousness' of the economic and political realities of that time, to be set alongside *völkisch* groups and the cult of Mazdaznan and colonic irrigation which Johannes Itten promoted at the Weimar Bauhaus. However, when Hitler became chancellor on 30 January 1933, any notion of a 'false consciousness' was replaced by an 'interpolation' of the Althusserian variety, in which the masses were included in the racist ideology of the swastika (and in the 'mission' of the sign) as the subjects of a mythical 'Aryan aristocracy'. Althusser's famous dictum was that ideology 'represents the imaginary relationship of individuals to their real conditions of existence', implying a privileging of ideology over reality, achieved by an 'interpolation' which addresses the masses as the subjects of that ideology.[11] The distinction between a 'true' and a 'false' consciousness then becomes problematic. This phenomenon was at work both in the armorial emblem of the swastika and in Hitler's typically eschatological proclamation, on 1 February 1933, of 'national awakening', a phantom coming to consciousness in which representations of racism took on the mantle of a revealed truth and a higher reality.[12]

In comparing the 'mission' of the Nazi swastika with the corporate mission symbolised in the contemporary logo, I am describing the logic of self-representation developing at different rates and in different circumstances, but which in the end both attempt to supply an ontological referent ('identity') to complete the visible image. And in both cases, the goal which is sought is collapsed into the image which ostensibly 'represents' it. The image is then maintained and displayed *as* the goal, which therefore remains phantasmagoric and unattainable. It should be noted, however, that when the Nazi swastika was the dominant icon in Germany, the corporate logo was still enmeshed in a productivist rather than subjective/psychological sign language. At this stage the logo was still a manufacturing template or archetype, rather than the sign of a direct and unmediated 'public address' from the corporate psyche to a community of consumers. In his guide to corporate identity, Wally Olins describes a pre-conscious state of capitalism outside the sphere of public concerns, citing as evidence the fact that companies such as Ford Motors kept up production in both America and Germany during World War II:

> Ford, Unilever, General Motors and others traded right through the Third Reich, working with even-handed willingness for both Allies and Nazis. Today such a situation would be unacceptable. Society does not reject the corporation; on the contrary, increasingly it welcomes it into its bosom. But it demands from it what it regards as socially acceptable behaviour.[13]

What Olins sees as an ethical question can more accurately be read as an issue of representation, and of the distinction separating the subjective signs of Nazism from the commodity and trademark signs of commerce. It is not that the consumer now asks more of the corporation, but that the corporation no longer communicates only via the object (brand identity) but instead speaks directly, 'person to person' using the corporate identity of the logo or logotype. Ethical issues such as ecology or racism that abound in contemporary advertising simply narrativise and extend this 'first-person' address: they give the corporation a human face. In 1942, when Ford was making trucks for both the American public and the *Wehrmacht*, the situation was somewhat different, insofar as politics and commerce had realised a 'non-aggression' pact, and their systems of representation did not as yet coincide. In the Nazi state, commodity distinctions such as company trademarks were allowed to exist alongside the totalitarian sign of race, but what the party did prohibit in its 'Laws for the Protection of National Symbols' of May 1933 was the use of the swastika as a commodity sign which could increase the value of mass-produced objects.

Because of this historical difference, many comparisons which have been made between the Nazi swastika and modern corporate identity are superficial. Such comparisons are made by designers in order to invest the modern logo with a borrowed potency, and simultaneously to 'tame' the Nazi image by a retrospective and patronising comparison. The truth is that the Nazi swastika was not 'just like' a corporate logo; it might be more accurate to say that the logo is an etiolated swastika. Corporate wars parallel the semiotic contest between swastika and hammer and sickle that took place in the Weimar republic, but no corporate identity has yet succeeded in moving beyond this system of differences and into the totalitarian environment which existed in Germany after 1933, where both ideological contest and electoral appeal were superfluous and only one sign was required, which therefore could no longer be read as a sign in the accepted sense of this term. A passive rather than dialogic 'reading' of the sign requires that it be placed within a structured set of differences, and it is such a reading which allows for and directs the pseudo-activity of 'consumer choice' between one product or service and another. With the Nazi swastika, this already illusory commercial 'choice' in which one element presents itself as a singular, rather than as a constitutive value, is replaced by what might be termed the radical singularity and enhanced passivity of race consciousness. The battlefield of contesting signs familiar from the marketplace is replaced by the corralling effect of the identical sign field of the swastika, which substituted siege warfare (Aryans within, non-Aryans without) for the ritualised engagements of commerce.

The rules of commercial engagement and the links between a particular company, its competitors and the economic sub-structure work to ensure that the assertion of autonomy and a projected 'state of being' in the corporate image or logo is provisional and rhetorical. The gravitational force exerted by an economy also ensures that the 'brand loyalty' promoted by the logo is normally seen as distinct from the 'company loyalty' which it also effects. The latter is something which normally only company employees have been persuaded to have, and the public or community created by the product has traditionally been seen as a beneficial side-effect rather than an end in itself. However, recent developments in advertising, such as the Benetton campaign, in which the product disappears and is replaced by 'event-images' bearing the company logotype, places the 'corporate personality' squarely in the midst of the public sphere and political concerns. What is on sale is the Benetton *Weltanschauung*, and the commodity (clothing) is hidden within the ultimate 'free gift' of charitable humanism: 'advertising in its new dimension invades everything, as public space ... disappears.'[14]

It is when this trans-economic ambition can be recognised that a comparison between the Nazi swastika and contemporary corporate identity becomes possible. In 1933, however, the image of the swastika was the site of a struggle between the commercial and commodifying values of mass production and the Nazi project of a *Gleichschaltung*, a public 'co-ordination' around the new national symbol. Goebbels' regulations of 19 May that year were intended to stop the wholesale application of the Nazi swastika to all manner of manufactured objects from paperweights to blackboard dusters as a sales gimmick. Paragraph one of the regulations states that 'it is forbidden to use the symbols of Germany history, of the German state and the National awakening in public in such a way that the dignity of these symbols is seen to be lessened'.[15] Couched in the tortuous rhetoric of National Socialism, these regulations instituted a system for policing uses of the swastika which provided for the immediate confiscation of unsuitable objects without compensation and the fining or jailing of anyone selling them. Supplementary regulations distinguished between mass-produced and 'art or applied art and craft' objects bearing the swastika, and thus become 'anti-commodity' laws, since factory-made objects were likely to have the swastika applied simply 'to adorn the object, or make it more saleable (*Absatszfähigkeit*)'. No restrictions were placed on craft objects whose form was that of the symbol itself, for example stickpins and badges:

> If the symbol is used on an object or in connection with it, it may only be used when the object itself has an inner relation (*innere Beziehung*) to the symbol ... The use of symbols for publicity purposes is in any case forbidden.[16]

These regulations imply a distinction between the elevation of the *object* as a commodity form and the elevation of the individual *subject* to race consciousness. Items such as flags and lapel badges were deemed to ennoble the person, whereas in the specifically forbidden instance of a children's ball, the addition of a swastika would increase the purchase price of an object only then to be unceremoniously kicked around the streets.[17] These laws insisted that the 'national awakening' of 1933 should be an experience collectively shared rather than an object privately possessed. The trans-economic is the realm not of having but of being, a domain which commerce was at that time imperfectly equipped to colonise.

Goebbels' laws against public display of the swastika, however, did not explicitly prohibit the commodification of the swastika in the form of a ready-mixed literary exegesis. After 1933, books on the origin and meaning of the swastika were legion, including pamphlets such as *5000 Year Swastika* by Dr Fritz Geschwendt, who set out to explain to German youth 'the history of the swastika and its meaning, in particular swastikas as the symbols of the Germans'.[18] Ulrich Hunger has noted that in the swastika literature of this period, the Germanic fantasies which filled the tantalising gap between image and meaning knew no bounds.[19] This is certainly true of Dr Geschwendt's book, which sought to satisfy childish curiosity as to why the swastika in particular should be the sign under which 'the new Germany marches'. He began by quoting Hitler's words on the swastika in *Mein Kampf*, in which the symbol is referred to as an anti-Semitic sign. Geschwendt then attempted to supply a Germanic history and meaning which could explain the position Hitler had adopted, and he was probably fully aware that only a child would have accepted the history of the swastika he presented. His account includes a description of Schliemann, the 'German explorer' who discovered swastikas at Troy, and the Trojan whorls are introduced to account for the 5000-year Germanic prehistory proclaimed in Geschwendt's title, a prehistory which is mapped onto an indefinite future.

Geschwendt's 'educational' material on the swastika appears to bear out Ulrich Veit's claim that: '[The Nazis] . . . integrated history at all levels, to the extent that even minor local periodicals of historical societies were turned into pamphlets of National Socialism.'[20] However, the party itself did not bother to question that the swastika was Germanic *because* it was anti-Semitic, without further evidence being necessary. Hitler's contempt for myths of origin and patched-up prehistory is a matter of record, and his view of the swastika was primarily architectural, a matter of Aryan form and Aryan space, with the word 'Aryan' being accorded its narrowest and least 'archaeological' or textually exact definition as the Germanic. Even the verbose and obfuscatory Rosenberg in his *Mythos* referred not to a prehistoric dispersal or an ancient meaning (the endless *Ursprungs* and *Bedeutungs* of Germanic swasticology) but instead placed his emphasis on the swastika as 'a new symbol' for a renewed existence, in the process demonstrating how the swastika neatly aggregated the texts of National Socialism. The swastika, said Rosenberg, was 'in accord with our new Mythos . . . Folk-honour, living space, national freedom, social equality, racial purity and a life-renewing fertility.'[21] Here yet again the swastika was used as the device which could draw together a set of disparate and inconsistent meanings in order to make them self-evidently and symbolically *meaningful*. This 'drawing together' via the swastika is simultaneously a process of drawing racial distinctions. Rosenberg's emphasis on renewal also shows that the Nazi Party did not intend the gap between image and meaning in the swastika to be filled by an explanatory text, but rather by a sudden revelation of race consciousness. It is this tradition of 'self-evidence' and an emotional recognition of and somatic involvement with the image which links Schliemann to Rosenberg, rather than the attempt to gather historical proofs for a racist ideology.

The official Nazi line on the swastika was national renewal through racial purge. Meaning, explanation and attribution were unnecessary, since an explanation of the swastika would have immediately introduced the ambiguity and interpretative freedom which accompanies texts. Goebbels' laws of 1933 existed to police the *uses* of a form, not to control the interpretations of that use. These laws might appear to be an example of ordinary copyright legislation enforced by extraordinary methods, but in the context of the Enabling Bill passed two months earlier on 23 March 1933, they can more accurately be seen as part of the attempt to Nazify all aspects of life in Germany. The passage of the Enabling Bill (The National Emergency Termination Bill), which gave the Nazi government the power to act without parliamentary sanction, ended the illusory promise of a bourgeois nationalist regime which might have replaced the weak democracy of Weimar, an illusion which the Nazi party had sought to foster. The clash between the purveyors of swastika cuff-links and party officialdom highlights the conflict between a bourgeois economy of difference and the imposition of unswerving totalitarian identity, since those selling Nazi kitsch were merely attempting to gain a competitive edge, whilst the party itself attempted to subsume the individual entrepreneurial instinct into the determinism of race. In May 1933, the *Berliner Illustrierte Zeitung* commented that since Hitler's assumption of the Chancellorship on 30 January that year, an 'entire industry' had set to work cashing in on the popular appeal of Nazism, a phenomenon which was 'more damaging to the community than it was helpful to the economy'.[22] This statement places race and commerce on opposite sides of a divide which ostensibly separated an elevated national interest from a low commercial self-interest. What was in fact happening was a struggle for the swastika between two systems, both attempting to absorb the other. Where Nazism tried to commodify the German subject as a member of the Germanic race, commerce carried on relentlessly with its traditional practice of commodifying the object.

The ultimate victor in this battle of wills has of course been commerce, in the form of those pulp publishers who still live by the dictum that 'nothing sells like sex and swastikas' on a book cover. In this economy-driven system, signs are interchangeable, and if they carry the same commercial value, it is immaterial whether they are swastikas or women's breasts. The pulp publishers of today follow in the footsteps of those purveyors of 'Nazi kitsch' who first saw the commercial potential of the swastika in 1933.

It is the unique characteristic of kitsch that it makes public, vulgarises or cheapens private experiences, usually of a transcendental, religious or sexual nature. Those who manufacture kitsch often find themselves in conflict with those organisations which have traditionally mediated between the private and the public realm, such as the Church. On the one hand these organisations see kitsch as a challenge to their authority; on the other they may realise that their own sacred symbols of communal transcendence stand a hairsbreadth away from vulgarity and profanity. This was certainly true of Nazism, since as Gillo Dorfles has pointed out, 'what could be more ... kitsch than ... Nazi myths?'[23] Dorfles has distinguished between what he terms the mythagogic or ersatz 'revelation' of Nazism and the mythopoetic character of literature and art. His notion of a *Kitsch-anschauung*, a 'kitsch consciousness' is persuasive, but there remains the question of precisely how this is effected. The kitsch object uses the emotionally catalytic symbol as a sales gimmick, a means to elicit a recognised and predictable 'effect' for which commercial gain is the underlying cause and through which consumer consciousness travels on a closed loop. In order for the consumer to personalise the emotion which the kitsch object has made public, she or he must make that same emotion a private possession once more through the act of purchasing the object. Nazism, to the contrary, was more concerned to maintain an elevated experience at the level of a public and communal participation, rather than returning it 'home' in the form of a sentimentalised object. The 'Laws for the Protection of National Symbols' specifically condemned 'pictures of artistically low value, with self-illuminating swastikas' whilst condoning images of the leading personalities of the new regime.[24] These pictures, when displayed in the home, had the effect of transforming the German living room into a public, rather than a private space, and were sanctioned by the anti-kitsch regulations under the heading of 'the object which is itself the symbol'. Nazism was concerned to protect the integrity of its self-representations at all costs. It saw its swastika as defensible *völkisch* space, a 'national symbol' which defined the Germanic ghetto, and which could not be allowed to fall into the wrong hands. Goebbels' regulations represent one step on the road to 14 July 1933, when German bourgeois democracy finally voted itself out of existence, the Nazi party was declared the only political party in Germany, and the swastika was established as the single dominant sign. In another sense, this curbing of commercialism had simply raised kitsch consciousness to a higher power. In Nazi race ideology, the signs of distinction, elevation and fulfilment did not have to be purchased, they were freely given to all 'Aryans'. The short cut to bliss that kitsch represented became shorter still, and the sign of distinction did not have to be mediated by a mass-produced object, since it could be possessed by all Aryo-Germans as their spurious 'birthright'.

THE MISSION STATEMENT

This hypertrophied singularity in which the subjective sign becomes an all-encompassing national symbol is absent from the corporate identity, the gestures of which towards subjectivity and ontology are provisional, positional and more easily referred to economic factors. The corporate mission is in one sense a market-driven goal; but in another sense the company is also driven by the logic of its own self-representation. It may then become difficult to sort out economically pragmatic from 'symbolic' gestures. On 21 March 1991, an article in *The Guardian* described a redesigned logo for British Telecom, 'part of the company's plans to redefine itself for the 1990s'. This was accompanied by the news that Telecom was to cut 40,000 jobs. In one sense, the new logo was being read as a piece of cosmetic surgery, a fragment of 'false consciousness' concealing harsh economic realities. This is the interpretation suggested by the headline 'BT unveils four million pound facelift and cuts 40,000 jobs'. However, these same job cuts are then described as one part of a redefinition for which the new logo is the material expression, the embracing and co-ordinating symbol. In an interview about the controversial new logo, its designer Wally Olins claimed that the debate provoked by the image had confirmed his intuition that 'symbolism is emotional and causes people to get worked up'.[25] Channelling emotions through the symbol in this way could also serve as a way of diverting attention from economic issues, both in the marketplace and within the company itself. However, Olins also revealed that his intention had been to create a cross-culturally recognisable image drawing on the classical symbolism of Mercury and Hermes: 'something ... immediately recognisable, in any culture, as a symbol of communication'.[26] This double colonisation of Classical symbolism and the global market, and the emphasis on subjective factors such as 'emotion' and the corporate psyche, typify the trans-economic and supra-material aspirations of the corporate identity.

The question of the cross-culturally identifiable image is particularly relevant to Nazism, which took the globally dispersed sign of the swastika, a sign which Norman Brown[27] had described in 1933 as 'common human property' and renamed it as a 'national symbol'. This annexing or copyright of a universal sign parallels the process described by Olins in which an 'internationally understood' symbol is simultaneously recognised as the property of a particular company. The global market is implicit in the selection of the symbol, whose sphere of semiotic influence defines the propositional space which will eventually be colonised. In this respect, the Germanically exclusive and globally inclusive sign of the swastika differed sharply from the communist hammer and sickle, which in global terms was the symbol of an 'export drive' on behalf of Marxist ideology. The hammer and sickle attempted to export a Western philosophy of productivity and labour as an international language of revolution. This attempt was criticised by Jean Baudrillard in *The Mirror of Production*, which suggested that both capitalism and Marxism were in the thrall of the same productivist ethic: 'When Marxism speaks of the mode of production of primitive societies, we ask to what extent this concept fails to account even for our own historical societies (the reason it is exported).'[28] When he wrote *The Mirror of Production*, Baudrillard was still preoccupied with the vision of a primitive 'symbolic exchange' which with its prodigality, waste and sacrifice could challenge both political economy and the economy of the code. In his later text on 'Symbolic Exchange and Death' this concept of a meaningless *dépense* (taken from the work of Marcel Mauss and Georges Bataille), was seen as haunting Western society in the form of 'an obsessive memory, a demand ceaselessly repressed by the law of value'.[29] It might seem plausible to suggest that Nazism, which in the name of representations of racial purity murdered human beings *en masse*, in secret and with no political, electoral or economic end in view, was participating in just such a 'symbolic exchange' which cancelled and negated all the laws of exchange and every human value. It could also be argued that the death camps of the Nazi Holocaust were only 'factories' insofar as this obscene realisation of a productivist concept was linked to the uneconomic and impossible project of a 'final solution'. This argument might be sustained were it linked to the disjunction between symbol and reality, the gulf between an anti-Semitic image and its phantom reference to an Aryan identity. It cannot, on the other hand, sustain any idea of an 'ecstasy of sacrifice'.[30]

The term 'final solution' (*Endlosung*) as employed by Reinhard Heydrich at the Wannsee conference on 20 January 1942 stands as a bland euphemism for an unspeakable act. The term also carries the connotations of a paradox or logical difficulty, a squaring of the circle in which all other realities and all previous standards of judgement were abandoned to maintain the economy and equilibrium of a racial representation, the one factor by which Nazism could name and distinguish itself. The 'sacrifice' here is of the possibility of an alternative view, and of a different logic than the logic of mass murder. According to the testimony of one member of the SS killing squads, 'the Jews were killed because they were Jews'.[31] This is not a tautology but a statement with its own pitiless internal logic, a sentence which is a killing machine in its own right: human beings at one end, and representations at the other.

Reality was sacrificed to racist logic in successive stages. In *Mein Kampf* Hitler had already subordinated the economic principle of labour to the trans-economic principle of race. In defining the swastika as the sign of 'creative work' he adds that creative work 'has been and always will be anti-Semitic'. In an earlier passage, Hitler had already established that 'work' should be done in the 'interests of the community', but this gesture towards a socialist ideal is undermined by his declaration that only the Aryan is capable of such selflessness.[32] All labour in the Aryan state, as Hitler makes clear in his statement on the swastika, is only a means towards a racial end. Even military goals were eventually sacrificed to Hitler's racial project: as J. P. Stern has pointed out, the murder of Jewish prisoners was carried out 'at considerable cost to the German war effort'.[33] In his identification of anti-Semitism as the guiding principle of Nazi policy from first to last, Stern has criticised the revisionist tone employed by Ernst Nolte, who whilst not denying the reality of the Holocaust, has interpreted it as a reaction to what he terms the 'annihilation' occasioned by the Russian revolution and a 'copy' of similar atrocities throughout history, thus making racism a peripheral rather than the central determinant of Nazi policy.[34]

Nolte's attempt to 'level out' Nazism relative to other forms of oppression is manifest in his *Three Faces of Fascism*, a book which compares *Action Française*, Italian fascism and Nazism.[35] In his adoption of a 'phenomenological' method of analysis for fascism, Nolte reifies an abstraction, since the differences between movements labelled generically as fascist outweigh the similarities which might reasonably be said to constitute a 'phenomenon'. However, his comparison of the Nazi swastika with the Italian fasces allowed for a radical difference in the 'extremity' of the visual rhetoric employed:

> What was genuinely new and typically transformed was the party flag. The swastika did not, like the lictors' bundle, recall a remote but nevertheless still tangible historical era: as an ancient and prehistoric symbol of salvation, it was supposed to proclaim the future victory of 'Aryan man.' Just as Mussolini's oratorical style, even in its worst outbursts, seemed controlled and moderate compared to Hitler's, so the recalling by the Fascists of the Roman Imperial tradition seemed ... concrete and historically valid when compared with this appeal to the prehistoric and the archaic. Not only in ideas; in sight and sound, too, the extreme nature of the young movement ... is easily recognizable.[36]

This passage is worth quoting at length as an example of an analysis of the swastika which does not accept its own implications. Nolte allows his general fascist comparison to repress an investigation of the 'phenomenon' of Nazi difference *qua* difference. Nazism was not fascism *in extremis*, it was the institution of racist extremism in the form of a fascist political programme. In other words, Nazism was fascism plus the swastika. Nolte is correct in identifying the Nazi swastika as ahistoric and archaic, but he shies away from identifying race as the ideology within which these elements functioned and for which the swastika was the emblem. The swastika differs from the fasces precisely in its explicit racism, not in its degree of fascism. Both the swastika and the lictor's bundle express the basic fascist equation of the many contained within the one, but the swastika accomplishes this in a more literal and less literary sense as a signifying surface of identical images, in which each singularity represents the whole as one uniform represents an army. However, in Nazism, this fascist principle is used to construct not a form of the state but a form of the person, or of the state founded on the principle of racial purity. This is why the swastika should be compared not to the lictor's bundle, but to Fichte's autokinetic state machine of 1807, whose motive power was derived from Aryan race energy. Nazism, the historian George L. Mosse has claimed, 'expressly reject[s] the Roman-law concept of the state as a separate corporate identity'.[37]

Georges Bataille also offered radically divergent interpretations of Italian and German fascism in his 'The Psychological Structure of Fascism', an essay which first appeared in the journal *Critique Sociale* on 10 November 1933.[38] Whilst suggesting that the principle of an aristocratic 'sovereign form of value' was common to both political movements, Bataille implied that Italian fascism had identified the state itself as the symbol of this highest value, whereas Nazism, with its exaltation of race above all else, had given the state only a secondary and contingent role. Bataille's central concept of fascist sovereignty as 'an existence for itself' was an elaboration of his theory of symbolic exchange that Baudrillard and Jacques Derrida were later to seize upon. Bataille himself had developed his theory as a reworking of Marcel Mauss' concepts of the gift and of 'Mana', the force in which Polynesian mythology unites the community represented in the symbol or totem. In Maussian anthropology, both the expenditure of the gift and the mysterious force of Mana work to stabilise a primitive social structure, but Bataille saw in Mana a potentially destructive and violent force. In his essay, Bataille claimed that the 'affective' symbols of fascism, like primitive totems, at once constitute and represent the community, and that like Mana, the reality created by fascism 'is that of a force or shock' which transcends the quotidian reality of the economy and the object.[39] At the centre of Bataille's argument is the opposition of a heterogeneous and fascist 'being for itself' to the homogeneous and relative 'having to be' of the bourgeois capitalist economy.

Written in 1933, at the moment of the Nazi victory, Bataille's essay seems both to anticipate and to defer the possibility of Auschwitz, since although he places race at the centre of the Nazi programme, Bataille's Marxism lights upon the proletarian soldier as the intended sacrificial victim. What has become clear since 1933 is that it was the repressive reality of Nazism that sustained the racial myth of an Aryan community, and not vice versa. The oppression and murder of 'the Jews' was the only means by which Nazism could constitute the 'sovereign form of value' called the Aryan. Within the terms of reference set by moral, ethical, military/industrial and political economies, what occurred in the concentration camps was indeed an 'unexplainable difference' and a one-way 'symbolic exchange'. However, this annihilating impulse was framed by an economy of logic, a logic which committed murder to maintain the structure of representations and the racial mission of the swastika.

BREAKING THE CHAIN: JOHN HEARTFIELD

Bataille's essay accurately describes the political utility of a racist appeal to the 'sovereign law of value' which, as I showed in my introduction, had a particular applicability in Germany.[40] However, what he could not show in 1933 was the Nazi attempt to convert the seizure of power under the sign of race into a form of the state founded on exactly the same sign. The coming to consciousness and aristocratic 'being for itself' promised by the swastika was a representation which could only be sustained by the negative action involved in boycotting Jewish shops, burning books, imprisoning and murdering opponents and finally declaring war. Although Nazi ideology privileged the *Volk* over the state, this same notional *Volk* could only be supported by state repression. Only a year after Bataille wrote his essay, this point was made clearly and forcibly by John Heartfield in one of his anti-Nazi photomontages, *The Old Slogan in the 'New' Reich: Blood and Iron* of 8 March 1934 (Plate 19). Heartfield's image, which strips away the autokinetic rhetoric of race to reveal the repressive political machinery that supported it, shows four axe blades bound crudely together in the shape of a swastika. This photomontage had appeared in the exiled Communist newspaper *AIZ (Arbeiter Illustrierte Zeitung* or Workers' Illustrated Paper), and Heartfield introduced a double historical reference, relating the recent beheading of four Communists by the Nazis to Bismarck's declaration of 1862 that 'Blood and Iron' were the means to German unity. Douglas Kahn has suggested that this photomontage was 'generalised to mean that nothing had changed since Bismarck, the stability of the nation-community was being gained only through barbarism'.[41] Heartfield meant this and much more, since he had succeeded in making the swastika *historical* and historically specific, thus annihilating the ahistoric illusion of Aryanism.

In examination of the semiotic potency of this photomontage, it is worth noting the distinctions that George L. Mosse has drawn between Bismarckian *Realpolitik* and Nazism. For Mosse, the message of Bismarck's 'Blood and Iron' bluntly asserted the power of the state in contrast to the more abstract and spiritual unity of the *Volk* sought by romantic nationalism.[42] In this respect, Heartfield's image functioned as an X-ray that revealed the apparatus of state terror supporting 'the struggle for the . . . victory of the Aryan man'. And in successfully subverting these illusions, Heartfield's image of protest co-opted the means and the scale of their dissemination. *AIZ* had the third largest circulation of any illustrated magazine in the Weimar republic and continued to publish from exile in Prague until Hitler's invasion of Czechoslovakia. In this way Nazi mass-media propaganda encountered anti-Nazi mass-media polemic. Heartfield was later to say that:

> My montage 'Blood and Iron' showing four bloody hatchets bound together in the form of a swastika, was one of the montages which became famous because of the little A-I-Z booklet and appeared as graffiti on stone walls and was reproduced on mimeographed pamphlets.[43]

The image 'caught on' in a wider sense, since Resistance movements in Germany began to deface Nazi swastikas by adding curved lines for the axe blades and jagged lines for the blood. The Nazi swastikas that had 'appeared on walls and bridges everywhere' had now met their match in the 'graffiti on stone walls' which became icons of anger and resistance.

Heartfield's image scored against Nazism on a number of counts, the most important of which is its visual rather than verbal iconoclasm. Heartfield was not interested in the issue of verbal content and cultural context for the swastika, since that would have left the visible image intact. Earlier in 1934, in the 25 January issue of *AIZ*, an article had appeared with the title 'A German Symbol?' showing the swastika on a Buddha, a Javanese Puppet and a Russian banknote: this represented a laudable attempt to replace the swastika within a structural signifying system, but it is a Marxist critique which might have been better addressed to Heinrich Schliemann, since by 1934 the swastika had become its own autonomous signifying system. The repression and dictatorship which supported the symbol of the swastika instituted a situation where both ideological and semiotic difference was superfluous and only one sign was required. In terms of visual politics at least, Bataille's 'sovereign law of value' had now been instituted in the structure of the sign, a 'being for itself' which was to be referred only to itself and not to its place ('having to be') in a signifying system. Goebbels' laws of 1933 were designed to shore up the self-referentiality of the swastika, and to protect the totalising 'National Symbol' from the economic relativism of the commercial sign and the commodity law of value. In these regulations, the connection between repression and racism is made explicit: the supersession of relative differences, whether economic, political or semiotic, introduced the rule of the singular and exclusive difference which is the illusion that racism requires.

To subvert Nazism required not the ascription of a different meaning to some ideal and non-Nazi swastika but a 'disfiguring' of the visual chain which linked image to image. The swastika would have to be made non-uniform and 'unlike itself'. This was precisely what was accomplished by the graffiti which followed the publication of the *Blood and Iron* photomontage. Heartfield not only introduced historical and representational codes into the self-identity of the Nazi swastika, he thereby reintroduced the proscribed politics of communism into Nazi Germany. The four axes became a reactionary, parodic and distorted version of the ideology of productive labour represented in the hammer and sickle. The labour of Nazism as shown in *Blood and Iron* is meaningless, destructive and unproductive: its sole function is to support the race 'idea'. The primitive machinery of the four axes prefigures the machinery of the death camps, and the blood on the axes becomes the blood of the victims of the Nazi terror rather than the Aryan blood promoted by National Socialist propaganda.

The polar opposite of John Heartfield's reworking of the Nazi swastika is provided by the chapter devoted to the swastika by the psychoanalyst Wilhelm Reich in *The Mass Psychology of Fascism*. Reich felt free to begin again with the swastika at the point where Schliemann started, using the image as a point of origin and the palimpsest for a self-interested interpretation and neo-Freudian 'free association'. Predictably, Reich's exegesis of the swastika devolved upon the question of sexuality, and the repression of sexual energies in the form of 'reactionary mysticism'. He claimed that the Nazis were aware of the lure of the secrecy in mysticism and religion, and that they knew how to manipulate it: 'an understanding of fascist ideology', he claimed, 'is not possible without a study of the psychological effect of mysticism in general.'[44] Reich argued that Nazi manipulation had amplified the potential 'Fascist psychology' of the individual into a mass movement. He referred to the deliberate use of ambiguity and obfuscation in National Socialist phraseology, the purpose of which was the 'management of the mystical feeling of the masses'.[45]

This theory was the starting point for Reich's discussion of the swastika, provoked by the question: 'why does the symbol lend itself so well to the provocation of mystical feelings?'[46] He attempted to answer this question by using the familiar idea of an 'original meaning' for the swastika, and in doing so merely reified the mystical secrecy he had wished to dispel. Again the swastika was described as an image with a hidden identity, and a secret purpose or intention. This identity, Reich claimed, was wholly sexual, a fact of which Hitler was unaware when he chose the image. By a circuitous route that recalls Schliemann's elaborate explanations, Reich's argument leads us from the original meaning to Hitler's 'victory of the idea of creative work':

> *The swastika, then, was originally a sexual symbol.* In the course of time, it took on diverse meanings, among others that of a mill-wheel, that is of work. The original emotional identity of work and sexuality

explains a finding of Bilmans and Pengerots on the mitre of St Thomas à Becket. It is a swastika with the following inscription, 'hail earth, mother of man. Grow great in the embrace of God, fruitful to nourish mankind'.[47]

This was a rather different interpretation of the 'machinery' of the Nazi swastika than that suggested by John Heartfield, although both Heartfield and Reich found a use for the autokinetic aspect of the image. Reich's analysis rapidly became more specific; he saw in the swastika not just a nexus of sexuality/work in general but the particular and 'unmistakable' representation of a copulating couple:

> A look at the swastikas on page eighty-six will show them to be a schematic but unmistakable presentation of two intertwined human bodies. The swastika at left represents the *sexual act* in the recumbent position, the one at right in the standing position.[48]

This apotheosis of absurd interpretations of the swastika was an attempt to expose the 'mass psychological problem' of mysticism as repressed sexuality, by exposing the true sexual meaning beneath the mystical allure. In the effectiveness of the image of the swastika, Reich saw a substratum at work; specifically sexual, but dependent on the model of a definite yet invisible 'symbolic content' completing the visible image. His theory does not encounter the possibility of a fetishistic and displaced eroticism of the surface rather than a 'symbolically' encoded depth. Reich also offered experimental evidence to support the theory that the swastika 'represents the sexual act':

> This effect of the swastika on unconscious emotional life is, of course, not the reason for the success of fascist mass propaganda: but it is a potent stimulant. Random tests with people of either sex and of various ages and social positions showed that only very few people failed to recognise the meaning of the swastika: most people recognised it sooner or later.[49]

Reich was prepared to go halfway with the swastika, recognising the role of mysticism, but as the censor of true meaning, not as a mystique of significance. He concluded by saying that he had no wish to broadcast his discovery of the swastika's sexual secret identity, since 'the moral disguise would act as a defence against our attempt'. Elsewhere in his text, Reich does provide a description of the mechanics of mystical feeling which could be applied to the Nazi swastika, when he claims that we experience the same psychic reaction to grotesque fairy tales, mystery thrillers, Church services and nationalistic display.[50] That his own interpretation of the swastika could be seen as the fetishisation of the 'mystery thriller' of unmanifest content, of an apparently absent meaningful identity, is unfortunately not discussed. The lie perpetrated by the Nazi swastika was that there existed an identity to be recovered and a meaning to be found, and the fetishisation of the image as a totalitarian 'sign field' postponed that moment of completion indefinitely. The fact that a completion is required already signals its impossibility: Nazism's answer was to continue to reproduce the sign and to extend the territorial boundary which it demarcated.

APOTHEOSIS OF THE GERMAN WORKER

Reich's analysis of the swastika does raise the pertinent question of the role of religious or pseudo-religious mysticism in the Nazi swastika. One way to approach this issue is to ask whether the Nazi swastika was intended to supplant the Christian cross. In one sense, the idea of a perverted *content* in the Nazi swastika, whether this was the archetypal meaning espoused by Jolande Jacobi or the sexual sub-text proposed by Wilhelm Reich, is challenged by the notion that the swastika was itself a perverted *image*, an abominable cross. Once again, this morphological and visual rather than literary approach to the swastika characterises Heartfield's attack on the Nazi *Gleichschaltung*. On 15 June 1933, *AIZ* carried an image showing an SA stormtrooper fixing extensions onto the cross of Thorwaldsen's Christ to turn it into a swastika, and on 27 December 1934, another of a Christmas tree twisted cruelly into the shape of a swastika, with the caption 'O little German Christmas tree, how bent your branches seem to be'. This image also shows the 'swasticised' tree standing on a swastika-shaped Christmas-tree base, one of the types of object cited in Rolf Steinberg's list of popular Nazi kitsch.[51]

To attack Nazi incursions into religious life by depicting the party as the violators of the cross was a powerful propaganda weapon, powerful because it had a basis in truth: Nazism was keen to annexe and surpass the influence of the Church with its own racist doctrine. A caption to Heartfield's *Tannenbaum* montage noted that the reproduction of the Christian version of the seasonal tree had been forbidden in 1934: one year earlier, the railway workers of Berlin had celebrated Christmas by gathering around a gigantic Christmas tree topped by an equally massive swastika (Plate 20). The caption that accompanied this photograph in the propaganda yearbook *Das Jahr* was 'Thus the German people can once again celebrate a truly German Christmas'.[52] However, if this image is seen alongside others in the book, the clear message is that the swastika was being insinuated into *all* existing social praxis in Germany, whether secular or sacred. In the photograph of the railwaymen's Christmas, the Christian cross still appears, but in a subsidiary role: Christianity has not been done away with, it has simply been made 'truly German'. Again, the strategy employed is that of a typographic over-stamping of the cross with the 'truly German' swastika. This tactic was prefigured in the attempts of nineteenth-century authors such as Emile Burnouf to 'Aryanise' Christianity. *Das Jahr* promoted the single 'swastika system' within which all other social relations are included and against which they are judged. This was made clear by party satrap Martin Boorman in 1942:

> Only the Reich leadership, together with the party and the organs and associations connected with it, has a right to lead the people. Just as the harmful influence of astrologists, soothsayers and other swindlers has been suppressed by the state, so it must be made absolutely impossible for the Church to exercise its old influence . . . Only then will the future of Reich and the Volk be secured for all time.[53]

Boorman's denunciation of 'astrologists and soothsayers' in the same breath as a condemnation of the Church borrows its tone from Hitler's railing against '*deutschvölkisch* wandering scholars' in *Mein Kampf*.[54] And in both cases, the denunciation stems from the need to eliminate rivals for the space of *nationalen Erhebung*. The militarised and explicitly politicised form of the swastika as the emblem of the 'nationalisation of the masses' contrasts sharply with the use of the swastika as a token of *völkisch* nostalgia in the Wilhelmine and Weimar years. Despite Hitler's attempts to assert a Nazi hegemony over other groups which had laid claim to the Aryan high ground, the same swastika which was at the centre of his ideological programme had been one of the key devices of *völkisch* sub-culture in Austria and Germany since 1875, when the 'runologist' and occultist Guido von List celebrated the summer solstice of that year by burying eight wine bottles in the shape of a swastika in the ruins of the Roman city of Carnuntum in Austria.[55] In the 1920s Hitler is said to have expressed an interest in excavating List's bottles as a precedent for his ambition to annexe Austria.[56] But what this anecdote also shows is that from the very first Hitler's concept of the swastika was *spatial*, and that his preference was for the rhetoric of conquest rather than for mystical or religious dogma. He conceived the search for an Aryan identity as a progress outwards, using the swastika as a landmark, rather than inwards towards an hermeneutic or interpretative depth.

Hitler's erasure of the last signs of romantic/nostalgic *völkisch* ideas from the swastika can be traced back to his intervention in and control over the political and propaganda programme of the DAP (Deutsches Arbeiter Partei) an organisation to which he had been sent as a military spy on 2 September 1919, and which was soon to become the National Socialist German Worker's Party. The DAP had been founded on 5 January 1919 as a working-class splinter group from the 'Thule Society', a *völkisch* organisation which had established itself in Munich the previous summer. The Thule Society was itself but one branch of the esoteric and neo-masonic Germanenorden (Germanic Orders), a secret lodge which had founded itself on the principle that 'only at least third generation pure blooded Germans are eligible for membership ... the principles of the "Altdeutsche" are to be extended to the entire German race'.[57]

At this time, *völkisch* groups were beginning to realise the possibilities for a broad-based anti-Semitism following the humiliation of the Versailles treaty, and they contributed to the spread of the fiction of *Der Dolchstoss* (the stab in the back) which hinted that Germany could have won the war if its fighting spirit had not been sapped by 'Jewish-Bolshevik' subversive elements. The Russian revolution and the Bavarian communist uprising also fanned the flames of a general anxiety which could be readily channelled into anti-Semitic feelings. The danger that a working-class revolution presented was effectively neutralised by propaganda which recognised only two class distinctions, the Aryan and the Jew. Nazism was to gather workers and *bourgeoisie* behind the swastika flag, homogenising class divisions in the 'sovereign law of value' of race.

The political impetus behind the foundation of the DAP was the desire for a *völkisch* doctrine which could appeal to the German worker; the difficulty was to translate the existing discourse of esoteric and exclusive racism into a movement with a generalised mass appeal. Obviously, all workers could not be screened for the presence of 'third-generation Germanic blood'. The 'nationalisation of the masses' could therefore only be accomplished ideologically, as a 'coming to consciousness' by the worker of his inner Aryanism. This populism was not to be achieved by the DAP until the unwonted intervention of Hitler in 1919, who changed the arcane language of initiation inherited from the Germanic Orders into one of militant action. The swastika then became a sign which was not read as an occult signifier promising an 'educated' depth of meaning but as an heraldic emblem, 'a symbol of our own struggle' and 'the outward sign of ... [a] common bond'.[58] Taking up position 'behind' the swastika in this way both immediately included the worker in the Aryan corral and precluded the need for a pseudo-theological, occult or (as with Marxism) complex ideological initiation.

REDESIGNING THE REICH

Before Hitler first joined and then assumed control of the DAP, the image of the swastika had been introduced to the party in 1919 by Friedrich Krohn, 'a dentist from Starnberg'.[59] Nicholas Goodrick-Clarke, in *The Occult Roots of Nazism*, claims that Krohn had proposed that the party adopt a leftward-turning swastika with curved arms as used by both theosophist groups and the Germanenorden.[60] Theosophy had adapted this leftward form of the swastika from Buddhism, but Goodrick-Clarke suggests that after joining and assuming control of the party, Hitler preferred and eventually insisted in committee discussions on a straight-armed, right-ward-turning swastika. In *Mein Kampf*, Hitler notes only that 'the one fault' of Krohn's version was 'that a swastika with curved legs was composed into a white disc', a design he eventually replaced with his own. His account of the design of the swastika is careful to place his own contribution centre-stage.[61]

The final form of the Nazi swastika severed the connections between the DAP and its 'occult roots', whilst retaining the swastika as the signifier of race *per se*. This last act of deracination marks the culmination of the morphological purge that began with Zmigrodski's isolation of the 'pure form' of the swastika in 1886. What is retained from Zmigrodski to Hitler is the status of the swastika as the symbol of anti-Semitism and therefore of the Aryan: what was expunged were the romantic Aryo-Germanic narratives that had sought to bridge the gap between image and identity, and to weave a new set of meanings around the image. The way in which Hitler finally made the swastika his own was by placing it within the white, red and black colours of the flag of the old Reich, a scheme which Bismarck had personally decided upon in 1866. This was no 'recontextualisation' of the swastika, but rather a montage in which the new movement and its symbol of an Aryan mission was seen to both renew and to challenge 'the old Reich that perished through its own errors'.[62] The false rhetoric of this aim was to be exposed in Heartfield's *Blood and Iron* counter-montage, which showed the 'new Reich' of Nazism supported by Bismarckian-style repression. This reversed the logic of Hitler's design by collapsing the old flag into the new swastika: as soon as the racist symbol of the swastika was rendered historical, the idea of race became meaningless.

In 1919, however, the first Nazi *Gleichschaltung*, the first 'co-ordination' of racism into an existing German order of meaning, was Hitler's incorporation of the swastika image within Bismarck's flag:

> I myself, after innumerable attempts, had laid down a final form; a flag with a red background, a white disk and a black swastika in the middle. After long trials I also found a definite proportion between the size of the flag and the size of the white disk, as well as the shape and thickness of the swastika.[63]

In adopting this colour scheme in preference to the red, black and gold of the 'November criminals' of the Weimar republic, Hitler had stressed that the flag of the old Reich could not simply be resurrected. What was needed was 'an expressive symbol of our own activity' which could distinguish Nazism from an out-of-date German nationalism: 'The movement which today fights Marxism with this aim ["to build a new state"] must therefore bear the symbol of the new state in its very flag.'[64] The swastika was from the very first the sole distinguishing mark of National

Socialism and its ambition to set up a state based on an ideology of racial purity. Hitler also saw design advantages in the swastika as well, as a distinctive device which would be self-identical and clearly and equally recognisable as poster, insignia, armband and flag: 'an effective insignia can in hundreds and thousands of cases give the first impetus towards interest in a movement.'

The most obvious and superficial comparison between Hitler's swastika and the contemporary corporate logo can be made at the 'design stage' in 1919. The way in which the final scheme of the Nazi flag was thrashed out in committee discussion and by sifting through various drafts recalls the process by which the contemporary corporate identity is designed, as does Hitler's expressed wish to find a sign which could be used to compete with the 'market share' gained by communism in Germany. Wally Olins has laid emphasis on the work of trial and error which links the first sketch for a corporate identity to the final form of the logo: 'a complex series of discussions, carried out through a mixture of talk and drawing ... working on a design which will be seen by millions'.[65] The initial audience for the completed version of the Nazi sign was not so large; the new insignia and flag made its first appearance on the banners of a Nazi rally in Munich in May 1920, and at this time the party was all but indistinguishable from the various right-wing and *völkisch* groups which plied their political trade in Munich in the aftermath of World War I. Anton Memminger, who in 1922 wrote a short comparative study of the swastika and the star of David, described the Nazi 'political children' who were at that time using the swastika as their 'talisman'.[66] Memminger's intention was to prove that the swastika, rather than being an anti-Semitic sign, was well known amongst Semitic nations. However, his familiar 'cross-cultural' argument against Nazi appropriation of the sign was being rapidly undermined by political and topographic realities. Memminger mentions that the swastika was at that time being applied to housefronts, doors and toilet walls, which reflects Hitler's references to the work of 'spreading the new symbol of the movement' after 1920, and shows that from the first the symbol was used territorially.[67] The strong self-identity of the swastika, and the fact that it could not be easily confused with any other symbol, made it an ideal device for mapping out the growing public space of Nazism between 1921 and the Kapp *Putsch* of 8–9 November 1923. After 1933, when the symbol of the party became the symbol of the nation, this expansionist trajectory was repeated on a European-wide scale.

When Hitler wrote of 'spreading the new symbol' he was in fact referring to his redesigned flag as a whole, but the swastika, as the one element of the flag which differentiated Nazism from a generalised nationalism, could be detached from the scheme without thereby losing its significance. This significance did not depend on a decoding of the historical reference of the black, white and red, but rather upon a cognitive and emotional *Gestalt*.

The 'conditions of recognition' for this revelation can be found in the discourse of Germanic difference and self-identity which I have traced in the writings of Zmigrodski, Worringer and others, and which by 1920 had established a cognitive framework within which Hitler's swastika could be seen as both disturbingly new, 'revolutionary' and yet authentically Germanic in the context of the flag of the old Reich. The swastika is at the centre of the propaganda discourse of re-cognition, of 'national awakening' in which the symbol is first of all seen as a 'foreign' and distinctive object, a challenge and a threat to the existing order, and then accepted as a revelation of the Germanic race consciousness within a German political context. Nazism posited the 'personality' of the German subject as the missing link between Bismarck's flag and Hitler's swastika, between nation and race. The hammer and sickle had to be learned as an ideological 'object lesson': the swastika, instead, was intended to be *seen* and meaningfully completed in the sudden *Erlebnis* in which, through the agency of a visionary image, the German citizen recognised what she or he was 'in truth'.

That Nazism wished to present itself as a discourse of political revelation is evident in Hitler's idealised references to sudden conversions on the part of communist agitators sent to break up Nazi meetings. This, coupled with his expressed contempt for the masses as stupid, easily led and 'feminine' explains Hitler's preference for the political 'short-cut' which the adoption of the swastika effected.[68] The swastika also facilitated the double-coding through which the red, white and black of the old Reich flag was 'revolutionised' into the red of socialism, and the white of nationalism using the black swastika of racism. As I mentioned in my introduction, the swastika was the device which made antagonistic sense of the equivocal and bet-hedging legend 'National Socialism', insofar as a difficult and radical ideological concept and a redundant nineteenth-century nationalism could be represented as a 'social' *Volk* community and a racial rather than geographic 'national' boundary. The Nazi 'revolution' was presented both as a homecoming and as the preservation of German identity in terms of Germanic racial difference. This appeal to a supposedly pre-existing but buried race consciousness made an effective contrast to the internationalist and homogenising ambitions of Marxism.

The 'coming to consciousness' effected by the swastika might appear in the light of a religious conversion to the Nazi racial 'mission'. However, if Nazism was a religion, it was a religion which offered no 'other place' to go to. In Nazi propaganda, the racial purge through which the German becomes the Germanic is ideologically accomplished in a 'future state' which is constructed, paradoxically, as a return to a pre-existing truth. The Nazi idea was not simply metaphysical, but ontological, which may account for Ernst Nolte's descriptive summary of Nazism as the practical and violent 'resistance to transcendence'.[69] Through this definition Nolte contrasts Hitler's idea or ideal of the material manifestation of an over-whelming will to the ideologies of monotheism and communism. Accord-ing to Nolte, Nazism was not an ideology in the traditional sense, since it made no appeal to the supra-material or personal transcendence, the greater good, of God or state. It desired itself:

> Its *Weltanschauung* ... is in a very primitive way a mere 'legend' which seeks, *by alluding to better blood* [my italics], not so much to legitimize as to establish the rule of the rulers in the eyes of the subjugated.

It is at this point, when Nolte moves away from his bogus comparative method and places the issue of race at the centre of his argument that his analysis becomes convincing. J. P. Stern has reached the opposite con-clusion, since for him, Nolte's 'anti-transcendental' theory applied to the fascist phenomenon is 'a disappointing conclusion to a remarkable book'.[70] For Stern, Nazi racial theories were conducted 'under the image and in the language of transcendence' but in the absence of the moral and social prohibitions which would normally forestall the attempt to realise a heaven on earth. However, Nolte's analysis, in which racism does not 'legitimise' power so much as 'establish' it, has the benefit of showing how Stern's 'moral and political safeguards' could be so easily waived. The rights of 'better blood' rendered civil rights null and void. The danger of the Nazi 'revelation' was that it alluded to an immanent or latent power, not to a transcendent one. This immediately abolished the traditional division between the secular and the sacred, and replaced the 'otherworldly' vision of religion with a heightened perception of an existing reality through communal experience. In this way, 'crowd behaviour' could be transformed into 'race consciousness' through the addition of the symbolic *Gestalt* of swastika or *Führer*.

The concept of an 'affective' and revelatory, rather than merely repres-entational, symbol is discussed in Daniel J. Boorstin's *The Image*, a book which in 1961 proposed a psychoactive model of corporate identity, in which the preceptual event takes precedence over the transmission of meaning. Boorstin suggested that the visual 'triggers' that identify us with the corporate persona do not so much convey information as catalyse an experience that lies somewhere between somatic sensation and the imagin-ation: 'The graphic revolution had made the hypnotic appeal of the image take the place of the persuasive appeal of the argument ... in a flash the entire corporate image is etched in the mind.'[71] In Boorstin's model, the reflective quality and semiotic complexities of symbolic interpretation are dispensed with. Contemporary explanations for such schematisation and simplification in corporate identity programmes often refer to the need for easily assimilated units of significance; in the flood of information, the argument goes, the image that requires reflection or interpretation will be lost. However, Boorstin argued that this kind of immediacy ('a new iconography of speed') had become the desired end, not simply the means; what was on sale was the corporate personality itself, and not its products. Boorstin also discussed the relationship between the visual hook of the 'identity' and the miasmic corporate image or 'persona'. He identified the importance of the factors of ownership and of conscious design in the modern logo, which is 'produced by specialists', and which therefore is not simply the traditional or historically sanctioned property of a guild.

Boorstin's concomitant appeal to the traditional 'ideals' which have been suppressed by the hypnotic and synthetic modern image was to be criticised by Guy Debord in 1967. He accused Boorstin of avoiding the logic of alienation implicit in his own argument, by attempting to isolate the 'pure commodity' or authentic private experience from the public representation of the spectacle: 'Boorstin describes the excesses of a world which has become foreign to us as if they were excesses foreign to our world.'[72] However, the manner in which Boorstin accords an 'affective' rather than merely representative status to the corporate logo corresponds closely to Debord's identification of the 'autonomous movement of the non-living'. Debord's more radical analysis showed how the law of the commodity first of all creates an artificial distinction between the public and the private (a world of work opposed to one of leisure, or the factory to the home), and subsequently employs the private sphere as the domain in which public representations are avidly consumed as authentically 'personal' experiences. It is a commonplace of contemporary life that the commodity injunction operates through advertising, and that we are encouraged to identify with images of personality and 'individuality' via the purchase of products: such blatant appeals to 'buy into' a lifestyle may appear harmless and naive. However, in case of the corporate logo, no purchase is necessary, and ontological rather than commercial ambitions reveal themselves. Like Kracauer's 'mass ornament', the logo 'hovers in mid-air', a phantasmagoric miracle with no visible means of support and no commercial strings attached. In the context of economic exchange, the trans-economic logo can only appear as a miraculous visitation from another world, the world of the 'free gift'.

Boorstin's account of the affective rather than representative qualities of the logo described the victory of its instantaneous event-image over the sequential character of language, economy and of the 'persuasive appeal of the argument' used by advertising. Linking Boorstin, Debord and Jean Baudrillard is a shared phenomenology of what is respectively termed the image, the spectacle and the simulation. In each case, the phenomenon is autonomous, unsupported by and unaccounted for within systems of exchange. Michael Schirner, in an essay on the logos and logotypes of the Franco-American designer Raymond Loewy, has claimed that the logo does not so much demand a decoding from the viewer as offer a visual supplement or gift in excess of commodity values and the ideological texts of advertising. The logo for Schirner is an instant tautology, 'the fastest form of communication we know',[73] a revelation which reveals itself. In this way the logo succeeds in distancing itself as a gift from the ideological and material purchase. Schirner claims that the consumer is being told 'the world as you know it still exists' in a kind of acknowledgement without reserve:

> Logos appear so far outside the context of products, and by communicating in seconds they seem so close to the most everyday experience that their purpose is clearly to take responsibility for the whole world, or at least claim a copyright in what they show us.[74]

Here Schirner identifies the ontological gap which the logo opens up, a space which current corporate advertising seems determined to colonise. In the future, we can anticipate more advertising in the 'papal' and philanthropic style of the Benetton campaign, and more largesse with no purchase necessary. It is more disturbing to consider that these gifts may be free from commercial taint but symbolically poisoned, than to assume that old-fashioned deception and the manipulation of sales figures will be the determining factor in every case. In a situation in which existing ideological positions are being compromised on every side, these corporate goals may become more explicitly political. Schirner's 'taking responsibility for the whole world' might appear as the summit of altruism when contrasted with a post-1989 scenario in which orthodox political practice has become increasingly factionalised and localised.

PROPAGANDA CONTINUED

Like the contemporary logo, the Nazi swastika had ambitions which were 'trans-economic' rather than transcendental. For the majority of those who voted Nazism into power and democracy out of existence in 1933, to escape the social and economic instability of the Weimar years was salvation and transcendence enough: heaven could wait. And despite being enthusiastically supported by industrialists, Hitler managed to make his ideological pitch outside the productivist language of capitalism and Marxism. The largesse which Nazism offered via the swastika was that of 'being', 'will' and the return of Germany to itself. The pure and economically 'innocent' salutation of the logo was preceded by the swastika, in which an ontological 'coming to consciousness' effected through the symbol is both the substance and the supplement of the message 'Germany awake'.

In *Mein Kampf*, Hitler appeared to reject the idea of social distinction based entirely on 'excessive wage differentials' and the commodity sign.[75] This superficially 'socialist' position was underpinned by his substitution of the single and dominant sign of race (the swastika) which was trans-economic rather than socialist, bringing about not equality, but merely a different kind of hierarchy. Hitler's answer to the substitution of signs of community for commodity signs was, in effect, to commodify the vision of a *Volk* community. He wrote of the state which would one day represent 'not an alien mechanism of economic concerns and interests, but a national organism: *a Germanic state of the German nation*'.[76] The final part of this sentence rhetorically returns Germany to 'itself' but does so using a single sign set above all others. Verbally this is accomplished by the substitution of the Germanic for the German: visually the transforming sign was the swastika. That an industrialised and urbanised mass could only be distinguished as a 'folk community' in representation and not in fact posed a problem which was solved, as it is in Michael Schirner's model of the logo, by Nazism's institution of tautology as the dominant cognitive principle: 'The first task of propaganda is to win people for subsequent organisation; the first task of organisation is to win men for the continuation of propaganda.'[77] Here all human energy is directed towards maintaining the status of the sign *as* a sign, which is also the point at which the word 'sign' in fact becomes inapplicable. Instead, the sign as exchange value aspires to the condition of the symbol: the image of limit, demarcation, territoriality. The tautology is a way of transforming a representation into a pseudo-absolute or pseudo-object by forcing it to exchange itself for itself. In a potentially infinite system of economy and exchange, tautology remains one of the few ways of exhausting sign-exchange and marking out its symbolic limit. As Peter Viereck suggested in *Metapolitics*, tautology is the dominant trope of Nazi propaganda: 'nothing is being said except that life is life, and nation is nation.'[78] Wilhelm Reich also noted that National Socialist texts 'seem to disclose no meaning' and J. P. Stern, employing a slightly different interpretation, has defined Nazi propaganda as 'a perlocutionary act ... through its very act of affirmation the claim is made good'.[79] Yet the tautology is productive, not of meaning, but of a self-representation.

As I noted in the previous section of this book, there is a form of exchange at work in Nazi propaganda which simulates the communicative and dialogic act, through the exchange of salutations: swastika, salute, 'Heil Hitler' *et al.* But these salutations merely establish their own existence through repetition: they acknowledge themselves as themselves. The perception of difference *within* a system of exchange is surpassed by an attempt to found an absolute 'difference from' dividing the Aryan from the Semite. The symbol is absolute, self-identical and above all non-exchangeable, which is why Goebbels' laws for the protection of the swastika were introduced to prevent the Nazi 'national symbol' becoming a sign which could be used to increase the value of a mass-produced object such as a hairbrush or a pair of cuff-links. Yet Nazism, for its part, used the swastika to place a higher 'value' on being, and on being German. In this sense, the Aryan is the commodity form of the German, and the swastika remains a commodity sign, just as the freely given saluation of the corporate logo is trans-economic, not post-economic. The logo, precisely, designates 'being for itself' as a value: it sells the consumer back to her/himself as an 'identity' without money ever changing hands. Nazism, similarly, sold the German back to her/himself as an Aryan, which is why Hitler described propaganda as both the means and the end of his 'movement'. The results of this tautology are inevitably destructive, since in the 'tautological state' all the resources of representation and economy are turned against themselves, in the attempt to realise the representation as a self-evident reality: 'the Jews were killed because they were Jews.' As I have suggested, this is no 'symbolic exchange' but an obscene economy of logic. The Nazi swastika, as a sign of distinction underwritten and guaranteed not by relative values but by the tautological 'fact' of being a Aryo-German, was, despite this difference, only the image of the symbol, only half of the *symbolum* whose two parts must be brought together. The fantasy of an undying race and an absolute value which the autokinesis of the Nazi swastika visually described was simply the kitsch solution of a self-representation, an indefinite and tautological loop travelling nowhere.

Tautology, which frames the infinite in an indefinite form, returns us to Hegel's definition of the symbol as the linear mimesis of an illimitable space. In Hegelian philosophy, the symbol cannot escape representation and substitution, because as it tries to abolish the distance between form and meaning, the symbol 'acts out' the Absolute which it purports to embody, and in so doing vulgarises itself, promising a dramatic revelation which ends in a melodramatic farce. This has been the trajectory of Nazism itself, from *Triumph of the Will* to *The Producers*. What has hitherto prevented the Nazi swastika from also becoming an object of ridicule is the history of its institution as symbol of race, and the crimes which Hitler commited to ensure the continuity of that representation. The danger of our current situation is that individual memories of Nazi terror will fade, but the swastika will continue to be used as a racist symbol uniting far-right groups across Europe. This is an unpleasant scenario, but at present it unfortunately appears a more realistic possibility than the naive optimism of those who believe in the gradual rehabilitation of the swastika as a 'symbol of peace'.

The Nazi swastika is a monument both to the immoral and violent actions which accompany racist thought and also to the corruption of meaning in an act of collective self-representation. That it is still being used as a racist symbol in 1994 is testimony to the desire that a racist way of thinking appears to fulfil. Racism creates community without responsibility: it is a magical representation which allows people to believe that they share a fellowship of 'blood' without the burden of social or civic obligations. It is therefore no accident that racist ideology often finds itself sharing a political platform with the prophets of free-market economics, since the sense of civic responsibility which unfettered capitalism erodes can then be retooled in the form of easily digestible representations of race or nation, which establish 'birthrights' rather than duties. Racism also accomplishes the same feat with language, privileging a 'common' speech over the act of communication; meaning then becomes something which is simply recognised, which need not be articulated or explained. It is this logic of the racist tautology, of the 'we are what we are', that accounts for the persistence of the swastika, which historically has represented not just the 'final solution' of Nazism but the solution to the problem of the sign of an imagined community, of a representation which must be *seen* to exist in spite of evidence to the contrary. From Michael Zmigrodski's heraldic swastika, through Nazism and on to the activities of the far-right in contemporary Europe, the attempt has been made to institute the swastika as a visual 'fact', an absolute and mutually recognised symbol which establishes the value of 'we are what we are' as a thing in the world. In this sense, the swastika is totemic, since it creates the group which it symbolises, a transforming power which it shares with the corporate identity. In another sense, both swastika and logo are fictions, which simply succeed in frustrating or short-circuiting language, and which then pass off their anti-representations as being 'beyond representation'. In Nazism, the symbol is constructed as an arrested and static sign: the death of representation artificially maintained by the exertion of totalitarian force.

Throughout this book, I have focused on the issue of the morphological cohesion and self-identity of a signifying form, not on the relationship between that form and a set of decodable references. In the modern and Occidental swastika, the notion of a form which is 'handed down' as an heirloom from the past to the present was used to construct the symbol of race, but insofar as the idea of race required a representation in the nineteenth century, it revealed only nostalgia, absence and lack. An unbroken continuity could be displayed by mimesis, through the elaboration and repetition of images, but this mimesis preserved only a sequence of signs, not a set of inherited characteristics or a common tradition. The 'tradition of the symbol' of the Aryan swastika can only continue to produce itself by reproducing the sign. Those racist groups who in 1994 are still attempting to add yet one more swastika to the Aryan corral are kept busy delimiting and fencing off a void.

NOTES

INTRODUCTION: READING THE SWASTIKA

1 Letter from Max Müller to Heinrich Schliemann, quoted in Schliemann, *Ilios*, London, 1880, p. 346.

2 *The Guardian*, London, 18 September 1993. The photograph was accompanied by the caption 'signs of the times ... a postbox on the isle of Dogs'. The BNP had won its first council seat in Tower Hamlets on 16 September 1993.

3 Chris White in *The Guardian*, London, 12 August 1993: 'Bunches of flowers steadily submerged the "Heil Hitler" at the entrance to Nijmegen's Allied War cemetery yesterday ... in one dark night the cemetery where 1,674 Second World War soldiers were laid to rest had been vandalised ... Nazi slogans, swastikas and neo-Nazi symbols were daubed and sprayed on 150 gravestones.'

4 See Beate Ruhm von Oppen, (ed.) *Documents on Germany Under Occupation*, Oxford, 1955, p. 9. This set of undated regulations was issued on the authority of the Allied Supreme Command. As well as abrogating the Law for the Protection of National Symbols, this order revoked the Reich Flag Law and the Law for the Protection of German Blood and Honour, both issued on 15 September 1935. An abstract of Goebbels' 'swastika laws' and their supplementary regulations is reproduced in Rolf Steinberg, *Nazi Kitsch*, Darmstadt, 1975.

5 Sergei Eisenstein, 'Open Letter to the German Minister of Propaganda, Dr Goebbels' (9 March 1934) in *S. M. Eisenstein: Selected Works*, vol. 1, ed. and trans. Richard Taylor, London, 1988, pp. 281 and 283: referring to Goebbels' praise for the 'realism' of his film *Battleship Potemkin*, Eisenstein had said that: 'truth and National Socialism are incompatible ... However hard you try, you cannot create a 'National Socialist realism. In this mongrel of lies there would be as much genuine truth and realism as there is socialism in National Socialism.'

6 J. W. Goethe, quoted in Hans Georg Gadamer, *Truth and Method*, trans. William Glen-Doepel, London, 1975, p. 68.

7 See Müller's letter to Schliemann, Schliemann, 1880, *op. cit.*, p. 351 and Count Goblet D'Alviella, *The Migration of Symbols*, Westminster, 1892, p. 45.

8 Ian Kershaw, *The Nazi Dictatorship: Problems and Perspectives of Interpretation*, London, 1989, pp. 4 and 106: 'Arguably, an adequate explanation is an intellectual impossibility ... faced with Auschwitz, the explanatory powers of the historian seem puny indeed.'

9 Adolf Hitler, *Mein Kampf*, trans. Ralph Mannheim, with an introduction by D. C. Watt, London, 1992, p. 452.

10 'Our race is a family of the highest nobility, and has for its armorial shield

the swastika', Michael Zmigrodski, *Histoire du Svastika*, Paris, 1891, p. 18. Naming the swastika as an 'armorial' device also employed the etymology of 'Aryan' from the Sanskrit *aryas* meaning 'noble'.

11 Edward Butts, *Statement Number 1: The Swastika*, Kansas City, Mo., 1908, p. 9. It is worth comparing Butts' visionary discourse with a more recent piece of North American swasticology, by the self-styled 'Man-Woman' which appeared in *Re-Search* no. 12 (1989), San Francisco, p. 41. In an interview for the magazine, Man-Woman revealed that the swastika had appeared to him in a dream:

> It was a dream in which a very beautiful, spiritual holy man was showing me a glowing symbol which he said was a symbol of god's love. It was a pure white swastika radiating light ... Then I had many more dreams about swastikas ... dreams where Florence Nightingale had swastikas on her uniform while the Edmonton Symphony Orchestra was applauding.

12 Ramasvamayya's booklet links Scandinavian, American Indian and Greek mythology using the concept of the diaphragm and the symbol of the swastika. The interpetation of Nazism in Walker's text (*Real History of the Swastika*, London, 1939) is discussed on p. 44.

13 See Christopher Hitchens, 'City of Cults', *The Guardian*, London, 19 August 1993: 'At his last parole hearing, Manson turned up with a freshly-cut swastika carved into his forehead and advised the parole board to keep him inside.'

14 Jane Pilling and Mike O'Pray (eds) *Into the Pleasure Dome: The Films of Kenneth Anger*, London, 1989, p. 16.

15 Dan Sperber, *Rethinking Symbolism* Cambridge, 1975, p. 33:

> to take the view suggested here is merely to follow the metaphorical expression that the Ndembu use to designate symbols ... 'a landmark'. A landmark is not a sign but an index which serves cognitively to organise our experience of space. This ... metaphor ... seems much more apposite and subtle to me than the Western metaphor which compares symbols to words.

See also Pascal Boyer (ed.), *Cognitive Aspects of Religious Symbolism*, Cambridge, 1993. In his introduction, Boyer cites Sperber's cognitive approach as differing from the Durkheimian position which sees psychological factors as trivial, and a rationalist interpretation or explanation of the symbol as paramount.

16 Ian Hodder, *The Present Past: An Introduction to Anthropology for Archaeologists*, London, 1982, pp. 204–7:

> The Nazi symbols were used [by punk] as being appropriately aggressive, but certain aspects of their meaning changed by being placed in a new context ... The meaning of the symbol is immediately altered by being placed in a new set.

17 *Ibid.*, p. 213.

18 Barbara G. Walker, *The Woman's Encyclopaedia of Myths and Secrets*, Harper and Row, London, 1983, p. 964.

19 Paul Gilroy, 'Mixing It', *Sight and Sound*, September 1993, p. 24.

20 'Critical Theory in Germany Today: An Interview with Axel Honneth', *Radical Philosophy*, Autumn 1993, p. 40.

21 Paul Virilio, *Speed and Politics*, trans. Mark Polizotti, New York, 1986, p. 117: 'Since fascism never died, it doesn't need to be reborn.'

22 Paul Virilio, *War and Cinema: The Logistics of Perception*, trans. Patrick Camiller, London, 1989, p. 54.

23 Steven Heller, 'Symbol of the Century', *Print*, vol. 46, January/February 1992, pp. 39–49. 'Girls Club' was a magazine published by Curtis in Philadelphia between 1914 and 1918, using the swastika as its emblem.

24 Virilio, 1989, *op. cit.*, p. 54: 'The swastika, for example, releasing potent affective associations, could not be confused with any other symbol – its stark simplicity still has an arresting power, as so much graffiti continues to prove.'

25 Wim Wenders, quoted in Jeffrey M. Peck, 'Rac(e)ing the Nation: Is there a German "home"?', *New Formations* 17, Summer 1992, p. 81.

26 Extract from the programme of the NSDAP (National Socialist German Worker's Party) February 1920, quoted in Barbara Distel and Ruth Jakusch (eds), *Concentration Camp Dachau 1933–45*, trans. Jennifer Vernon, Munich, 1978, p. 20. See also Hitler, *op. cit.*, p. 596: 'Just as Germany's frontiers are fortuitous frontiers, momentary frontiers in the current political struggle of any period, so are the boundaries of other nations' living space.'

27 During World War I an orange swastika on a red field was the shoulder patch of the American 45th Division.

28 Thomas Wilson, *The Swastika, the Earliest Known Symbol and its Migrations*, Washington, 1896, p. 764. Wilson's publication was an extract from the report of the US National Museum for 1894, pp. 757–1011.

29 *Ibid.*, p. 794.

1 SYMBOL

1 Michael Zmigrodski, *Histoire du Svastika*, Paris, 1891, p. 3.

2 Count Goblet D'Alviella, *The Migration of Symbols*, Westminster, 1892, p. 44, n. 3: 'Mr Michael Smigrodski [*sic*] who in his essay 'Zur Geschichte der Svastika' (Branscwig, 1890, extracted from the Archiv für Anthropologie) has classified, chronologically a considerable number of gammadions [swastikas] belonging to monuments of the most different periods and nations.'

3 Zmigrodski, *op. cit.*, p. 16: with reference to the archaeological import of the swastikas which Schliemann had discovered at Hissarlik, Zmigrodski writes 'Is not an insect trapped in amber which has remained there for millions of years a document for etymology?'

4 See *Congrés International des Traditions Populaires, Première Session Paris 1889*, Paris, 1891. See also Thomas Wilson, *The Swastika, the Earliest Known Symbol and its Migrations*, Washington, 1896, p. 792: 'I met Mr Zmigrodski at the tenth International Congress of Anthropology and Prehistoric Archaeology in Paris, and heard him present the results of his investigations on the swastika.'

5 Letter to H. Schliemann from Emil Burnouf, 29 January 1872, in Heinrich Schliemann, *Briefwechsel*, vol. 1, Ernst Meyer, Berlin, 1953, p. 201. In his letter, Burnouf goes on to say that the Jews may have adopted the swastika from Aryan races and used it for mystical purposes, but this concurs with the 'refutation of Judaic originality' in his vehemently anti-Semitic *The Science of Religions* of 1874.

6 See Pierre Bourdieu, *Distinction*, trans. Richard Nice, London, 1992, p. 2: 'the capacity to see (*voir*) is a function of the knowledge (*savoir*), or concepts, that is, the words, that are available to name visible things, and which are, as it were, programmes for perception.'

7 Renan had said that 'one does not have the right to go through the world fingering people's skulls, and taking them by the throat saying "You are of our

blood; you belong to us!" ' The quotation is from Renan's lecture 'Qu'est-ce qu'un nation?' delivered at the Sorbonne on 11 March 1882, trans. Martin Thom in *Nation and Narration*, ed. Homi K. Bhabha, London, 1990, p. 15. In this lecture, Renan warned of the dangers of politicising race: however, Thom ('Tribes Within Nations', p. 23) sees in this speech a specifically anti-German rather than a generally enlightened or anti-racist sentiment.

8 See Müller's letter to Heinrich Schliemann, Schliemann, *Ilios*, London, 1880, p. 351. Also G. F. W. Hegel, *Aesthetics*, vol. 1, trans. T. M. Knox, Oxford, 1975, p. 308: 'when we first enter the world of the old-Persian, Indian, Egyptian shapes and productions, our footing is not really secure; we feel that we are wandering amongst *problems*.'

9 D'Alviella, *op cit.*, p. 45.

10 'Closure is the circular limit within which the repetition of difference infinitely repeats itself. That is to say, closure is its playing space . . . in its closure, representation continues.' Jacques Derrida, 'The Theatre of Cruelty and the Closure of Representation' in *Writing and Difference*, trans. Alan Bass, Chicago, 1978, p. 250.

11 Michael Zmigrodski, *Die Mutter bei den Völkern des Arischen Stammes*, Munich, 1886, p. 406. Zmigrodski was referring to the discovery by Schliemann of a single swastika on a fragment of pottery found at a depth of 16 metres at the Hissarlik site, 'a pure and religious Symbol'. See Heinrich Schliemann, *Troy and its Remains*, London, 1875, p. 157:

> I must also draw attention to the fact that I have found the [image of swastika] twice on fragments of pottery, one of which was discovered at a depth of 16 meters (52½ft) and the other at a depth of 14 meters (46ft). The primitive Trojans, therefore, belonged to the Aryan race, which is further sufficiently proved by the symbols [swastikas] on the round terracottas.

This same fragment is repositioned in his *Ilios, op. cit.*, p. 350, n. 1:

> This potsherd as well as another one with a [swastika] having been picked up in 1872 at a much greater depth in my excavations, I held them to belong to the first city. But after carefully examining the clay and fabric of these fragments, I feel convinced that they belong to the third or burnt city.

Schliemann's eventual conviction that the swastika was the sign of the 'third city' above all may have led Zmigrodski to change his idea of 'pure swastika' in his later text from an image which was physically, to one which was perceptually, 'framed'.

12 See Peter Levi, *Atlas of the Greek World*, Oxford, 1980, p. 54: 'Suppose that the stories from which the *Iliad* grew had their roots not only in other stories and in experience, as all stories do, but also in ruins and beliefs about ruins.'

13 Zmigrodski, 1891, *op. cit.*, p. 5. See also Wilson, *op. cit.*, p. 809. Wilson's misreading of this list gives a total of 420, omitting ten 'pure' swastikas and ninety 'three-branched' ones.

14 Schliemann, 1880, *op. cit.*, p. 350, n. 1.

15 See Maurice Pope, *Decipherment*, London, 1975, p. 103.

16 Michel Foucault, *The Order of Things*, London, 1989, p. 252.

17 *Ibid.*, p. 296.

18 Saussure's critique of Indo-European language theory itself was that it employed a synchronic method as 'but a means of reconstructing the past'. See Ferdinand

de Saussure, *Course in General Linguistics*, trans. Wade Baskin, New York, 1966, p. 82.

19 Quoted in Heinrich Schliemann, *Troja: the Results of the Latest Discoveries on the Site of Homer's Troy*, London, 1884, p. 128.

20 See Leo Deuel, *Memoirs of Heinrich Schliemann*, London, 1978, p. 309. Deuel claims that Bötticher and his 'deadly necropolis theory' represented a serious threat to the archaeologist's peace of mind.

21 Schliemann, 1884, *op. cit.*, p. 129.

22 *Ibid.*, p. 125: 'Mr Greg has since informed me that he has found a [swastika] on a Hittite cylinder, which, in his belief, shows probably that the Hittites had an Aryan origin or cult.' On p. xxi, Sayce is quoted as saying that the swastika 'must . . . have originated in Europe and spread eastward through Asia Minor, or have been disseminated westward from the primitive home of the Hittites'.

23 *Ibid.*, pp. 357–8.

24 Foucault, *op. cit.*, p. 297:

> Since language was becoming an object of science, a language had to be invented that . . . would for that reason be transparent to thought in the very movement that permits it to know. One might say in one sense that *logical algebra and the Indo-European languages* are two products of the dissociation of *general grammar*: the Indo-European languages express-ing the shift of language in the direction of the known object, logical algebra the movement that makes it swing towards the act of knowing, stripping it in the process of its already constituted form.

25 Max Müller, *Biographies of Words and the Home of the Aryas*, London, 1888, p. 82. Müller's attack on 'brachycephalic grammar' echoes a phrase from Renan's speech of 1882 (see Renan, *op. cit.*, p. 14): 'Words such as Brachycephalic or Dolichocephalic have no place in either history or philology.'

26 *Ibid.*, p. 127.

27 Foucault, *op. cit.*, p. 286.

28 Johann Gottlieb Fichte, *Addresses to the German Nation*, 1806, trans. with an introduction by R. F. Jones and G. H. Turnbull, London, 1922.

29 *Ibid.*, p. 56.

30 *Ibid.*, p. 68.

31 Léon Poliakov, *The Aryan Myth: A History of Racist and Nationalist Ideas in Europe*, trans. Edmund Howard, London, 1974, p. 76. He quotes Hildegard of Bingen as having written that Adam and Eve 'teutonica lingua Loquebantur, quae, in diversa non dividitur ut Romana'.

32 *Ibid.*, p. 85.

33 *Ibid.*, p. 91.

34 *Ibid.*, p. 91. Poliakov notes that Grimmelhausens' German *Heldensprache* (heroic speech) was distinguished from the collaged or 'patched-up' (*zusammengeflickt*) quality of other languages.

35 Guido von List (b. 1848) was a Viennese occultist and runologist whose texts on Germanic ancestral speech and Germanic signs exemplified the hybrid of Theosophical mysticism and Pan-Germanism which became popular in Austria and Germany in the early twentieth century. In his *Geheiminis der Runen*, 1907, List identified the swastika as the 'mysterious eighteenth rune' and said 'only there, uniquely and alone, understand the thrice-high-holy secret of constant generation, constant life, and uninterrupted recurrence'. See Stephen E. Flowers' translation of this text as *The Secret of the Runes*, Rochester, VT, 1988, p. 63.

36 See p. 75.

37 Andrew Lang, writing about the swastika in his *Custom and Myth*, 1910, quoted in Donald A. Mackenzie, *The Migration of Symbols, and their Relation to Beliefs and Customs*, London, 1926, p. 53.

38 Schliemann, 1875, *op. cit.*, p. 102.

39 Glyn Daniel and Colin Renfrew, *The Idea of Prehistory*, Edinburgh, 1988, p. 67, and Hugh Kenner, *The Pound Era*, London, 1972, p. 42: 'Schliemann had been to Troy, and a cosmos had been altered.'

40 Accounts of the current excavations at Troy may be found in *Studia Troica* (von Zabein, Mainz).

41 Paul Virilio, *Speed and Politics*, trans. Mark Polizotti, New York, 1986, p. 106.

42 Georg Lukács, *The Destruction of Reason*, trans. Peter Palmer, London, 1980, p. 12: 'the line of development from Schelling to Hitler.' Palmer concedes that this book is 'by general consensus his worst, and by far his silliest, Stalinist tract'.

43 Deuel, *op. cit.*, p. 168.

44 *Ibid.*, p. 309.

45 *Ibid.*, p. 9. Arnold had said: 'Homer was eminently rapid, eminently plain and direct, and eminently noble, and Schliemann was the contrary of all of these – a slow, cautious, complex, devious man, often pompous and ill-tempered, with no natural nobility in him.'

46 Gianni Vattimo, *The End of Modernity: Nihilism and Hermeneutics in Post-modern Culture*, trans. Jon R. Snyder, London, 1988, p. 161.

47 Schliemann, 1875, *op. cit.*, pp. 119–20.

48 Chris Tilley, *Material Culture and Text*, London, 1991, p. 154.

49 See also James Fentress and Chris Wickham, *Social Memory*, Oxford, 1992, pp. 70–1: referring to the image of the magic tree in the folk-tale of 'The Juniper Tree' they claim that the tree is

> less of a symbol than a connecting thread in a series of metamorphoses . . . All that is necessary is that the audience grasps that the tree is a magic tree . . . it no longer matters exactly *how* the tree does what it does – it simply does it by *magic*.

50 Bertram Fulke Hartshorne, 'Dr Schliemann's Trojan Collection', *The Archeological Journal*, vol. XXXIV, London, 1877, p. 269.

51 Eric Hobsbawm, 'Mass Producing Traditions: Europe 1870–1914' in Eric Hobsbawm and Terence Ranger, *The Invention of Tradition*, Cambridge, 1983, p. 278.

52 *Ibid.*, p. 7.

53 Kossinna (b. 1858) was trained as a philologist, but turned eventually to the study of prehistoric 'Germanic' material culture. See Ulrich Veit, 'Ethnic Concepts in German Prehistory: a Case Study on the Relationship between Cultural Identity and Archaeological Objectivity' in Stephen Shennan (ed.), *Archaeological Approaches to Cultural Identity*, London, 1989, p. 37. In his introduction (p. 2), Shennan suggests that

> as far as reconstructing and explaining the past is concerned, traditional origin myths are as good as archaeology, which is, in fact, simply a way of producing origin myths which are congenial to the way of thinking of a particular kind of society.

54 *Ibid.*, p. 61.

55 Daniel and Renfrew, *op. cit.*, p. 120.

56 *Ibid.*, p. 45.

57 In *Black Athena*, Martin Bernal describes the construction of Homer as an oral poet in the eighteenth century, offering as an example Robert Wood, whose *Essay on the Original Genius and Writings of Homer* of 1775 'Stressed Homer's oral status and made him "A primitive and almost Northern bard" '. Bernal, *Black Athena: The Afroasiatic Roots of Classical Civilization*, vol. 1, London, 1991, p. 210.

58 Schliemann, 1875, *op. cit.*, p. 16.

59 *Ibid.*, p. 101.

60 *Ibid.*, p. 105.

61 Schliemann, 1880, *op. cit.*, fig. 226 and pp. 337–8:

> I now pass to the description of the very remarkable figure no 226, which is of lead, and was found in the burnt city at a depth of twenty-three feet . . . The two hands touch the breasts, probably as a symbol of generative power. The navel is also well indicated. The vulva is represented by a large triangle, in the upper side of which we see three globular dots; we also see two lines of dots to the left and right of the vulva. The most curious ornament of the figure is a [image of swastika] which we see in the middle of the vulva.

See also p. 353, where Schliemann quotes A. H. Sayce as claiming: 'the fact that it [the swastika] is drawn within the vulva of the leaden image of the Asiatic goddess seems to show that it was a symbol of generation.'

62 Herbert Schmidt, *Heinrich Schliemann's Sammlung Trojanischer Altertürmer*, Berlin, 1902, p. 255 and Fig. 6446. Schmidt says of this figure: 'Gefunden nach Schl. in der "verbrannten" Stadt. Abg. Schl. Ilios S.380 No.226, hier fälschlicher Weise mit Hakenkreuz im Dreieck und ringsum gesetzen Buckeln.'

63 See Phillip Smith's introduction to Schliemann, 1875, *op. cit.*, p. xix:

> It seems quite natural for a simple and religious race, such as the early Aryans certainly were, to stamp religious emblems and sentences on objects in daily use, and then to consecrate them as *ex voto* offerings, according to Dr Schliemann's suggestion.

See also Hartshorne, *op. cit.*, p. 296: 'the actual purpose served by the spindle whorls is not very clear, unless they were used, as Dr. Schliemann suggests, as ex voto offerings; this explanation, however, does not seem to be founded on anything but supposition.'

64 *Illustrated London News*, 29 December 1877.

65 *Illustrated London News*, 5 January 1878.

66 Karl Marx, *Surveys From Exile; Political Writings Vol. 2*, ed. David Fernbach, London, 1973, p. 319.

67 Karl Marx, *Surveys From Exile; Political Writings Vol. 1*, ed. David Fernbach, London, 1973, p. 10: 'Marx claimed that Germany had to "think what others had done".' See also Edward W. Said, *Orientalism*, London, 1978, p. 19: 'What German Oriental scholarship did was to refine and elaborate techniques whose application was to texts, myths, ideas and languages almost literally gathered from the Orient by imperial Britain and France.' Said thus concludes that German Orientalism was academic rather than nationalist in intent until the late nineteenth century. Said's argument does not take account of how this German version of India 'at one remove' allowed greater scope for a romantic/ nationalist 'ancestralisation' of the East, of a kind which would have seemed implausible in Britain or France.

68 Marx, *vol. 2, op. cit.*, p. 320.

69 George Waring, *Ceramic Art in Remote Ages*, quoted in *op. cit.*, Wilson, p. 776.

70 John Ruskin, *The Two Paths*, 1859, quoted in Partha Miller, *Much Maligned Monsters: A History of European Reactions to Indian Art*, Oxford, 1977, p. 245.

71 *Ibid.*, p. 246.

72 Hegel, *op. cit.*, p. 77: 'This may be taken to be the first form of art, the symbolic form with its quest, its fermentation, its mysteriousness, and its sublimity.'

73 Charles Karelis, 'Interpretative Essay' in *Hegel's Introduction to Aesthetics*, trans. T. M. Knox, Oxford, 1979, p. xiv.

74 Hegel, *op. cit.*, p. 81.

75 *Ibid.*, p. 76: In discussing 'the symbolic form of art' Hegel declares that

> Perceived natural objects are, on the one hand, primarily left as they are, yet at the same time the substantial Idea is imposed on them as their meaning . . . and so are to be interpreted as if the Idea itself were present in them.

76 *Ibid.*, p. 305, see also p. 308.

77 Hegel, quoted in Miller, *op. cit.*, p. 215.

78 Hegel, *op. cit.*, p. 334.

79 Marx, *vol. 1, op. cit.*, p. 46.

80 Marx, *vol. 2, op. cit.*, p. 325.

81 Fichte, *op. cit.*, p. 166.

82 Schliemann, 1875, *op. cit.*, p. xv.

83 Walter Liefer, *India and the Germans: 500 Years of Indo-German Contacts*, Bombay, 1977, p. 1.

84 See Poliakov, *op. cit.*, p. 100: 'The contradiction [between an old Aryan race and an eternally young one] was reflected, from about 1870 onwards, in polemics between upholders of the "aryan immigration" theory and the partisans of the new theory of autochthonism.'

85 Colin Renfrew, *Archaeology and Language: The Puzzle of Indo-European Origins*, Harmondsworth, 1987, pp. 178–90.

86 *Ibid.*, p. 187.

87 *Ibid.*, p. 189.

88 Schliemann, 1880, *op. cit.*, p. 346.

89 *Ibid.*, p. 516. On p. 517, Schliemann writes 'I wish I could have proved Homer to have been an eye-witness to the Trojan war! Alas, I cannot do it!'

90 Renfrew, *op. cit.*, p. 187.

91 Rudolf Virchow, preface to Schliemann, 1880, *op. cit.*, p. xv.

92 Revd Norman Walker, *The Real History of The Swastika*, London, 1939.

93 Norman Brown, *The Swastika, A Study of Nazi Claims of its Aryan Origin*, New York, 1933.

> Adolph Hitler [*sic*] and the Nazis use the swastika as their emblem. They claim that it is a pure 'Aryan' symbol, that it originated in Europe amongst the 'Aryans,' that it is a special characteristic of the 'Aryan' peoples as a whole and the Germanic people in particular.

94 *Ibid.*, p. 8.

95 *Ibid.*, p. 30.

96 Poliakov, *op. cit.*, p. 100.

97 Emile Burnouf, *The Science of Religions*, trans. Julie Liebe, with a preface by E. J. Rapson, London, 1888. In his preface (p. v) Rapson writes: 'The present work of Burnouf . . . was written with the object of proving that Christianity

is essentially an Aryan religion . . . That it is possible at the present day is due almost entirely to the revelations of comparative philology.'

98 *Ibid.*, p. 111: 'The reader must also bear in mind this fact: that the more we learn about the old Germanic and Scandanavian religions . . . the plainer we see their bond of unity with Asia.'

99 *Ibid.*, p. 76.

100 *Ibid.*, p. 243: 'We must ever bear in mind that the operations of the intellect, which are the theme of philosophers, wholly and solely apply to the Aryan – to the adult, perfected and civilised Aryan.'

101 *Ibid.*, p. 153.

102 Max Müller in Schliemann, 1880, *op. cit.*, p. 348.

103 Bourdieu, *op. cit.*, p. 3.

104 Jean-François Lyotard, *The Differend: Phrases in Dispute*, trans. Georges van den Abbeele, Manchester, 1988, p. 4.

105 See Michael Holquist, *Dialogism: Bakhtin and his World*, London, 1990, p. 43.

106 V. N. Volosinov, *Marxism and the Philosophy of Language*, trans. Ladislav Matejka and I. R. Titunik, London, 1977.

107 See Holquist, *op. cit.*, p. 8: '[Bakhtin] would later claim that he published some work . . . under the names of his friends Mendevev . . . Volosinov ('Freudianism, a Critical Sketch' 1927, 'Marxism and the Philosophy of Language' 1929).' For a more detailed exegesis of this claim, see Tzvetan Tordorov, *Michael Bakhtin, the Dialogical Principle*, trans. Wlad Godzich, Minneapolis, 1984.

108 Graham Pechey, 'Bakhtin, Marxism and Post-Structuralism' in Francis Barker *et. al.* (eds), *The Politics of Theory*, Essex, 1983, p. 234. However, where Bakhtin's 'post-structuralism' differs from contemporary varieties is in its neo-Kantian and developmental model of the social self as *zadnie*, a given element (*dan*) whose task is to conceive (*zadan*) itself as a social and discursive being. For Bakhtin, the self is like an egg, inert *in itself* but which when fertilised by language, can fulfil its destiny as a social 'dialogic' entity. In contrast, later critiques of structuralism have presented a 'chicken-and-egg' paradox of the relationship between self and society which in its fastidious rejection of origins excludes the temporal sequence implied by *zadnie*, in favour of the post-Saussurean synchrony of *différance*. See Holquist, *op. cit.*, p. 23, and also Pechey, p. 238, who suggests a closer affinity between Bakhtinian and Derridean deconstruction.

109 Volosinov, *op. cit.*, p. 73.

110 Robert Stam in Robert Stam, Robert Burgoyne and Sandy Flitterman-Lewis, *New Vocabularies in Film Semiotics*, London, 1992, p. 13.

111 Volosinov, *op. cit.*, p. 74. See also Dan Sperber, *Rethinking Symbolism*, Cambridge, 1975, p. 22: 'many societies have a symbolism but not a known key to it. Among those that have a key, many reserve it to a minority, while the majority are witnesses of and even actors in the symbolic activity.'

112 Volosinov, *op. cit.*, p. 75.

113 Wilson, *op. cit.*, p. 443. The quotation is attributed to one Professor Holmes, in the Second Annual Report of the Bureau of Ethnology.

114 Said, *op. cit.*, p. 246. Describing the change from an academic to an 'instrumental' attitude, through which Orientalism was transformed into a set of Western reflexes, Said says that '[The Orientalist] need no longer see himself – as Lane, Sacy, Renan, Caussin, Müller, and others did – as belonging to a sort of guild community with its own internal traditions and rituals.' However, this does not obviate the role of the guild member as the mediator or 'translator' described by Bakhtin.

115 Volosinov, *op. cit.*, p. 73.
116 Zmigrodski, 1891, *op. cit.*, p. 5.
117 Saussure, *op. cit.*, p. 9.
118 See note 11.
119 Zmigrodski, 1886, *op. cit.*, p. 242.
120 *Ibid.*, p. 406.
121 *Ibid.*, p. 316: 'In der Germania ... finden wir unverkennbare Spuren der Mut-terepoche bei den Germanen, doch müssen wir gleich bemerken, dass es schon ein Ubergangsperiode zur neueren, zur Vaterepoche ist.' Zmigrodski cites chap-ter 40 of the 'Germania', where Tacitus states that: 'There is nothing noteworthy about these tribes individually, but they all share a common worship of Nerthus, or Mother Earth.' Tacitus, *The Agricola and the Germania*, trans. H. Mattingley and S. A. Handford, London, 1970.
122 Zmigrodski, 1886, *op. cit.*, p. 406.
123 Jacques Derrida, 'Différance' in *Margins of Philosophy*, trans. Alan Bass, Chi-cago, 1982, p. 9:

> According to this classical semiology, the substitution of the sign for the thing itself is both *secondary* and *provisional*: secondary due to an original and lost presence from which the sign thus derives; provisional as con-cerns this final and missing presence towards which the sign in this sense is a movement of mediation.

124 Homi K. Bhabha, 'Difference, Discrimination and the Discourse of Colonial-ism' in Barker, *op. cit.*
125 *Ibid.*, p. 195.
126 Karl Abraham, 'Restrictions and Transformations of Scopophilia in Psycho-Neurotics', 1913, in *Selected Papers of Karl Abraham*, trans. Douglas Bryan and Alex Strachey, London, 1979.
127 *Ibid.*, p. 213.
128 *Ibid.*, p. 223.
129 Zmigrodski, 1891, *op. cit.*, p. 17: 'Il y a dans ces ornements un sentiment inconscient de leur origine.'
130 G. B. Waring, *Ceramic Art in Remote Ages*, quoted in Wilson, *op. cit.*, p. 780.
131 Sigmund Freud, 'Fetishism', 1927, quoted in Bhabha, *op. cit.*, p. 205: 'affection or hostility in the treatment of the fetish ... are mixed in unequal proportions in different cases, so that the one or the other is more clearly recognisable.'
132 Martin Bernal (*op. cit.*, p. 1) divides Aryanism into two phases, an early nine-teenth-century 'Broad' Aryanism, and an 'Extreme' Aryanism 'which flourished during the twin peaks of anti-semitism in the 1890's and again in the 20's and 30's'.
133 Bhabha, *op. cit.*, p. 195.
134 Zmigrodski, 1891, *op. cit.*, p. 11: Zmigrodski refers to the 'Deus Ignotus' of St Paul the Areopagite.
135 D'Alviella, *op. cit.*, pp. 72–83.
136 *Ibid.*, p. 74.
137 *Ibid.*, p. 75.
138 Wilson, *op. cit.* See also Sir E. A. Wallis Budge, *Amulets and Superstitions*, Oxford, 1930, p. 335. 'Thomas Wilson, who ... seems to have collected all the available information about the sign [of the swastika].'
139 *Ibid.*, p. 763.
140 *Ibid.*, p. 759.
141 *Ibid.*, p. 764.

142 See Daniel and Renfrew, *op. cit.*, pp. 82 and 90. '[Bastian] argued that by a general law the psychical unity of man everywhere produced similar ideas.'

143 *Ibid.*, p. 893.

144 *Ibid.*, p. 820.

145 See Dan Sperber, *On Anthropological Knowledge*, Cambridge, 1985, p. 53:

> Human beings ... rather than reject information which they cannot represent propositionally, they try to salvage it by using semi-propositional representations. These play a role not only as temporary steps towards full propositionality, but also as [a] source of suggestion in creative thinking.

146 Wilson, *op. cit.*, p. 951.

147 *Ibid.*, p. 771.

148 *Ibid.*, p. 952.

149 Alfred Gell, 'The Technology of Enchantment and the Enchantment of Technology' in I. Coote and A. Shelton (eds), *Anthropology, Art and Aesthetics*, Oxford, 1992, p. 44.

150 *Ibid.*, p. 46.

151 See A. David Napier, *Masks, Transformation and Paradox*, Berkeley, Ca., 1986, p. 216. Referring to the magic 'Semut sadular' writing on the Balinese Barong mask, Napier comments:

> The semut sadular is, like the ongkara, or word of words, a sign that is at least as old as the philosophy of Brahminism ... a sign, that is in its own right a source of power ... The mangala symbols are, therefore, not only auspicious signs, but signs that 'promote the preservation of the contents.'

The notion of at once 'promoting' and 'preserving' meaning content is common to the talismanic, the occult and the heraldic device.

152 Sperber, 1975, *op. cit.*, p. 7: 'It is hard to see what symbolic discourse adds – very expensively – to that which any speaker already knows and can explain much more simply; or else symbolic categories constitute a proper language and this language only speaks of itself.'

153 Dan Sperber, 'Is Symbolic Thought Pre-Rational?' in Mary LeCron Foster and Stanley H. Brandes (eds), *Symbol as Sense*, London, 1980.

154 *Ibid.*, p. 39.

155 Fentress and Wickham, *op. cit.*, p. 8.

156 'The Phatic Function corresponds to the contact or the channel; it is specifically geared to establishing an initial connection and ensuring a continuous and attentive reception. In short, it keeps the channels open.' Stam, Burgoyne and Flitterman Lewis, *op. cit.*, p. 16.

157 Susanne Küchler and Walter Melion (eds), *Images of Memory: On Remembering and Representation*, Washington, 1991.

158 *Ibid.*, p. 7.

159 Andrew Lang, *Custom and Myth*, 1910, quoted in A. Mackenzie, *op. cit.*, p. 53.

160 Wilson, *op. cit.*, p. 771.

161 Augustus Pugin, *Glossary of Ornament*, quoted in Wilson, *op. cit.*, p. 776. The work that Pugin cited was the *Alphabetum Tibetarium* of Augustini Antonii Georgi, Rome, 1762, pp. 211, 460 and 275.

162 Bernal (*op. cit.*, p. 220) says that the term 'Aryan' was being used from the 1790s onwards.

163 Wilson, *op. cit.*, p. 784: Goodyear claimed that 'There is no proposition in

archaeology which can be so easily demonstrated as the assertion that the swastika was originally a fragment of the Egyptian meander, provided Greek geometric vases are called in evidence.' However, Wilson also cites Sir George Birdwood's claim in his *Industrial Arts of India* that the swastika was 'the origin of the key pattern ornament of Greek and Chinese decorative art'.

164 Robert Phillips Greg, quoted in Wilson, *op. cit.*, p. 796. The reference was taken from Greg's 'Fret or Key Ornamentation in Mexico and Peru', *Archaeologia*, XLVII, pt 1, p. 159.

165 Mackenzie, *op. cit.*, p. x.

166 *Ibid.*, p. xvi.

167 Raymond Firth, *Symbols Public and Private*, London, 1973, p. 22. See also Umberto Eco, *Semiotics and the Philosophy of Language*, Basingstoke and London, 1984, p. 132: 'In his exhaustive survey of all the possible uses of *symbol*, Firth remarks that this term is used in place of *sign* when there is a certain *ineffectuality*: "a *symbolic* gesture does not attempt to get immediate concrete effects." ' I would argue that Eco here places too much emphasis on the negative aspect of 'ineffectuality' and too little on the positive 'excess' value of the rhetorical gesture as described by Firth.

168 Otto Grabowski, *Das Geheimnis der Hakenkreuzes und die Wiege des Indoger-manentums*, Berlin, 1921. Grabowski began his text (p. 4) with a four-point programme for a reading of the swastika:

> inasmuch as the attempt is made here to trace the original of the swastika and its true meaning, we become aware that we are also confronted with the great question of the Indo-Germanic people, and that we are also not spared a few ethnological excursions. The issue separates into four topics. We look at the swastika: 1: In terms of its distribution and its prehistoric age. 2: In relation to the theory of Indo-Germanic colonisation. 3: In relation to the symbols and symbolism of prehistory. 4: to question its origins and original meaning.

169 *Ibid.*, p. 132.

2 ORNAMENT

1 Robert A. Pois, 'German Expressionism in the Plastic Arts and Nazism: A Confrontation of Idealists', *German Life and Letters*, vol. XXI, no. 3 (April 1968), pp. 205–6: 'it was the youthful Expressionist artists of the 1930s who reacted to the Nazi revolution rather than vice versa . . . the vicissitudes of this relationship . . . manifested the unsettled character of intraparty relations during the years of 1933–4.'

2 'Der Deutsche Bauer ist der Urquell alles Lebens.' Rosenberg writing in 'Der Weltkampf' (November 1923), quoted in Pois, *op. cit.*, p. 207.

3 *Ibid.*, p. 210: '[Schardt was] a defender of the Expressionists . . . with its roots in the bronze works and religious woodcuts of pre-15th century German mediaeval art [Expressionism] represented for him a synthesis in the dialectical development of German national art.' For a case study of Nazi attitudes to the Expressionist/medievalist aesthetic of one artist, see Elizabeth Tumasonis, 'Bernard Hoetger's Tree of Life' in the *Oxford Art Journal*, vol. 51, no 1, Spring 1992, pp. 81–91. Tumasonis shows how Hitler's primary motivation in such disputes over aesthetic propriety was to turn the situation to his political and financial advantage, in this instance the alternate intimidation and placation of the industralist Ludwig Roselius, whose 'Haus Atlantis', built by the

Expressionist Hoetger, had been deemed inadmissible on 'cultural political grounds' by the regime.

4 The Rosenberg vs Goebbels debate is echoed in the internecine warfare in 1933–7 between the Rosenberg Office and Heinrich Himmler's *Ahnenerbe* over Germanic prehistory. And the outcome was similar: both parties were ridiculed by Hitler as 'crack pot otherworldly apostles' peddling 'home made Germanic myths'. See Bettina Arnold, 'The Past as Propaganda: Totalitarian Archaeology in Nazi Germany', *Antiquity*, vol. 64, no. 224, September 1990, p. 469.

5 Donald Kuspit, 'Diagnostic Malpractice: the Nazis on Modern Art', *Artforum*, vol. 25, November 1986, pp. 90–8. Kuspit's thesis is that Nazism sought to repress the alienation and anxiety revealed in modern art, and substitute 'archaic symbols of power and unity'. See also Matthias Winzen, 'The Need for Public Representation and the Burden of the German Past', *New York Art Journal*, vol. 48, no. 4, Winter 1989, p. 310: 'Between 1933 and 1945 the Nazis managed to exploit the fear of chaos many Germans had built up during the economically unstable Weimar Period. In the eyes of many, the products of avant-garde art embodied this chaos.'

6 Adolf Hitler, 18 July 1937, quoted in Kuspit, *op. cit.*, p. 98.

7 Steven Heller has pointed out that in the 1930s the swastika 'was as common as a graphic design motif as the lozenge, leader dot, and sawtooth rule are in contemporary postmodern design'. Steven Heller, 'Symbol of the Century', *Print*, vol. 46, Janaury/February 1992, p. 41.

8 Helen Boorman, 'Rethinking the Expressionist Era: Wilhelmine Cultural Debates and Prussian Elements in German Expressionism', *Oxford Art Journal*, vol. 9, no. 2, 1986, pp. 3–15.

9 *Ibid.*, p. 12. 'The expressionist social utopia remained, one might conclude, one which was envisaged within the emotional and ideological constraints of male martial codes.'

10 Douglas Kellner, 'Expressionism and Rebellion' in *Passion and Rebellion*, quoted in Boorman, *op. cit.*, p. 13.

11 In their brief polemical history of Nazi Germany, Hermann Mau and Helmut Krausnik suggest that Hitler 'divined the tactical advantages of a potential anti-Semitic bias in a movement setting out to appeal to sections of the population which had been forced down the social scale by inflation and economic crisis'. H. Mau and H. Krausnik, *German History 1933–45*, London, 1978, p. 69.

12 See Hermann Glaser, *The Cultural Roots of National Socialism*, trans. with an introduction and notes by Ernest A. Menze, London, 1978, p. 236:

> [Nazism] served the purpose because its collectivist view of life released the individual from responsibility and thereby seemed to safeguard bourgeois quiet and self-satisfaction ... The apolitical subject of the Second Empire and the unpolitical 'citizen' of the Weimar republic represented stages in the development of the apolitical *Volksgenosse*.

13 Adolf Hitler, *Mein Kampf*, trans. Ralph Mannheim with an introduction by D. C. Watt, London, 1992, p. 403.

14 'German Army Confronts its Dark Past', *The Guardian*, London 3 September 1993. General von Scheven was speaking at the inauguration of the new German defence ministry at the 'Bendler-Block' in Berlin on 2 September 1993.

15 Adolf Loos, 'Ornament and Crime', 1908, in *The Architecture of Adolf Loos*, London, 1986, pp. 100–3. In his notes to the 1931 edition of his essays, Loos remarked that 'the first battle cry against ornament' was delivered in his article on 'The Luxury Vehicle' in the *Neue Freie Presse* of 3 July 1898: 'to

seek beauty in form and not in ornament is the goal towards which all humanity is striving.' See Loos, *Spoken Into the Void: Collected Essays 1897–1900*, Cambridge, Ma., 1982, p. 40.

16 Hans Georg Gadamer, 'The Ontological Foundation of the Occasional and the Decorative' in *Truth and Method*, trans. William Glen-Doepel, London, 1975, p. 141: 'Ornament is not primarily something by itself that is then applied to something else, but belongs to the self-presentation of its wearer. Ornament is part of the presentation. But presentation is an ontological event: it is a representation.'

17 Loos, 1986, *op. cit.*, p. 100: 'the man of our time who daubs the walls with erotic symbols to satisfy an inner urge is a criminal or a degenerate ... such symptoms of degeneration most forcefully express themseves in public conveniences.'

18 Adolf Loos, 'Review of the Arts and Crafts', *Die Wage*, 1 October 1898, in Loos, 1982, *op. cit.*, p. 104.

19 *Ibid.*, p. xi.

20 See Hal Foster's definition of a 'postmodernism of reaction' in his introduction to Hal Foster (ed.), *Postmodern Culture*, London, 1985, p. x. See also Peter Eisenmann, quoted in Andreas Papadakis, Catherine Cooke and Andrew Benjamin, *Deconstruction*, London, 1989, p. 150: 'What has been called Post-Modernism in Architecture, a blatant nostalgia for the lost aura of the authentic, the true and the original.'

21 Brandon Taylor, 'Nazism and Post-Modernism' in Brandon Taylor and Wilfred van der Will (eds), *The Nazification of Art, Design, Music, Architecture and Film in the Third Reich*, Winchester, 1990, pp. 128–93: 'The art of the third Reich in its "mature" form of 1936 and 1937 came to employ a host of formal and aesthetic devices which Modernism itself had invented.'

22 Ernest Nolte, *Three Faces of Fascism*, trans. Leila Vennewitz, London, 1965, p. 368: 'Although the [Nazi] flag was blood-red, that alarming expanse of a single colour was now embellished with a symbol (albeit strange) of salvation and hope in the middle ... Great swastikas appeared on house walls and bridges everywhere.' Nolte has been criticised by historians such as J. P. Stern for expounding a quasi-revisionist view of Nazism and the Holocaust which, whilst not denying the existence of the camps, interprets Nazi anti-Semitism as a 'reaction, born of fear, to the process of annihilation of the Russian revolution'. (Nolte quoted in J. P. Stern, *Hitler, the Führer and the People*, London, 1990, p. 186.)

23 Lukács, *The Destruction of Reason*, trans. Peter Palmer, London, 1980, p. 6.

24 Eisenmann, 'En Terra Firma: In Trails of Grotextes', in Papadakis, Cooke and Benjamin, *op. cit.*, p. 153. In this essay, Eisenmann defines the grotesque as an inappropriate relationship, 'the manifestation of the uncertain in the physical' which is nonetheless indefinable as a concrete form: 'whilst the concept of the grotesque or the uncanny can be conceptualised and imagined, it cannot be designed.' This echoes Wilhelm Worringer's invisible force of the Gothic, which is manifest in architectural morphology whilst itself being indefinable either as form or historically situated 'style'.

25 See Loos, 1986, *op. cit.*, pp. 102–3. In 'Ornament and Crime' Loos contrasts the mass-produced ornament which is 'no longer organically related to our culture' with folk ornament: 'I suffer the ornament of the Kaffir, that of the Persian, that of the Slovak farmer's wife ... because they all have no other means of expressing their full potential.' What Loos stressed was the abscence

in the modern era of an ontological link between human beings and their ornaments.

26 Winzen, *op. cit.*, p. 311.

27 Julia Kristeva, *Desire in Language: A Semiotic Approach to Literature and Art*, ed. Leon S. Roudiez, Oxford, 1980, p. 143: 'the obscene word, lacking an objective referent . . . mobilizes the signifying resources of the subject, permitting it to cross through the membrane of meaning where consciousness holds it, connecting it to gesturality, kinaesthesia.'

28 Loos, 1986, *op. cit.*, p. 102: 'the tortured, laboriously extracted and pathological nature of modern ornament'. This colonisation and profitable exploitation of tradition characterises National Socialist attitudes towards the past. See Arnold, *op. cit.*, p. 469: 'there was no real respect for the past or its remains . . . while party historians . . . distorted the facts, the SS destroyed archaeological sites like Biskupin in Poland.'

29 Wilhelm Worringer, *Form in Gothic* (*Formprobleme der Gotik*) trans. with an introduction by Herbert Read, London, 1927, p. 76.

30 *Ibid.*, p. 41.

31 Loos, 1982, *op. cit.*, p. 2. Jacob Grimm (1785–1863), as well as collecting fairy tales with his brother Wilhelm, was the author of works on German grammar and a definitive dictionary of the German language. In his dictionary, the initials of non-proper nouns are the lower case, even those beginning sentences.

32 *Ibid.*, p. 3.

33 Nicholas Goodrick-Clarke, *The Occult Roots of Nazism: the Ariosophists of Austria and Germany 1840–1935*, Wellingborough, 1985, pp. 60–1.

34 Paul Frankl, *The Gothic: Literary Sources and Interpretations Through Eight Centuries*, Princeton, 1960, pp. 669–79. Frankl notes that a year after the publication of *Formprobleme*, an essay on German late Gothic appeared by Kurt Gerstenberg who claimed that

> every style, considered as to its expressive content, poses a problem not merely of history but also of race . . . the irrationality of the sudden explosion of pent-up force is German, also its desultory (*sprunghafte*) manner. The Germanic spirit is characterised by mood.

In his comprehensive survey of interpretations of the Gothic, Frankl has shown that the notion of the style as specifically Germanic is an old one: what his work also reveals is the extent to which this view was championed by German romanticism.

35 Herman Weyl, *Symmetry*, Princeton, 1952, p. 67.

36 See Chapter 1, note 35.

37 Worringer, *op. cit.*, p. 54.

38 Heller, *op. cit.*, p. 34.

39 Rudolf Koch, *The Book of Signs*, London, 1930, p. 18: 'the swastika, or fylfot cross, derived from the sun wheel by breaking the circumference of the circle'. Koch also describes the *triquetrum* or *triskelion* as a 'revolving wheel'.

40 Worringer, *op. cit.*, p. 38.

41 *Ibid.*, p. 38.

42 Herbert Read, *A Concise History of Modern Painting*, London, 1980, p. 218.

43 Worringer, *op. cit.*, p. 11.

44 Wilhelm Worringer, *Abstraction and Empathy: A Contribution to the Psychology of Style*, trans. Michael Bullock, New York, 1980, p. 51.

45 Worringer, 1927, *op. cit.*, p. 7.

46 *Ibid.*, p. 42. Referring back to Weyl's 'Medusa's head' motif, we here have

another example of 'swastikal' symmetry being associated with the freezing or holding of the gaze.

47 Guy Debord, *Society of the Spectacle*, Exeter, 1987, theses 2 and 3.

48 *Ibid.*, thesis 2.

49 E. H. Gombrich, *The Sense of Order: A Study in the Psychology of Decorative Art*, New York, 1984, p. 202.

50 See Worringer, 1980, *op. cit.*, p. vii.

51 *Ibid.*, pp. 114–15. See also his 'Foreword to the New Impression', pp. vii-viii.

52 Gombrich, *op. cit.*, p. 138. See also Dorothy Washburn and Donald Crowe, *Symmetries of Culture: Theory and Practice of Plane Pattern Analysis*, Seattle and London, 1988, p. 20: 'Individuals assign a "top" and "bottom" and "sides" to figures in their environmental contexts. Shifts in position of the objects of 45 or 90 degrees makes recognition more difficult . . . these results confirm the primary importance of bilateral symmetry.'

53 Worringer, 1980, *op. cit.*, p. 109.

54 Worringer, 1927, *op. cit.*, p. 105.

55 Gombrich, *op. cit.*, p. 213:

> Thus, while we must give up the search for the laws of history which could explain every stylistic change, we are still entitled to watch out for sequences and episodes which we can hope to explain in terms of the logic of situations . . . A configuration can be clear and asymmetrical, indistinct but flat . . . What remains true is that any one of these features can become dominant, a focus of interest and competition.

56 Thomas Wilson, *The Swastika, the Earliest Known Symbol and its Migrations*, Washington, 1986, p. 785.

57 Roland Barthes, 'Réquichot and His Body' in *The Responsibility of Forms: Critical Essays in Music, Art and Representation*, trans. Richard Howard, Oxford, 1986, p. 218:

> The symbolism of the spiral is the opposite of that of the circle: the circle is religious, theological; the spiral, a kind of circle distended to infinity, is dialectical; on the spiral, things recur, but at another level; there is a return in difference, not a repetition in identity.

58 See Frankl, *op. cit.*, p. 669. Frankl notes the difficulty of translating *Kunstwollen* and suggests the alternatives of 'art-will, artistic volition, artistic intention, artistic aim'. Of Lipps, he says 'through him, empathy became, at the beginning of the twentieth century, the ruling concept of all psychologically orientated aesthetics'.

59 *Ibid.*, p. 630. See also p. 634: 'It is everywhere a matter of the relation between individual and collective unity.'

60 *Ibid.*, pp. 417–18. Frankl calls Goethe's essay 'a masterpiece of the highest rhetoric. Even one who does not entirely understand it on a first reading is nevertheless carried away by enthusiasm.'

61 *Ibid.*, p. 418.

62 *Ibid.*, p. 469. Goethe had expressed these sentiments in a letter to C. E. von Reinhard, dated 14 May 1810.

63 *Ibid.*, p. 465. Christian Ludwig Steiglitz, *Von altdeutsche Baukunst*, Leipzig, 1820.

64 *Ibid.*, p. 472.

65 *Ibid.*, p. 472.

66 *Ibid.*, p. 450.

67 *Ibid.*, p. 595. Hippolyte Adolphe Taine, *Philosophie de l'Art*, Paris, 1865. Frankl says that 'what he [Taine] says is absolutely unoriginal, and shockingly superficial... according to Taine, Gothic is bound up with race, milieu and historical moment.'

68 *Ibid.*, p. 674.

69 *Ibid.*, p. 737.

70 *Ibid.*, pp. 735–8. 'Freely copying Worringer, Schelfler jettisons the "academic" concept of Gothic.'

71 *Ibid.*, p. 738.

72 Oswald Spengler, *The Decline of the West*, London, 1959, p. 58.

73 *Ibid.*, p. 167.

74 *Ibid.*, p. 261.

75 *Ibid.*, pp. 342–3.

76 *Ibid.*, p. 261. 'In race there is nothing material... but the metaphysical force and power of the ideal.'

77 Karl Radek, October 1930, quoted in Wilhelm Reich, *The Mass Psychology of Fascism*, trans. Theodor P. Wolfe, New York, 1946, pp. 9–10.

78 Ernest A. Menze, introduction to Hermann Glaser, *op. cit.*, p. 14. See also p. 9: 'German culture, regardless of the period in question... cannot be made responsible for the year 1933... The concluding phase of the Romantic age actually paralleled the rise of its earliest unimaginative imitators.'

79 Gadamer, *op. cit.*, p. 67. See also p. 64: 'It is not the genuineness of the experience or of the intensity of the expression, but the ingenious manipulation of fixed forms and modes of statement which makes its work of art a work of art... as late as the eighteenth century, we find poetry and rhetoric side by side in a way that is surprising to modern consciousness.'

80 *Ibid.*, p. 68: 'It is only in the correspondence between Schiller and Goethe, that we have the beginnings of the new form of the concept of the symbol. Goethe's letter of 17 August 1797 speaks of the "properly symbolic" as "eminent examples which stand, in characteristic multiplicity, as representative for many others, and embrace a certain totality".'

81 Umberto Eco, *Semiotics and the Philosophy of Language*, London, 1984, p. 142.

82 J. W. Goethe, quoted in Gadamer, *op. cit.*, pp. 60–9.

83 *Ibid.*, p. 69.

84 C. G. Jung, quoted in Anthony Stevens, *Archetype: a Natural History of the Self*, London, 1982, p. 43: 'The revival of the possibilities of ideas that have always existed, that can be found in the most diverse minds and in all epochs, and are therefore not to be mistaken for invented ideas.'

85 *Ibid.*, p. 35.

86 *Ibid.*, pp. 52 and 46.

87 *Ibid.*, p. 29.

88 J. P. Stern, *Hitler, the Führer and the People*, London, 1990, p. 92. 'This claim Jung's essay takes entirely seriously and enjoins its readers to accept as sincere and valid. The religious dimension of National Socialism is for Jung not a matter of propaganda, but the psychic *donnée* of contemporary Germany.' See also G. L. Mosse, *Nazi Culutre: Intellectual, Cultural and Social Life in the Third Reich*, trans. Salvator Attenasio *et al.*, London, 1966, p. xxxi.

89 Alfred Bauemler, 'Nietszche and National Socialism' in George L. Mosse, *Nazi Culture: Intellectual, Cultural and Social Life in the Third Reich*, trans. Salvator Attenasio *et al.*, London, 1966, p. 97. See also p. 93: 'As Professor at the University of Berlin, he [Bauemler] became the chief liaison man between

the German Universities and Alfred Rosenberg's office, which was charged with the ideological education of the Nazi party.'

90 Kurt Gauger, 'Psychotherapy and Political World View: Extracts from a Lecture given at the Medical Congress for Psychotherapy, Bad Nauheim', 1934, quoted in Mosse, *op. cit.*, p. 224. As well as his role as a psychotherapist, Gauger worked with a government office in charge of educational films.

91 C. G. Jung, *The Archetypes and the Collective Unconscious*, trans. R. F. C. Hull, London, 1959, pp. 47–8.

92 Terry Smith, 'A State of Seeing, Unsighted: Notes on the Visual in Nazi War Culture', *Block* 12, London, 1986/7, p. 51: 'The danger with this sort of analysis is, of course, that it attributes responsibility to a cause beyond the control and even the perception of most people ("we wuz brainwashed").'

93 C. G. Jung in *Memories, Dreams, Reflections*, recorded and edited by Aniela Jaffé, trans. Richard and Clara Winston, London, 1983, p. 202: 'First I formulated the things as I had observed them, usually in "high-flown language" for that corresponds to the style of the archetypes. Archetypes speak the language of rhetoric, even of bombast.'

94 Jolande Jacobi, *Complex, Archetype, Symbol in the Psychology of C. G. Jung*, London, 1959, p. 112.

95 Mme Helena Petrovna Blavatsky, 'The Relation of the Seen and the Unseen', 1888, quoted in Fred Gettings, *A Dictionary of Occult, Hermetic and Alchemical Signs*, London, 1981, p. 257. Blavatsky was a Russian occultist who was one of the founders of the Theosophical movement: 'her work comprises a sustained and frequent plagiarism of about one hundred contemporary texts, chiefly relating to ancient and exotic religions, demonology, Freemasonry and the case for spiritualism' (Goodrick-Clarke, *op. cit.*, p. 18).

96 Goodrick-Clarke, *op. cit.*, p. 1. Citing George L. Mosse, 'The mystical origins of National Socialism', *Journal of the History of Ideas*, 22, 1961, pp. 81–96, Goodrick-Clarke notes that 'theosophy typified the wave of anti-positivism sweeping Europe at the end of the century, and ... its outré notions made a deeper impression in Germany than in other European countries'.

97 Worringer, 1927, *op. cit.*, p. 40: 'On the other hand, to thus cite the Germanic peoples in particular is in any case in accordance with our view that a disposition to Gothic is only found where Germanic blood has mingled with that of the other races.'

98 *Ibid.*, p. 181.

99 *Ibid.*, p. 180.

100 Worringer, 1980, *op. cit.*, p. 59: 'The symbolic value of the motif vanishes beneath the higher will to form.'

101 Gombrich, *op. cit.*, pp. 151 and 217–50.

102 Walter Benjamin, afterword to the Frankfurt 1961 edition of *Illuminations*, quoted in Karsten Witte, 'Introduction to Siegfried Kracauer's "The Mass Ornament", *New German Critique*, no. 5, Spring 1975, p. 62.

103 Taylor, *op. cit.*, p. 136: 'Over and above the correspondence of Nazi Classicism to the Classicism of Imperial Rome, it must be clear that the very forms and angles of National Socialist architecture were imbued with the values of the harsh, the expressive and the coercive.'

104 Worringer, 1927, *op. cit.*, p. 43.

105 Loos, 1982, *op. cit.*, p. 2.

106 Dan Sperber, *Rethinking Symbolism*, Cambridge, 1975, pp. 86–7.

107 Ian Hodder, *Reading the Past: Current Approaches to Interpretation in Archaeology*, Cambridge, 1986, p. 141. It should be noted that Hodder (p. 151)

stresses that 'context' can be seen as a *langue* of fixed meanings which attempts to suppress the *parole* of individuals creating 'their own, shifting, foot-loose schemes'. But this does not suggest how an authoritarian structure of contextual differences might itself become destabilised.

108 Henrietta Moore, 'Ricoeur: Action, Meaning and Text' in Christopher Tilley (ed.), *Reading Material Culture*, London, 1990, p. 113.

109 See Ekrem Akurgal, *The Art of the Hittites*, trans. Constance McNab, London, 1962, plate 7:

> We cannot be sure whether the swastikas in a lozenge shaped standard, revolving partly to the right and partly to the left, should be interpreted as the rising and setting sun; but the total aspect of these standards permits us to assume that it somehow represents the universe.

110 The Karatay Medrese is a Seljuk monument. Derek Hill, in his *Islamic Architecture and its Decoration AD 800–1500*, London, 1969, writes that: 'The Seljuks had already accepted the Muslim religion in the tenth century, but had certainly felt the influence of Christian Armenian architecture . . . the Armenians in their turn being equally influenced by Byzantium.'

111 See Oleg Grabar, *The Formation of Islamic Art*, New Haven and London, 1973, p. 131:

> Early Islam seems on the whole to have avoided visual symbols . . . Whether this was a negative result of the power of symbols in Christian art, or whether some internal Islamic reason brought it about, the new culture did not endow its novel forms with liturgical and symbolic meanings.

See also p. 179:

> On the visual level, the difference can be defined as a modification in the signifying value of forms; this is easiest to observe in architectural decorations, where the majority of themes do not have a meaning independent of the monument itself.

112 Titus Burckhardt, *Sacred Art in East and West*, London, 1967, p. 110.

113 Worringer, 1927, *op. cit.*, p. 53: 'When comparing the two styles [northern and Classical] of ornament, the first point that strikes one is that Northern ornament lacks the concept of symmetry, which from the beginning was so characteristic of all Classical ornament.'

114 Worringer, 1927, *op. cit.*, p. 55.

115 Paul Klee, *Pädagogisches Skizzenbuch* (Pedagogical Sketchbooks): 'Dynamisches auf Grund der Quadrat – Dreiecksschemata, zum Teil auf den Kreis bezogen' (Dynamics Based on the Square and the Triangle, in part Related to the Circle) in Heinz Schutz, 'Transformation und Wiederkehr: Zur Kunstlerisches Rezeption nationalsozialistische Symbole und Asthetik', *Kunstforum International*, no. 95, June-July 1988, pp. 70–1.

116 *Ibid.*, p. 71.

117 Wulf Bley, *Das Jahr 1*, Berlin, 1934, p. 70.

118 Smith, *op. cit.*, p. 55.

119 Wulf Bley, *Das Jahr 2*, Berlin, 1935, p. 112.

120 Susan Sontag, 'Fascinating Fascism' in *A Susan Sontag Reader*, Harmondsworth, 1982, p. 316.

121 See Smith, *op. cit.*

122 Worringer, 1980, *op. cit.*, p. 109.

123 Ilse McKee, 'Skepticism and Participation' in George L. Mosse, *op. cit.*, p. 279.

124 Kate Linker, *Love For Sale: the Words and Pictures of Barbara Kruger*, New York, 1990, p. 27: 'for Kruger, power implements its impositions through the imagistic stereotype, the pose.'

125 Jean Baudrillard, 'Symbolic Exchange and Death' [L'Echange symbolique et la mort, 1976] in *Selected Writings*, ed. Mark Poster, Cambridge, 1988, p. 144: 'The code's disjunction supplants the centralist injunction. Solicitation is substituted for the ultimatum [and evolves into] a total, environmental model made up of incessant spontaneous responses, joyful feedback and irradiated contact.'

126 *Ibid.*, p. 144.

127 Alfred Rosenberg, *Mythos des 20. Jahrhunderts*, Munich, 1938, pp. 111 and 252–9.

128 Siegfried Kracauer, 'Der Ornament der Masse', 1927, translated as 'The Mass Ornament', *New German Critique*, no. 5, Spring 1975, pp. 67–76.

129 Spengler, *op. cit.*, p. 340: 'there are streams of being which are "in form" in the same sense in which the term is used in sports.'

130 Andrew McNamara, 'Between Flux and Certitude: The Grid in Avant-Garde Utopian Thought', *Art History*, vol. 15, no. 1, March 1992, n. 73:

> This is a very similar judgement to that Kracauer made of the 'officially fabricated mass ornaments' of the Nuremberg rallies. In a retrospective determination, he too readily equates these forms as one (or as one leading to the other), a resolution which his initial analysis tends to work against.

131 Kracauer, 1975, *op. cit.*, p. 68.

132 *Ibid.*, p. 68.

133 Antonio Gramsci, ' "Animality" and Industrialism' in *Antonio Gramsci, Selections from Prison Notebooks*, ed. and trans. Geoffrey Nowell Smith and Quintin Hoare, London, 1971, p. 298. See also D. N. Rodowick, 'The Last Things Before the Last: Kracauer and History', *New German Critique*, no. 41, (Spring–Summer 1987), p. 115:

> If there is a fundamental idealism which pervades Kracauer's thought, it resides . . . in the equation of humanity with nature and a lost organic presence . . . the problem of 'nature' must be understood in relation to Lukács' ideas concerning 'second-nature' as the false, mythical reality created by man though not understood by him because he has lost sight of his historical origins.

134 Benjamin, quoted in Witte, *op. cit.*, p. 62.

135 Kracauer, 1975, *op. cit.*, p. 75.

136 *Ibid.*, p. 74.

137 *Ibid.*, p. 64.

138 Siegfried Kracauer, 'Masse und Propaganda: Eine Untersuchung über die fascistische Propaganda', Paris, 1936, quoted in Witte, *op. cit.* This essay was written by Kracauer for the Frankfurt Institute of Social Research, but never published.

139 *Ibid.*, p. 62.

140 *Ibid.*, p. 66.

141 *Ibid.*, p. 62.

142 *Triumph des Willens* was financed by Riefenstahl's own company and filmed between 4 and 10 September 1934. After painstaking editing by Riefenstahl, the film received its première on 28 March 1935 at the Ufa-Palast-am-Zoo,

Berlin's largest theatre. Its propaganda purpose from Hitler's point of view was to present the image of a unified party after the Röhm purge.

143 See Richard Meran Barsam, *Filmguide to Triumph of the Will*, Bloomington, 1975, p. 65. Writing of the final scene of the film, Barstam notes that

> the sequence closes with a long shot of the entire hall, followed by a medium shot of the swastika which dissolves to a close-up of the swastika which then dissolves to the final shot [also of a swastika into which the ranks are marching].

144 Barsam, *op. cit.*, p. 26: 'Hitler liked the film ... While Ufa had good success with the film in the larger cities of Germany, it was not successful with the general public and was not widely used as propaganda.'

145 Siegfried Kracauer, *From Caligari to Hitler: a Psychological History of the German Film*, Princeton, 1947, p. 301: 'the convention was planned not only as a spectacular mass meeting, but also as spectacular film propaganda.' Kracauer's claim is refuted by Barsam, *op. cit.*, p. 4: 'The 1934 meeting was not staged solely for Riefenstahl's cameras. Since the rally was an annual event, it was staged for the cameras only to the extent that political conventions in the US are staged for the tv cameras.'

146 Rodowick, *op. cit.*, p. 112.

147 Kracauer, 1947, *op. cit.*, p. 73.

148 *Ibid.*, p. 287.

149 *Ibid.*, p. 300.

150 *Ibid.*, p. 149: 'In Nibelungen, [Lang's] decorative scheme was rich in meaning; in Metropolis, the decorative not only appears as an end in itself, but even belies certain points made throughout the plot.' Here Kracauer describes the way in which an ornamental order and narrative meanings can pull in different directions.

151 *Ibid.*, caption to Figure 38.

152 Prof. Hans Speier, 'Magic Geography', *Social Research*, September 1941, quoted in Kracauer, *ibid.*, p. 279: 'maps ... resemble graphs of physical processes, they show how all known materials are broken up, penetrated, pushed back and eaten away by the new one.'

153 *Ibid.*, p. 279.

154 *Ibid.*, p. 279.

3 SWASTIKA

1 Dr Felix Marti-Ibanez, 'Symbology and Medicine' in Elwood Whitney (ed.), *Symbology: the Use of Symbols in Visual Communication*, New York, 1960, p. 161.

2 Wally Olins, *Corporate Identity: Making Business Strategies Visible Through Design*, London, 1989, p. 186.

3 *Ibid.*, p. 29.

4 See Judith Williamson's discussion of 'Magic' in *Decoding Advertisements: Ideology and Meaning in Advertising*, London, 1978, p. 143. According to Williamson, magic is a 'pre-scientific ordering of nature, not by an actual organisation of the elements of nature but by an assumption that some organisation does exist, some inherent causality.' Williamson also describes magic as 'a point of translation and exchange' (p. 144) which 'draws us into its non-being'.

5 Michael Schirner, 'Loewy and the Logo' in Angela Schönberger (ed.), *Raymond Loewy: Pioneer of American Industrial Design*, Munich, 1990, p. 183.

6 See J. P. Stern, *Hitler, the Führer and the People*, London, 1990, p. 176: 'Hitler discovered that *he* was *not* a Jew ... Not being a Jew meant that he was not, after all, nothing, a Nobody, and that his "race" was, or could become, everything.'

7 On 3 December 1938, as the climax to an increasingly repressive regime of anti-Semitic legislation, an ordnance was passed pertaining to the forced sale of Jewish businesses. The proceeds of these sales were kept in frozen accounts and confiscated during the war.

8 Rose de Neve, 'Whatever Happened to Corporate Identity?', *Print* 43, May/June 1989, p. 92.

9 *Ibid.*, p. 96.

10 The Wannsee conference was held on 20 January 1942 at the villa Am Großen Wannsee, Berlin. At the conference, Reinhard Heydrich, Chief of Security Police, announced 'the final solution (*Endlosung*) of the Jewish question'.

11 Louis Althusser, 'Ideology and Ideological State Apparatuses (Notes Toward an Investigation)' in *Lenin and Philosophy and Other Essays*, trans. Ben Brewster, New York, 1971, p. 162.

12 Hitler's 'Proclamation to the German People' of 1 February 1933, when the phrase 'national awakening' (*nationalen Erhebung*) was first used, followed his assumption of the chancelllorship on 30 January that year. This was followed by a 'day of national awakening' on 21 March, inaugurated at the tomb of Frederick the Great in the Garrison Church at Potsdam. The swastika is described as a symbol of the 'national awakening' in Goebbels' swastika laws of 19 May 1933. See Rolf Steinberg, *Nazi Kitsch*, Darmstadt, 1975, p. 80.

13 Olins, *op. cit.*, p. 204: 'nobody, not even the most radical anti-Nazi, even hinted that the major multinationals should withdraw from Hitler's Germany. The thought simply never occurred to anybody.'

14 Jean Baudrillard, 'The Ecstasy of Communication' in Hal Foster (ed.), *Postmodern Culture*, London, 1983, p. 129.

15 Steinberg, *op. cit.*, p. 80: 'Es ist verboten, die Symbole der Deutschen Geschichte, des Deutschen Staates und der nationalen Erhebung in Deutschland öffentlich in einer Weiss zu verwenden, die geeignet ist, das Empfinden von der Würde dieser Symbole zu verletzen.'

16 *Ibid.*, p. 81.

17 Also specifically forbidden were moneyboxes, paper, cuff-links, chocolate and tobacco packaging bearing the swastika.

18 Fritz Geschwendt, *5000 Jahre Hakenkreuz*, Breslau, *circa* 1933.

19 Ulrich Hunger, *Die Runenkunde im Dritten Reich*, Frankfurt, 1984, p. 98: 'Ab 1933 erseichen eine zahlenmäßig unübersehbare Konjunturliteratur über das Hakenkreuz.'

20 Ulrich Veit, 'Ethnic Concepts in German Prehistory: A Case Study on the Relationship between Cultural Identity and Archaeological Objectivity', quoted in Stephen Shennan (ed.), *Archaeological Approaches to Cultural Identity*, London, 1989, p. 61.

21 Hunger, *op. cit.*, p. 98.

22 Steinberg, *op. cit.*, p. 5.

23 Gillo Dorfles (ed.), *Kitsch: An Anthology of Bad Taste*, London, 1968, p. 37. Dorfles traces the etymology of the word 'kitsch' in the German verb *etwas verkitschen*, to 'knock off cheaply'.

24 Steinberg, *op. cit.*, p. 81.

25 Wally Olins, quoted in 'The BT affair: Wally Olins Talks to Deyan Sudjic', *Design Review* 1, Spring 1991, p. 36.

26 *Ibid.*, p. 41.

27 Norman Brown, *The Swastika, A Study of Nazi Claims of its Aryan Origin*, New York, 1937, p. 30.

28 Jean Baudrillard, 'The Mirror of Production', 1973, in *Selected Writings*, ed. M. Poster, Cambridge, 1988, p. 115.

29 *Ibid.*, p. 119. 'L'Echange symbolique et la mort' was published in 1976.

30 See Jean-François Lyotard, *The Differend: Phrases in Dispute*, trans. Georges van den Abbeele, Manchester, 1988, p. 142. Referring to Bataille, Lyotard says: 'an intellectual [as distinct from a philosopher] is someone who helps forget differends, by advocating a given genre, whichever it may be (including the ecstasy of sacrifice) for the sake of political hegemony.'

31 This statement of one of the *Einsatzkommandos* is taken from a review by D. H. Goldhagen in *The New Republic*, 17 April 1979, p. 43, quoted in Stern, *op. cit.*, p. 187.

32 Adolf Hitler, *Mein Kampf*, trans. Ralph Mannheim, with an introduction by D. C. Watt, London, 1992, p. 270:

> The Aryan is not greatest in his mental abilities as such, but in the extent of his willingness to put all his abilities in the service of the community ... The most wonderful elucidation of this attitude is provided by his word 'work' by which he does not mean an activity for maintaining life in itself, but exclusively a creative effort which does not conflict with the interests of the community.

33 Stern, *op. cit.*, p. 198.

34 *Ibid.*, p. 186. Against Nolte's thesis, Stern says ' "The Jews" were Hitler's political and ideological target at all times ... The regime itself could not have existed without the Jews as its adversarial rallying point.'

35 Ernst Nolte, *Three Faces of Fascism*, trans. Leila Vennewitz, London, 1965.

36 *Ibid.*, p. 370.

37 G. L. Mosse, *Nazi Culture: Intellectual, Cultural and Social Life in the Third Reich*, trans. Salvator Attenasio *et al.*, London, 1966, p. 321.

38 Georges Bataille, 'The Psychological Structure of Fascism', 1933, in *Visions of Excess: Selected Writings 1927–39*, ed. Allan Stoeckl, Manchester, 1985.

39 *Ibid.*, p. 143. Bataille argued that the 'heterogeneous reality' of fascism displaced power from the object to the image: 'the symbols charged with affective value thus have the same importance as the fundamental elements, and the part can have the same value as the whole.'

40 *Ibid.*, p. 155:

> The mystical idea of race immediately affirmed itself as the imperative of the new fascist society ... the necessity of maintaining a racial value above all others obviated the need for a theory that made the State the principle of all value.

41 Douglas Kahn, *John Heartfield: Art and the Mass Media*, New York, 1985, p. 91.

42 George L. Mosse, *The Nationalisation of the Masses*, New York, 1975, p. 18.

43 John Heartfield, quoted in Kahn, *op. cit.*, p. 91.

44 Wilhelm Reich, *The Mass Psychology of Fascism*, trans. Theodore P. Woolfe, New York, 1946, p. 98.

45 *Ibid.*, p. 83.

46 *Ibid.*, p. 85. See also p. 83: 'We must turn our attention to the symbolism which

the Fascists use in putting the revolutionary structures of the masses into reactionary fetters.'

47 *Ibid.*, p. 86.

48 *Ibid.*, p. 87.

49 *Ibid.*, p. 87.

50 *Ibid.*, p. 117.

51 Steinberg, *op. cit.*, p. 84, no. 67.

52 Wulf Bley *Das Jahr 1*, Berlin, 1934, p. 78.

53 M. Boorman, 'Kirchliches Jahrbuch für die evangelische Kirche in Deutschland', quoted in Mosse, 1966, *op. cit.*, p. 247.

54 Hitler, *op. cit.*, p. 326–7: 'If anything is unfolkish, it is this tossing around of old Germanic expressions ... I had to warn again and again against those *deutschvölkisch* wandering scholars whose positive accomplishment is always practically nil, but whose conceit can scarcely be excelled.'

55 Guido von List, 'Das Geheimnis der Runen', 1907, trans. and ed. with an introduction by Stephen E. Flowers, as *The Secret of the Runes*, Rochester, Vt, 1988, p. 4. List, who was born in Vienna in 1848, was a journalist and occultist, who throughout his long career produced articles and books on 'the runes' and other esoteric topics.

56 Nicholas Goodrick-Clarke, *The Occult Roots of Nazism: The Ariosophists of Austria and Germany, 1840–1935*, Wellingborough, 1985, p. 199. Goodrick-Clarke attributes this anecdote to Elsa Schmidt-Falk, who was in charge of a genealogical research group in Munich during the 1920s. 'Hitler was so intrigued by List's burial of the wine bottles ... that he wanted to exhume this "first swastika" once he had annexed Austria.'

57 Barbara Distel and Ruth Jakusch (eds), *Concentration Camp Dachau 1933–45*, trans. Jennifer Vernon, Munich, 1978, p. 18. 'Julius Streicher, Rudolf Hess, Alfred Rosenberg, Gottfried Feder, Dietrich Eckhardt and Hans Frank belonged to this "Thule Society" circle.'

58 Hitler, *op. cit.*, pp. 450 and 448.

59 Nicholas Goodrick-Clarke (*op. cit.*, p. 151) dates Khron's intervention to May 1919, in the form of a memorandum entitled 'Ist das Hakenkreuz als Symbol nationalsozialistischer Partei geeignet?' (Is the swastika a suitable symbol for the National Socialist Party?). In a note to his translation of *Mein Kampf* (*op. cit.*, p. 451, n. 1) Ralph Mannheim places this introduction of the swastika in August the same year. Both of these datings precede Hitler's arrival on 12 September 1919.

60 Goodrick-Clarke, *op. cit.*, p. 151.

61 Hitler, *op. cit.*, p. 451.

62 *Ibid.*, p. 450: 'we do not desire to awaken from death the old Reich that perished through its own errors, but to build a new state.'

63 *Ibid.*, p. 451–2.

64 *Ibid.*, p. 450.

65 Olins interviewed in *Design Review*, 1991, *op. cit.*, p. 37.

66 Anton Memminger, *Hakenkreuz und Davidstern*, Wurzburg, 1922, p. 1.

67 Hitler, *op. cit.*, p. 452.

68 *Ibid.*, p. 39: 'Like the woman whose psychic state is determined less by grounds of abstract reason that by an indefinable emotional longing ... the masses love a commander more than a petitioner.'

69 Nolte, *op. cit.*, pp. 429 and 422.

70 Stern, *op. cit.*, p. 80.

71 Daniel J. Boorstin, *The Image, or What Happened to the American Dream*,

Harmondsworth, 1961, pp. 197–8: 'An image is ambiguous. It floats somewhere between imagination and the senses, between expectation and reality.'

72 Guy Debord, *Society of the Spectacle*, Exeter, 1987, thesis 199.

73 Schirner, *op. cit.*, p. 183.

74 *Ibid.*, p. 185.

75 Hitler, *op. cit.*, p. 403.

76 *Ibid.*, p. 299.

77 *Ibid.*, p. 530.

78 Peter Viereck, *Metapolitics: From the Romantics to Hitler*, New York, 1941, p. 26.

79 Stern, *op. cit.*, p. 26–7. Discussing Hitler's speeches before and after 1933, Stern notes that one characteristic is constant: 'Solidarity and agreement are *expressed and thus achieved* even before it has become quite clear what precisely the agreement is about. The audience is not being informed, it is made to perform; and its performance "makes history".'

SELECT BIBLIOGRAPHY

THE SWASTIKA

Brown, Norman W. (1933) *The Swastika, a Study of Nazi Claims of its Aryan Origin*, New York, Emerson Books.

Butts, Edward (1908) *Statement Number 1: The Swastika*, Kansas City, Mo., Franklin Hudson.

Doering, Frederick (1936) *The Swastika: A Link Between the Old World and the New?*, London, Kitchener Press.

Geschwendt, Fritz (c. 1933) *5000 Jahre Hakenkreuz*, Breslau, Heinrich Handel Verlag.

Grabowski, Otto (1921) *Das Geheimnis der Hakenkreuzes und die Wiege des Indogermanentums*, Berlin, Verlaganstalt für Vaterlandische Geschichte und Kunst.

Greg, Robert Phillips (1884) 'On the Meaning and Origin of the Fylfot and Swastika', *Archaeologia*, vol. XLVIII: 293–326.

Heller, Steven (1992) 'Symbol of the Century', *Print* 46: 39–49.

Loewstein, Prince John (1942) *Swastika and Yin Yang*, London, China Society Occasional Papers.

Memminger, Anton (1922) *Hakenkreuz und Davidstern*, Würzburg, Gebruder Memminger Verlag.

Pennick, Nigel (1975) *The Swastika*, Cambridge, Bar Hill.

Ramasvamayya, N. (1943) *Swastika: The Symbol of Ancient Wisdom, Religion, Physiology and Medicine Known to Man some Thousands of Years Ago*, Madras, Cornwallis Press.

Schutz, Heinz (1988) 'Transformation und Wiederkehr: zur Künstlerisches Rezeption Nationalsozialistische Symbole und Asthetik', *Kuntsforum International* 95: 69–72.

Walker, Revd Norman (1939) *The Real History of the Swastika*, London, Lutterworth Press.

Wilson, Thomas (1896) *The Swastika, the Earliest Known Symbol and its Migrations, with Observations on the Migration of Certain Industries in Prehistoric Times*, Washington, US National Museum.

Zmigrodski, Michael (1891) *Histoire du Svastika*, Paris, Bibliothèque des Annales Economiques.

ARCHAEOLOGY, ANTHROPOLOGY AND ARYANISM

Arnold, Bettina (1990) 'The Past as Propaganda: Totalitarian Archaeology in Nazi Germany', *Antiquity*, vol. 64, no. 224: 464–78.

Bernal, Martin (1991) *Black Athena: the Afroasiatic Roots of Classical Civilization*, vol. 1, London, Free Association Books.

Bourdieu, Pierre (1984) *Distinction: a Social Critique of the Judgement of Taste*, trans. Richard Nice, London, Routledge.

Boyer, Pascal (1993) (ed.) *Cognitive Aspects of Religious Symbolism*, Cambridge, Cambridge University Press.

Childe, Vere Gordon (1926) *The Aryans: A Study of Indo-European Origins*, London, Kegan Paul & Co.

Daniel, Glyn and Renfrew, Colin (1988) *The Idea of Prehistory*, Edinburgh, Edinburgh University Press.

Deuel, Leo (1978) *Memoirs of Heinrich Schliemann: A Documentary Portrait Drawn from his Autobiographical Writings, Letters and Excavation Reports*, London, Hutchinson.

Fentress, James and Wickham, Chris (1992) *Social Memory*, Oxford Basil Blackwell.

Gell, Alfred (1992) 'The Technology of Enchantment and the Enchantment of Technology' in J. Coote and A. Shelton (eds) *Anthropology, Art and Aesthetics*, Oxford, Oxford University Press.

Hodder, Ian (1982) *The Present Past: An Introduction to Anthropology for Archaeologists*, London, Batsford.

—— (1986) *Reading the Past: Current Approaches to Interpretation in Archaeology*, Cambridge, Cambridge University Press.

Küchler, Susanne and Melion, Walter (eds) (1991) *Images of Memory: On Remembering and Representation*, Washington, Smithsonian Institute Press.

List, Guido von (1988) *The Secret of the Runes*, trans. Stephen E. Flowers, Rochester, Vermont, Destiny Books.

Mackenzie, Donald A. (1926) *The Migration of Symbols, and their Relation to Beliefs and Customs*, London, Kegan Paul, Trench, Turner & Co.

Miller, Daniel (1991) *Material Culture and Mass Consumption*, Oxford, Basil Blackwell.

—— and Tilley, Christopher (eds) (1984) *Ideology, Power and Prehistory*, Cambridge, Cambridge University Press.

Müller, Max (1888) *Biographies of Words and the Home of the Aryas*, London, Longman, Green & Company.

Napier, A. David (1986) *Masks, Transformation and Paradox*, Berkeley, University of California Press.

Poliakov, Léon (1974) *The Aryan Myth: A History of Racist and Nationalist Ideas in Europe*, trans. Edmund Howard, London, Chatto and Windus; Heinemann for Sussex University Press.

Pope, Maurice (1975) *Decipherment: From the Egyptian Hieroglyphics to Linear B*, London, Thames and Hudson.

Renfrew, Colin (1982) *Towards an Archaeology of Mind*, Cambridge, Cambridge University Press.

—— (1987) *Archaeology and Language: The Puzzle of Indo-European Origins*, Harmondsworth, Penguin.

Schliemann, Heinrich (1875) *Troy and its Remains: A Narrative of Researches and Dscoveries made on the Site of Ilium and in the Trojan Plain*, Phillip Smith (ed.), London, John Murray.

—— (1880) *Ilios: the City and Country of the Trojans: The Results of Researches and Discoveries on the Site of Troy and Throughout the Troad in the Years 1871–1879*, London, John Murray.

—— (1884) *Troja: The Results of the Latest Discoveries on the site of Homer's Troy*, London, John Murray.

—— (1886) *Tiryns: The Prehistoric Palace of the King of Tiryns: the Results of the Latest Excavations*, preface by F. Adler, contributions by W. M. Dorpfeld, London, John Murray.

Schmidt, Herbert (1902) *Heinrich Schliemann's Sammlung Trojanischer Altertümer*, Berlin, George Reiner.

Sperber, Dan (1975) *Rethinking Symbolism*, Cambridge, Cambridge University Press.

—— (1980) 'Is Symbolic Thought Pre-Rational?' in M. LeCron Foster and S. Brandes (eds) *Symbol as Sense: New Approaches to the Analysis of Meaning*, London, Academic Press.

—— (1985) *On Anthroplogical Knowledge*, Cambridge, Cambridge University Press.

Tilley, Christopher (1990) 'Foucault: Towards an Archaeology of Archaeology', in Tilley (ed.) *Reading Material Culture*, Oxford, Basil Blackwell.

—— (1991) *Material Culture and Text: the Art of Ambiguity*, London, Routledge.

Veit, Ulrich (1989) 'Ethnic Concepts in German Prehistory: A Case Study on the Relationship between Cultural Identity and Archaeological Objectivity' in Stephen Shennan (ed.) *Archaeological Approaches to Cultural Identity*, London, Unwin Hyman.

Volosinov, V. N. (1977) *Marxism and the Philosophy of Language*, trans. Ladislav Matejka and I. R. Titunik, London, Seminar Press.

Zmigrodski, Michael (1886) *Die Mutter bei den Völkern des Arischen Stammes*, Munich, Theodor Ackermann.

SYMBOL, ORNAMENT AND INTERPRETATION

Abraham, Karl (1979) 'Restrictions and Transformations of Scopophilia in Psycho-Neurotics' in *Selected Papers of Karl Abraham*, trans. Douglas Bryan and Alex Strachey, London, Maresfield.

Akurgal, Ekrem (1962) *The Art of the Hittites*, trans. Constance MacNab, London, Thames & Hudson.

Baudrillard, Jean (1988) *Selected Writings*, ed. Mark Poster, Cambridge, Polity Press.

Budge, E. A. Wallis (1930) *Amulets and Superstitions*, Oxford, Oxford University Press.

Burckhardt, Titus (1967) *Sacred Art in East and West*, London, Perennial Books.

—— (1976) *Art of Islam, Language and Meaning*, London, World of Islam Publishing.

Cassirer, Emile (1957) *The Philosophy of Symbolic Forms*, New Haven, Ct, Yale University Press.

Derrida, Jacques (1978) *Writing and Difference*, trans. Alan Bass, Chicago, University of Chicago Press.

—— (1982) 'Différance' in *Margins of Philosophy*, trans. Alan Bass, Chicago, University of Chicago Press.

Eco, Umberto (1984) *Semiotics and the Philosophy of Language*, Basingstoke and London, Macmillan Press.

Eisenmann, Peter (1989) 'En Terra Firma: In Trails of Grotextes' in Andreas Papadakis, Catherine Cooke and Andrew Benjamin, *Deconstruction*, London, Academy Editions.

Firth, Raymond (1973) *Symbols Public and Private*, London, George Allen & Unwin.

Foucault, Michel (1989) *The Order of Things*, London Tavistock/Routledge.

Frankl, Paul (1960) *The Gothic: Literary Sources and Interpretations Through Eight Centuries*, Princeton, Princeton University Press.

Gadamer, Hans Georg (1975) *Truth and Method*, trans. William Glen-Doepel, London, Sheed & Ward.

Georgi, Augustini Antonii (1762) *Alphabetum Tibetarium*, Rome, Sacred Congregation for the Propagation of the Faith.

Gettings, Fred (1981) *A Dictionary of Occult, Hermetic and Alchemical Signs*, London, Routledge & Kegan Paul.

Goblet, Count D'Alviella (1894) *The Migration of Symbols*, Westminster, A. Constable & Co.

Gombrich, Ernst (1984) *The Sense of Order: A Study in the Psychology of Decorative Art*, New York, Cornell University Press.

Hegel, G. F. W. (1975) *Aesthetics: Lectures on Fine Art* (vols 1 and 2), trans. T. M. Knox, Oxford, Oxford University Press.

Jung, Carl Gustav (1959) *The Archetypes and the Collective Unconscious*, trans. R. F. C. Hull, London, Routledge & Kegan Paul.

—— (1983) *Memories, Dreams, Reflections*, recorded and edited by Aniela Jaffé, trans. Richard and Clara Winston, London, Flamingo.

Kracauer, Siegfried (1975) 'The Mass Ornament', *New German Critique*, no. 5: 67–76.

Loos, Adolf (1982) *Spoken Into the Void: Collected Essays 1897–1900*, Cambridge, Ma., MIT Press.

—— (1986) *The Architecture of Adolf Loos*, London, Arts Council.

McNamara, Andrew (1992) 'Between Flux and Certitude: the Grid in Avant-Garde Utopian Thought', *Art History*, vol. 15, no. 1: 60–79.

Miller, Partha (1977) *Much Maligned Monsters: A History of European Reactions to Indian Art*, Oxford, Oxford University Press.

Moore, Henrietta (1990) 'Ricoeur: Action, Meaning and Text' in Christopher Tilley (ed.) *Reading Material Culture: Structuralism, Hermeneutics and Post-Structuralism*, Oxford, Basil Blackwell.

Rodowick, D. N. (1987) 'The Last Things Before the Last: Kracauer and History', *New German Critique*, no. 41: 109–39.

Saussure, Ferdinand de (1966) *Course in General Linguistics*, trans. Wade Baskin, New York, McGraw Hill.

Spengler, Oswald (1959) *The Decline of the West*, London, George Allen and Unwin.

Vattimo, Gianni (1988) *The End of Modernity: Nihilism and Hermeneutics in Postmodern Culture*, trans. Jon R. Snyder, London, Polity Press.

Wade, David (1976) *Pattern in Islamic Art*, London, Studio Vista.

Walker, Barbara G. (1983) *The Woman's Encyclopedia of Myths and Secrets*, London, Harper & Row.

Washburn, Dorothy and Crowe, Donald (1988) *Symmetries of Culture: Theory and Practice of Plane Pattern Analysis*, Seattle and London, University of Washington Press.

Weyl, Hermann (1952) *Symmetry*, Princeton, Princeton University Press.

Witte, Karsten (1975) 'Introduction to Siegfried Kracauer's "The Mass Ornament" ', *New German Critique*, no. 5: 59–66.

Worringer, Wilhelm (1927) *Form in Gothic*, trans. with an introduction by Herbert Read, London, G. P. Putnam's Sons Ltd.

—— (1980) *Abstraction and Empathy: a Contribution to the Psychology of Style*, trans. Michael Bullock, New York, International Universities Press.

NAZISM, RACISM AND NATIONALISM

Barsam, Richard Meran (1975) *Filmguide to Triumph of the Will*, Bloomington, Indiana University Press.

Bataille, Georges (1985) 'The Psychological Structure of Fascism' in *Visions of Excess: Selected Writings 1927–39*, ed. Allan Stoekl, Manchester, Manchester University Press.

Bhabha, Homi K. (1990) (ed.) *Nation and Narration*, London, Routledge.

Bley, Wulf (1934) *Das Jahr 1*, Berlin, Freiheitsverlag.

Boorman, Helen (1986) 'Rethinking the Expressionist Era: Wilhelmine Cultural Debate and Prussian Elements in German Expressionism', *Oxford Art Journal*, vol. 9, no. 2: 3–15.

Burnouf, Emile (1888) *The Science of Religions*, trans. Julie Liebe, with a preface by E. J. Rapson, London, Swan, Sonnerschein, Lowrey & Co.

Dorfles, Gillo (ed.) (1968) *Kitsch: An Anthology of Bad Taste*, London, Studio Vista.

Drescher, Seymour and Sabean David (eds) (1982) *Political Symbolism in Modern Europe: Essays in Honour of George L. Mosse*, London, Transaction Books.

Fichte, Johan Gottlieb (1922) *Addresses to the German Nation*, trans. with an introduction by R. F. Jones and G. H. Turnbull, London, Open Court Publishing Company.

Glaser, Hermann (1978) *The Cultural Roots of National Socialism*, trans. with an introduction and notes by Ernest A. Menze, London, Croom Helm.

Goodrick-Clarke, Nicholas (1985) *The Occult Roots of Nazism: The Ariosophists of Austria and Germany, 1840–1935*, Wellingborough, Aquarian Press.

Heskett, John (1980) 'Modernism and Archaism in Design in the Third Reich', *Block* 3: 13–24.

Hitler, Adolf (1992) *Mein Kampf*, trans. Ralph Mannheim, with an introduction by D. C. Watt, London, Pimlico.

Hobsbawm, Eric, and Ranger, Terence (1983) *The Invention of Tradition*, Cambridge, Cambridge University Press.

Hull, David Stewart (1969) *Film in the Third Reich 1933–45*, Berkeley, University of California Press.

Hunger, Ulrich (1984) *Die Runenkunde im Dritten Reich, ein Beitrag zur Wissenschafts- und Ideologiegeschichte des Nationalsozialismus*, Frankfurt, Lang.

Kahn, Douglas (1985) *John Heartfield: Art and the Mass Media*, New York, Tanam Press.

Kershaw, Ian (1989) *The Nazi Dictatorship: Problems and Perspectives of Interpretation*, London, Edward Arnold.

Kracauer, Siegfried (1947) *From Caligari to Hitler: A Psychological History of the German Film*, Princeton, Princeton University Press.

Kristeva, Julia (1980) *Desire in Language: A Semiotic Approach to Literature and Art*, ed. Leon S. Roudiez, Oxford, Basil Blackwell.

Kuspit, Donald (1986) 'Diagnostic Malpractice: The Nazis on Modern Art', *Artforum*, vol. 25: 90–8.

Liefer, Walter (1977) *India and the Germans: 500 Years of Indo-German Contacts*, Bombay, Shakantala Publishing House.

Lukács, Georg (1980) *The Destruction of Reason*, trans. Peter Palmer, London, Merlin Press.

Lyotard, Jean-François (1988) *The Differend: Phrases in Dispute*, trans. Georges van den Abbeele, Manchester, Manchester University Press.

Marx, Karl (1973) *Surveys from Exile; Political Writings*, vols 1 and 2, ed. David Fernbach, London, Pelican.

Mosse, George L. (1966) *Nazi Culture: Intellectual, Cultural and Social Life in the Third Reich*, trans. Salvator Attenasio *et al.*, London, W. H. Allen.

—— (1975) *The Nationalisation of the Masses: Political Symbolism and Mass Movements in Germany, from the Napoleonic Wars through the Third Reich*, New York, Howard Fertig.

Nolte, Ernst (1965) *Three Faces of Fascism*, trans. Leila Vennewitz, London, Encounter Books, Weidenfeld and Nicholson.

Peck, Jeffrey M. (1992) 'Rac(e)ing the Nation: Is there a German Home?' *New Formations*, no. 17: 75–84.

Pois, Robert A. (1968) 'German Expressionism in the Plastic Arts and Nazism: A Confrontation of Idealists', *German Life and Letters*, vol. XXI, no. 3: 204–14.

—— (1982) 'Man in the Natural World: Some Implications of National Socialist Religion', in S. Drescher and D. Sabean (eds) *Political Symbolism in Modern Europe: Essays in Honour of George L. Mosse*, London, Transaction Books.

Reich, Wilhelm (1946) *The Mass Psychology of Fascism*, trans. Theodor P. Wolfe, New York, Orgone Institute Press.

Ruhm von Oppen, Beate (ed.) (1955) *Documents on Germany Under Occupation 1945–1954*, Oxford, Oxford University Press.

Smith, Terry (1986/7) 'A State of Seeing, Unsighted: Notes on the Visual in Nazi War Culture', *Block* 12: 50–70.

Sontag, Susan (1982) 'Fascinating Fascism' in *A Susan Sontag Reader*, Harmondsworth, Penguin Books.

Steinberg, Rolf (1975) *Nazi Kitsch*, Darmstadt, Melzer Verlag.

Stern, J. P. (1990) *Hitler: the Führer and the People*, London, Fontana Press.

Tumasonis, Elizabeth (1992) 'Bernard Hoetger's Tree of Life: German Expressionism and Racial Ideology', *Oxford Art Journal*, vol. 51, no. 1: 81–91.

Viereck, Peter (1941) *Metapolitics: From the Romantics to Hitler*, New York, Alfred A. Knopf.

Virilio, Paul (1986) *Speed and Politics*, trans. Mark Polizotti, New York, Semiotext(e).

—— (1989) *War and Cinema: The Logistics of Perception*, trans. Patrick Camiller, London, Verso.

Winzen, Matthias (1989) 'The Need for Public Representation and the Burden of the German Past', *New York Art Journal*, vol. 48, no. 4: 309–14.

Young, Robert (1990) *White Mythologies: Writing History and the West*, London, Routledge.

CORPORATE IDENTITY

Boorstin, Daniel J. (1961) *The Image, or What Happened to the American Dream*, Harmondsworth, Penguin Books.

Bourdieu, Pierre (1986) 'The Production of Belief: Towards an Economy of Symbolic Goods' in Richard Collins *et al.* (eds) *Media, Culture and Society: a Critical Reader*, London, Sage Publications.

Debord, Guy (1987) *Society of the Spectacle*, Exeter, Aim Publications.

Marti-Ibanez, Felix (1960) 'Symbology and Medicine' in Elwood Whitney (ed.) *Symbology: The Use of Symbols in Visual Communication*, New York, Communications Arts Books.

Neve, Rose de (1989) 'Whatever Happened to Corporate Identity?', *Print*, vol. 43: 92–9 and 157.

Olins, Wally (1978) *The Corporate Personality: An Enquiry into the Nature of Corporate Identity*, London, Design Council.

—— (1989) *Corporate Identity: Making Business Strategies Visible Through Design*, London, Thames and Hudson.

—— (1991) 'The BT Affair: Wally Olins Talks to Deyan Sudjic', *Design Review* 1: 34–41.

Schirner, Michael (1990) 'Loewy and the Logo' in Angela Schönberger (ed.) *Raymond Loewy: Pioneer of American Industrial Design*, Munich, Prestel.

Williamson, Judith (1978) *Decoding Advertisements: Ideology and Meaning in Advertising*, London, Marion Boyars.

INDEX